W9-BAS-583

DISCARD

410.72
Au82s

ELLIS HORWOOD SERIES IN ARTIFICIAL INTELLIGENCE

Series Editor: **Professor John Campbell**, University of Exeter

COMPUTER GAME PLAYING: Theory and Practice
M. A. BRAMER, The Open University, Milton Keynes

MACHINE INTELLIGENCE 8: Machine Representations of Knowledge
Edited by E. W. ELCOCK, University of Western Ontario, and D. MICHIE, University of Edinburgh

MACHINE INTELLIGENCE 9
Edited by J. E. HAYES, D. MICHIE, University of Edinburgh, and L. I. MIKULICH, Academy of Sciences, USSR

MACHINE INTELLIGENCE 10: Intelligent Systems: Practice and Perspective
Edited by J. E. HAYES and D. MICHIE, University of Edinburgh, and Y-H. PAO, Case Western Reserve University, Cleveland, Ohio

IMPLICATIONS OF COMPUTER INTELLIGENCE
Edited by M. YAZDANI and A. NARAYANAN, University of Exeter

AUTOMATIC NATURAL LANGUAGE PARSING
Edited by K. SPARCK JONES, University of Cambridge, and Y. WILKS, University of Essex

COMMUNICATING WITH DATA BASES IN NATURAL LANGUAGE
M. WALLACE, ICL, Bracknell, Berks

AUTOMATIC NATURAL LANGUAGE PARSING

Edited by
KAREN SPARCK JONES
Senior Research Associate
Computer Laboratory
University of Cambridge

and

YORICK WILKS
Professor, Cognitive Studies Centre
University of Essex

ELLIS HORWOOD LIMITED
Publishers · Chichester

Halsted Press: a division of
JOHN WILEY & SONS
New York · Brisbane · Chichester · Ontario

First published in 1983 by
ELLIS HORWOOD LIMITED
Market Cross House, Cooper Street, Chichester, West Sussex, PO19 1EB, England

The publisher's colophon is reproduced from James Gillison's drawing of the ancient Market Cross, Chichester.

Distributors:

Australia, New Zealand, South-east Asia:
Jacaranda-Wiley Ltd., Jacaranda Press,
JOHN WILEY & SONS INC.,
G.P.O. Box 859, Brisbane, Queensland 40001, Australia

Canada:
JOHN WILEY & SONS CANADA LIMITED
22 Worcester Road, Rexdale, Ontario, Canada.

Europe, Africa:
JOHN WILEY & SONS LIMITED
Baffins Lane, Chichester, West Sussex, England.

North and South America and the rest of the world:
Halsted Press: a division of
JOHN WILEY & SONS
605 Third Avenue, New York, N.Y. 10016, U.S.A.

© 1983 K. Sparck Jones and Y. Wilks/Ellis Horwood Limited

British Library Cataloguing in Publication Data
Automatic natural language parsing. —
(Ellis Horwood series in artificial intelligence)
1. Language data processing
I. Sparck Jones, Karen   II. Wilks, Yorick
418   P98

Library of Congress Card No. 83-8601

ISBN 0-85312-621-6 (Ellis Horwood Limited)
ISBN 0-470-27460-3 (Halsted Press)

Typeset in Press Roman by Ellis Horwood Limited.
Printed in Great Britain by R. J. Acford, Chichester.

COPYRIGHT NOTICE —

All Rights Reserved. No part of this publication may be reproduced, stored in a retrieval system, or transmitted, in any form or by any means, electronic, mechanical, photocopying, recording or otherwise, without the permission of Ellis Horwood Limited, Market Cross House, Cooper Street, Chichester, West Sussex, England.

Table of Contents

410.72
au 825

Preface

This book is aimed at research students and research workers interested in current views on the problems and techniques of automatic natural language parsing. Parsing is a key element of natural language processing as a whole, and the design of natural language processing systems is an important area on the one hand of information technology, and on the other of language studies. Information technology oriented research, concerned with both language-based systems for purposes like summarising and with language subsystems as components of, for example, expert systems, needs effective parsing procedures. Linguistics oriented research needs effective parsing models. The book is intended to exhibit the state of the art in automatic natural language parsing, at the intersection of these two concerns. Research and development in language processing over the last decade has explored specific approaches to parsing in some depth, has consolidated practical experience, and has emphasised some trends, for example towards phrase structure grammar and deterministic parsing, and towards the closer integration of syntax and semantics. The papers collected here, spread across the whole area of parsing, represent the present thinking of active workers in the field on issues and possibilities stemming from the last decade's work.

ACKNOWLEDGEMENT

This book is based on papers presented at a Workshop on Automatic Natural Language Parsing held at the University of Essex in April 1982. The Workshop was supported by the United Kingdom Science and Engineering Research Council, and we wish to thank the Council for funding the meeting and so encouraging work in this area.

Contributors

B. K. BOGURAEV   Computer Laboratory, University of Cambridge, Cambridge, UK.

E. J. BRISCOE   Department of Linguistics, University of Cambridge, Cambridge, UK.

A. CATER   Department of Computer Science, University College Dublin, Dublin, Republic of Ireland.

E. CHARNIAK   Department of Computer Science, Brown University, Providence, RI, USA.

T. CHRISTALLER   Research Unit for Information Science and Artificial Intelligence, University of Hamburg, Hamburg, Germany BRD.

G. GAZDAR   Cognitive Studies Programme, University of Sussex, Brighton, UK.

R. L. JOHNSON   Centre for Computational Linguistics, UMIST, Manchester, UK.

M. KAY   Xerox Palo Alto Research Centre, Palo Alto, CA, USA.

C. S. MELLISH   Cognitive Studies Programme, University of Sussex, Brighton, UK.

D. METZING   Department of Linguistics and Literary Studies, University of Bielefeld, Bielefeld, Germany, BRD.

S. G. PULMAN   Linguistics, School of English and American Studies, University of East Anglia, Norwich, UK.

C. K. RIESBECK   Department of Computer Science, Yale University, New Haven, CT, USA.

G. D. RITCHIE   Department of Computer Science, Heriot-Watt University, Edinburgh, UK.

K. SPARCK JONES   Computer Laboratory, University of Cambridge, Cambridge, UK.

M. STEEDMAN   Department of Psychology, University of Warwick, Coventry, UK.

J. I. TAIT Computer Laboratory, University of Cambridge, Cambridge, UK

H. THOMPSON Department of Artificial Intelligence, University of Edinburgh, Edinburgh, UK

Y. WILKS Department of Computer Science, University of Essex, Colchester, UK

PART I

The field: structure, relations and applications

Introduction: a little light history

Y. Wilks and **K. Sparck Jones,** University of Essex; University of Cambridge

The papers in this book present, or comment on, recent ideas in automatic natural language parsing, using "parsing" to cover both the syntactic *and* the semantic analysis of a text in order to build a meaning representation for it. The purpose of this introduction is to set the papers in their historical context, and to motivate the way in which they are grouped.

It would be convenient, and intellectually tidy, if *automatic* natural language parsing could be discussed without any extended reference to the history of theoretical linguistics, as if computational analysis had its own autonomous life; and it is true that at times artificial intelligence workers have disregarded the concerns of contemporary theoretical linguistics. For others, however, autonomous parsing must be intellectually disreputable, mere amateur posturing: for them computational parsing ought to be the application of (well-founded) linguistic theory.

In fact, the historical relations between computational analysis and theoretical linguistics have been much more complex, with periods in which the two have essentially gone their own ways, and others where the connection has been much closer. Even in the latter, the flow of ideas has not always been in the direction theoretical linguists might take to be the natural one. It is true that the concerns of some research on parsing have been theoretical *ab initio* (for example the work on Generalised Phrase Structure Grammar). But in other cases (of which the Augmented Transition Network and Marcus's deterministic approaches *may* be examples (Woods, 1970; Marcus, 1980)), it is possible that the much publicised connection between the practical parsers and the theoretical results is *post hoc:* the procedural idea motivating the parsers preceded the search for theoretical justification. If this interpretation is correct, and we believe it is, then work on automated natural language parsing has a logic and motivation of its own, and one may as well look for evidence of the influence of parsing practice on linguistic theory as the reverse.

There are indeed good reasons for looking at work on automatic natural language processing in its own right, not merely as a source of practical tips, but as an intellectual tradition. From the earliest days of machine translation in the nineteen-fifties, attempts to build parsers have adopted a 'procedural view of language', not simply as a consequence of the fact that one is writing programs, but in the more fundamental sense foreshadowed by Wittgenstein's advice: don't ask for the meaning, ask for the use. The distinctive emphasis on the activity of parsing as opposed to its formally possible products has had unexpected consequences, leading to views of grammar and linguistic knowledge very different from those of many linguists. It would be surprising if the by now extensive work on automatic natural language processing had had no impact on theoretical linguistics, and some influence is indeed detectable.

Research on automatic natural language processing has gained in strength and self-confidence in the last ten years, as it has been clearly shown that working systems can be built, even if they are only very modest ones. We have suggested that automatic parsing ideas have influenced theoretical linguistics; but theoretical linguistics has also manifestly affected automatic parsing. However, this has sometimes emerged as negative rather than positive affect: automatic parsing research has developed and emphasised ideas in opposition to those of theoretical linguistics. The semantic parsers of Riesbeck (1975) and Wilks (1975), for example, were largely motivated by a rejection of the assumptions of the dominant theoretical orthodoxy.

The rest of this introduction will look in a little more detail at the development of automatic natural language parsing, and hence at the sources of the specific interests and 'schools' represented by the groups of papers in this book. For this purpose, and to make explicit what has been tacitly assumed so far, we will simply state, without further elaboration, that parsing is formally a computational process, and hopefully an actual working program on some (non-human) computer, that takes sentences in a natural language (but preferably texts) and converts them by rules to some representational structure useful for further processing as might be required, for example, for translation or question-answering. Parsing is thus not confined to syntactic operations, but can include semantic ones: indeed the definition does not exclude operations applying pragmatic information (whether "pragmatic" is used to refer, in the manner familiar to linguists, to e.g. speaker/hearer features, or, in the manner familiar to workers in artificial intelligence, to e.g. real world facts). This 'definition', moreover, makes no commitments about the 'depth' of the resulting representation, using "depth" as a shorthand for a whole gamut of possibilities covering the types of concept used for the representation, the degree of abstraction of the representation from the text, the amount of explicit filling-in of implicit items, and so on.

Increasing depth may be viewed as a progression from a purely syntactic representation to an extended situational description, not explicit at all in the given text, However, this progression is only valid as a very crude approximation, since e.g. syntactic representations, or semantic ones, may themselves be more or less abstract, and may not necessarily exhibit uniform abstraction: for example a representation may be more abstract in its treatment of input lexical items than in its treatment of the input sentence structure. The definition makes no commitment either about whether the parsing process is reversible, i.e. whether it could be run the other way round to produce sentences from representations.

Strictly, the nature of the output representation produced by a parser is not relevant to any discussion of parsing. Parsing is a formally defined process, and the proper concerns of parsing are therefore the abstract mechanisms for applying structure-determining rules to input strings. However, it has been found very difficult to confine the discussion of parsing and the development of parsing techniques to those proper concerns, and views of parsing have been heavily influenced by beliefs about the substantive content of the rules applied, and even more by beliefs about the nature of the text representation to be supplied by the parser.

The 'neutral' definition of parsing given is intentional: it brings all the current approaches within the scope of the book. But it has not been adopted merely for editorial convenience: as the papers show, what the scope of parsing is or ought to be is a matter of argument, or at least discovery. The characteristic inputs, processes and outputs of parsing are objects of research; the nature of the representations to be built is a major problem and issue in the field. The book is thus as much about what workers in the field believe are the problems to be tackled and promising-looking ways of approaching them as about tried, tested and agreed solutions to problems. However, as the chapters show, work in automatic natural language parsing in the last twenty years has provided research workers and practitioners with a range of implementational and investigative techniques, at both the programming and the analytic levels.

Without wishing to be aggressively archaeological, it is necessary, in looking at the background to the current state of parsing research, to make a brief reference to the Stone Age of automated parsing represented by the early work on machine translation. In a general way, for the lack of an autonomous tradition of its own, this research on translation *de facto* tended to be within the then dominant structuralist paradigm of theoretical linguistics. It was predominantly syntactically, and surface, oriented, though inevitably, as translation was the task, the problem of how to tackle text meaning determination and specifically lexical sense selection could not be neglected. The solutions proposed by those most directly involved were felt at the time to be distinctly *ad hoc:* for example, assuming given universes of discourse (e.g. chemistry), or providing special-purpose interpretive routines as parts of lexical entries. It is therefore of some interest to note that somewhat more sophisticated versions of these ideas (in the form of frames, procedural semantics, word expert parsing) have since appeared and have been accorded more respectful attention.

However, the main line of work was being attacked long before the public assault that the ALPAC Report of 1964 constituted, and both from within and from without. Some of those engaged in machine translation research were maintaining that semantics should be given a much more dominant role in parsing, effectively as the driver rather than as the finisher and polisher, and semantic primitives and semantic preference were already being advocated as parsing devices, though they were applied somewhat simplistically. At the same time, the phrase structure approach to syntactic description was being subjected by the theoretical linguists to the full weight of the Transformational Grammar juggernaut.

The relation of parsing to theoretical linguistics is brought out very clearly by reference to Transformational Grammar (TG) in its then Standard Theory (ST) form. From the beginning, for those concerned with parsing, the problems with the transformational approach were decidability and parsability: indeed these concepts are closely related in that, putting it crudely, only decidable systems can be reliably parsed. In its initial form, TG had neither of these properties. Much of the subsequent work within the TG paradigm (e.g on constraints) can be seen as an attempt to limit the power of TGs so that they would be decidable (at least as regards the class of structures generated, if not of strings).

Practical parsing workers were somewhat sceptical about these efforts to 'control' TG, because they were well aware that theoretical decidability and parsability in no way guarantee that a system will actually parse real sentences it is offered within a medically finite lifetime. Moreover, irrespective of the relation between decidability and parsability as a matter of principle concerning grammars, the intrinsic generative character of ST meant that, in a much more important and real, engineering sense, transformational grammars were not for parsing (nor, to be fair, had they been offered as such by linguists). This is indeed shown by the contortions and compromises found necessary in the building of ST parsers seeking a more respectable linguistic foundation for their efforts than any hitherto plausibly on offer.

It was here that the augmented transition network (ATN) was so important: here was a formalism of the same power as a transformational grammar, as a means of characterising sentence structures and structural relationships, but one whose operational claims could be clearly stated, and which, in addition, provided a 'surface grammar', i.e. provided a means of obtaining a sentence surface structure from the given input string.

This parsing capacity was crucial, for ST grammars could never be parsing systems in their standard form simply because they operated on and generated phrase markers: ST provided no mechanisms by which a parser could map, in the reverse direction, from sentence strings to deep structures. Although ST was claimed to be non-directional, it had, from the beginning, a deep-to-surface virtual machine associated with it. In the transformational parsing systems that were built this was the crux: *ad hoc,* heuristic links between surface trees and candidate deep sources had to be provided to guide the parsing-by-generation process.

In relation to TG, therefore, parsing workers found themselves in the awkward position of being offered a linguistic theory of manifestly superior status to anything they had tried to apply before, but one which was of such an abstract, descriptive character that it could not itself be applied to a processing task in any perspicuous way. Thus to those parsing workers concerned with syntax, the main consequence of ST was that it presented, in a well-founded way, an important general idea, namely that of deep structure, supported by a large body of specific structural observations and analyses. The felt semantic inadequacies of TG were major sources of concern to adherents of what may be described as the alternative tradition, which gives priority in parsing for discourse interpretation to semantic rather than syntactic processing, as will be seen below. But the problem of getting a procedural grip on the abstractions of TG was a challenge even to the adherents of the syntactic tradition in parsing, and so for them, ATNs were manna in the wilderness.

The ATN idea has had considerable staying power, and it has provided a useful tool largely because of the attractive way in which it explicates left-to-right processing, and because of the way in which, while largely separating the parsing interpreter from the grammar being applied, it encourages the grammar writer to think about his rules in a procedural way. More specifically, ATNs, in contrast to ST, provided a set of structure-building actions offering a procedurally neat way of linking the surface structure of the network path with the deep structure held in some structure register(s).

There have been subsequent developments of ATNs, for example island parsing, and cascading, which have extended the range of application of ATN parsers. There are also problems with ATNs: as linguistic description systems they fail to capture certain generalisations, for example in relation to conjunctions; and as programmable systems they suffer, for example, from a lack of properly scoped variables. The papers on ATNs in this volume illustrate some of the concerns for those who find the ATN model a useful one. It is worth noting that, although ATN parsing has been primarily applied in syntax-driven mode, it has also been successfully applied in semantically-driven analysis, illustrating its hospitality as a formalism. The ATN tradition is still a currently active one in automated parsing.

More recently, developments of TG itself, from the Standard Theory to the Extended Standard Theory, have found procedural explication in parsing implementations of TG, notably Marcus's PARSIFAL. Marcus claims that his deterministic parser is a theoretically-motivated implementation of the Extended Theory, and not merely a programmed hack, in the sense in which earlier attempts to implement transformational parsing were, theoretically speaking, unmotivated.

To be that, PARSIFAL must show in its operation the kind of universal constraints on the theory of grammar that Chomsky advocates. For him, though, these constraints are declaratively expressed and a component of the theory of grammar rather than procedurally explained.

The interest aroused by Marcus's 'determinism hypothesis' has been focussed more on the psychological claim being made than on the practical application of the model. The clear challenge is whether, within a syntactic framework, parsing can be done deterministically, given the definition of determinism Marcus offers, in terms of no building of (ultimately) unused structures. This is obviously a matter of importance for those who find it convenient to do syntactic processing before semantic processing. However, it has been suggested that the deterministic strategy will sometimes fail on sentences other than 'garden paths', and will require semantics in support of syntax. Marcus concedes the latter, and this has given comfort to those who advocate a larger role for semantics: both those who argue for its necessity as an aid to syntax (and so deny any useful autonomy to syntax), and those who have claimed effective determinism for semantic parsing. What is therefore of interest for computational parsing, rather than psycholinguistics, is the extent to which Marcus-style syntactic parsing can be usefully combined with semantics for a more powerful parser overall: this is currently an open question.

An important theoretical development in recent years has been the astonishing change in the intellectual climate implied by the re-evaluation of Chomsky's long-accepted argument that Finite State Grammars (FSGs) and Phrase Structure Grammars (PSGs) are inadequate for natural languages. Some theoreticians (for instance Harman, 1963) never accepted these arguments, at least as far as PSGs are concerned; computationalists were often unconvinced (see Wilks, 1967), and formalists (like Joshi and Levy, 1982) produced convincing counter-arguments. In the last few years a noticeable revival of interest in PSGs has occurred, most obviously connected with Gazdar's work on Generalised Phrase Structure Grammars (GPSGs) (see this volume).

GPSG has many attractions as a linguistic theory, notably the fact that phrase structure offers a firm anchoring of underlying structures in the realities of actual text, which in turn implies a potentially firm grounding for surface semantics as well as syntax. More to the point in the present context, it is easy to see the attractions of GPSG for computational parsing: unlike TG, GPSG can easily be given limitations to make it decidable, and so parsable; and the formal semantic theories which at least some computationalists believe offer the right kind of tools for their purposes assume a correspondence between syntactic and semantic rules of a sort that is readily available in GPSG. It is not surprising, therefore, that GPSG should currently be an object of intensive investigation by both linguistic and computational communities.

It is hardly surprising either, given all this, that some should want to reverse the historical process yet further and re-examine the relation between PSG and the even simpler and more tractable FSGs. There are good reasons for doing this, both theoretical and practical: there is some evidence, Pulman argues (see this volume), that humans have little capacity for recursive processing, which may be taken as an argument against recursive rules, such as NP → NP S. The practical result is that the ensuing version of PSG can be parsed by a Finite State Machine, though this implies a much stronger role for semantics, which indeed many would like to see.

Steedman's revival of a form of categorial grammar can also be placed within the move to a syntax weaker than TG, accompanied by a very strong, psychologically plausible, semantics (in this volume).

Within the syntactic tradition there has thus been a movement over the last decade in favour of approaches that are more hospitable to semantics, though it has to be recognised that these are still definitely approaches which imply primacy for syntax in parsing. Further, the work that has been done on semantics within this context has on the whole been of a fairly abstract character supplemented by limited, illustrative application, so workers on computational parsing who are down in the dust of the arena trying to build actual language processing systems are reserving judgement until they have some evidence as to how such semantics works out in detail. What the work on GPSG has done, therefore, is give research in theoretical linguistics a credibility in the eyes of workers on automatic parsing which the original TG could not sustain.

We now turn briefly to the 'alternative' tradition: semantic parsing. As we noted, the reasons for the earlier rejection of the syntactic tradition, and specifically of the ST syntactic tradition, are not hard to find.

Semantic parsing, in its most aggressive form, claims that there need be no separate syntactic processes, and that there can be a direct mapping from surface text sentences to their interpretive meaning structures. On this view, so-called syntactic regularities are either expressed in other ways, for example the assertion that adjectives precede nouns is replaced by the assertion that qualifier words precede entity names, or are held irrelevant to parsing as a performance process and so are not expressed, for example redundant gender agreement in languages other than English. Moreover, some practitioners have sought generalisations of a type not normally found in syntactic work (though see Steedman, this volume), such as the "preference" generalisations of Wilks.

The reasons for adopting this semantics-based approach are both principled and practical: it seems self-evident that *meaning* is what really counts in language understanding, and it certainly becomes evident in system building that one will get nowhere without semantics. Those drawn into system building in the later nineteen-sixties were therefore forced, like their scorned machine translation predecessors, to grapple somehow, anyhow, with the determination and representation of meaning.

The semantic parsing tradition has been widely misunderstood as, for example, claiming that no information about word order is necessary, or, contradictorily, as giving syntactic concepts fancy semantic names to no obvious gain. The semantic tradition is more properly viewed as one giving processing primacy to semantics, reversing the relative status accorded to syntax and semantics in the practice of the theoretical linguists. In the systems of Riesbeck and Wilks (Riesbeck, 1975; Wilks, 1975) syntax was exploited (and was recognised as such, though syntactic concepts might sometimes be unconventionally labelled), and at the lowest level of processing could be called in support of semantics; but much more wholehearted use was made of semantics as the essential ingredient of the parsing process, to drive it at higher constituent levels, and to characterise sentential structures. The rejection of contemporary linguistics was perhaps more noisy than real, since semantic processing drew heavily on Case Grammar and shared common concerns with the Generative Semanticists. Workers like Riesbeck and Wilks were not, however, shackled by the excessively simple view of process, namely as derivation from deep to surface tree, that dominated the thinking of the Generative Semanticists: and Riesbeck's more recent expectation-based parsing, in particular, has implemented a genuinely performance-oriented procedural approach to sentence analysis.

Thus if Woods's ATN work can be regarded as inaugurating a Copper Age in automated parsing, the more semantically-oriented work of Riesbeck, Wilks and Winograd (Winograd, 1972) can be taken as inaugurating the successor Bronze Age, as far as the development of useful computationally-relevant intellectual tools for parsing is concerned. The essence of this semantic tradition has been the view that whether syntactic processing is pushed as far as the building of a full sentence parse tree and is then followed by semantic processing on that tree, or whether the two are done concurrently, is not a mere matter of pragmatic choice motivated by local machine power or particular application requirements. Concurrent, interleaved, or other combined processing is more efficient because, given the huge range of syntactic and semantic possibilities for text constituents, semantics can squelch inappropriate syntactic options and vice versa: this is a theoretical position supported, for all but specialised cases, by practical observation. The result is that in these systems, little attempt is made to provide a detailed narrowly syntactic characterisation of the complete sentence structure, and specifically not a characterisation of this structure as an independent entity.

There is naturally variation within the semantic tradition: the work it subsumes ranges from approaches relying on syntax for mechanical driving with heavy and frequent semantic filtering (in which sense Winograd's SHRDLU must be included on the basis of its early noun-phrase reference), to approaches exploiting essentially semantic categories and structures as a means of driving parsing, subject to syntactic refinement. The intermediate position is occupied by approaches strengthening conventional syntax through semantically flavoured or restricted categories.

Perhaps as importantly, this semantically-oriented work, along with Woods's more syntactically-oriented LUNAR project, demonstrated convincingly that real language processing systems could be built. These successes have stimulated a large mass of work within the semantic tradition which, interestingly, has captured ATNs through the development and application to parsing of purpose-built, domain-specific semantic grammars. The semantic tradition has been a major force in the last decade with the many developments of Riesbeck's semantic expectation-based approach at Yale, like the ELI and CA parsers (Birnbaum and Selfridge, 1979; Riesbeck and Schank, 1976). These expectation-driven parsers constitute an interesting semantic parallel to the syntactically-based determinism of Marcus. These parsers have depended on general semantics, but the more bottom-up approach they, and Wilks's system, embody has been complemented by the top-down application of more specialised semantic information expressed in scripts and other large-scale knowledge structures; for some purposes, like those of FRUMP (deJong, 1979), these have been used to bypass detailed parsing altogether.

Much semantic parsing work, and especially that of Schank and his colleagues, as the term 'expectation' suggests, has drawn conspicuously on psychological argument in its support: this has always been available to show that humans seem relatively indifferent to surface syntactic structure (though they are sensitive to segment boundaries); and to show that humans may exploit enormous amounts of semantic (and pragmatic) information for processing even within the limits of the syllable, without leaving semantic operations until syntactic ones have identified potential phrase and clause boundaries. Steedman, in this volume, makes use of such evidence to justify a semantics—syntax combination for parsing in which syntax plays a minimal role, so that semantics can be immediately brought to bear on syntactic ambiguity.

Unfortunately, at the level of fine detail, we have no reliable experimental evidence as to human parsing strategies: thus it is quite possible that some backtracking occurs for sentences other than garden paths. All that does seem plausible is that human discourse processing is very inhomogeneous, so that any computer program which is tidy in its principles, in the sense of always doing X before doing Y, systematically, is not likely to constitute a good psychological model.

Computational parsing workers are thus, to use the old theoretical distinction, performance rather than competence oriented, and by necessity, unless one is prepared to restrict oneself to general computational principles, independent of any implementation or system. Some AI workers, like McCarthy, have felt able to adopt this position, but it remains an extreme one. It is this opposition, rather than the syntax/semantics one, which is the really important contrast: at the Workshop from which this book stems it was observed that the current automatic parsing slogan is "Bring *all* the information you've got to bear as soon as you can"; but this is not a constructive recipe as far as assembling the ingredients or mixing them in the right order is concerned. The current state of the art in automatic parsing, as the many contemporary variations on the characterisation of semantic information shows, is at least as much a matter of facing up to problems as of exploiting a consensus technology.

There has, nevertheless, been significant progress in automatic parsing: the papers in this book do not detail it, but rather focus on current research problems. Yet the problems identified, and the style in which they are approached, reflect many common assumptions, and, more·importantly, considerable common experience. Thus one cannot usefully address a specific parsing problem, like conjunctions, without some experimental parsing experience, and the community has now gained this experience. It is true that the semanticist, faced with Jane Robinson's call for semantic help to deal with the problems produced by syntactically parsing "I will sing and dance" as conjoined declarative and imperative clauses does not feel any too confident; but he can start from the consolidated experience of those who have been engaged with syntax.

The papers in this book show that, in the present state of automatic natural language parsing, many constructions in English can be parsed, and that syntactic and semantic, and even pragmatic, information can be effectively combined to interpret sentences in a way that leads to further research and development questions. Enormous experience has also been gained in the more theoretical areas of types of grammar, and with grammar-testing tools like the chart parser. These gains are of great importance: automatic parsing has been established as a craft, implying the ability to write, quickly, grammars for specific purposes, or interpreters for these grammars. Those in the field have also provided themselves with general-purpose utilities which may be exploited for a range of different natural language processing applications and tasks: the DIALOGIC system at SRI (see Grosz *et al.*, 1982), for example, is a component of very different language processing systems.

Practical developments like these have served to reduce the polarisations set out earlier in this Introduction: Kaplan and Bresnan's Lexical–Functional Grammar (Kaplan and Bresnan, 1982), and Hudson and McCord's Daughter Dependency Grammar (McCord, 1982) can be set alongside GPSG as developments in linguistic theory friendly to computational parsing. Equally, some operational syntax-driven systems, like those of SRI and BBN, because they have to be practical, are more friendly to semantics than earlier systems founded in the syntactic tradition. Finally, Kay's work (see this volume) on the theory of grammar and on the theory of parsing has done much to bring theoretical linguistics and computational analysis together.

However, although this convergence is visible, and useful operational systems are now being built, they are still Bronze Age systems: the really intractable problems, such as when exactly inference can be usefully called during parsing, have scarcely been formulated, and we still have a long way to go in applying to everyday systems, the theoreticians' developments in this area.

One final point should be made about the papers in this book: the contributors were originally invited to provide short position papers for the Workshop, on the assumption that fuller expositions of their findings and views were available elsewhere. We believe that the active interchange of views is encouraged by brief, clear position statements, and that a set of such statements may be of interest to a wider audience. However, some authors took the opportunity to revise and extend their statements for publication, accounting for the difference, in length and style manifested by the papers as they are now.

REFERENCES

Birnbaum, L. and Selfridge, M. (1979) Problems in conceptual analysis of natural language. Research Report No. 168, Department of Computer Science, Yale University.

deJong, G. F. (1979) Skimming stories in real time: an experiment in integrated understanding. Research Report No. 158, Department of Computer Science, Yale University.

Grosz, B. *et al.* (1982) DIALOGIC: a core natural language processing system. In *COLING 82,* Proceedings of the Ninth International Conference on Computational Linguistics. Amsterdam: North-Holland.

Harman, G. (1963) Generative grammars without transformation rules. *Language* **39,** 597–616.

Joshi, A. K. and Levy, L. S. (1982) Phrase structure trees bear more fruit than you would have thought. *American Journal of Computational Linguistics* **8,** 1–11.

Kaplan, R. M. and Bresnan, J. (1982) Lexical–functional grammar: a formal system of grammatical representation. In J. Bresnan (ed.) *The Mental Representation of Grammatical Relations.* Cambridge, Mass.: MIT Press.

Marcus, S. P. (1980) *A Theory of Syntactic Recognition for Natural Language.* Cambridge, Mass.: MIT Press.

McCord, M. (1982) Using slots and modifiers in logic grammars for natural language. *Artificial Intelligence* **18,** 327–367.

Riesbeck, C. K. (1975) Conceptual analysis. In R. C. Shank (ed.) *Conceptual Information Processing.* Amsterdam: North-Holland.

Riesbeck, C. K. and Schank, (1976) Comprehension by computer: expectation-based analysis of sentences in context. Research Report No. 78, Department of Computer Science, Yale University.

Wilks, Y. A. (1967) Transformational grammars again. Memo SP-2936, System Development Corporation, Santa Monica, California.

Wilks, Y. A. (1975) An intelligent analyser and understander of English. *Communications of the ACM* **18,** 264–274.

Winograd, T. (1972) *Understanding Natural Language.* Edinburgh: Edinburgh University Press.

Woods, W. A. (1970) Transition network grammars for natural language analysis. *Communications of the ACM* **13,** 591–606.

Natural language processing: a critical analysis of the structure of the field, with some implications for parsing

H. Thompson, University of Edinburgh

ABSTRACT

I present here a diagnosis of the somewhat incoherent state of Natural Language research nowadays. I draw a division between Computational Linguistics proper and Computational Psycholinguistics. Orthogonal to this distinction lies the scale from applied to theoretical concerns. At the applied end of the scale, where most of what is now being done lies, there is little distinction between Computational Linguistics proper and Computational Psycholinguistics. Much of the confusion in the field lies in a mistaken claim of theoretical significance for such work. I introduce a third term into the classification – Theory of Linguistic Computation, which is the correct label for much AI work on natural language. I close with some predictions about how the three theoretical areas will progress, what we can reasonably expect on the applied side in the near future, and what the implications for parsing are within each of the divisions.

I. NATURAL LANGUAGE PROCESSING: ITS DISPUTATIOUS PAST

A few years ago a vigorous debate was waged in the pages of *Cognition* on the general subject of the relationship of work done within AI on natural language as against work done within theoretical linguistics (of the Chomskian persuasion) (Dresher and Hornstein, 1976; Dresher and Hornstein, 1977a; Dresher and Hornstein, 1977b; Winograd, 1977; Schank and Wilensky, 1977). Considerable heat and perhaps some light were generated, but one suspects that in the end both sides retired from the field secure in the knowledge they had won (the naively optimistic ones) or at least supposing they had demonstrated the internal consistency of their own and their friends' position (the realists).

Overt interest in this issue has since died down almost as quickly as it blew up, but I fear that on the AI side of the fence this is a classic case of repression, and we are suffering the predictable consequences: schizoid neurosis.

On the one hand we find people who stoutly maintain that their work is of no (linguistic/psychological) theoretical significance – they are simply tool-builders, constructing artefacts which incidentally manipulate English words and sentences. Yet such folk can rarely resist the temptation to indulge in a bit of speculation as to the *possible* theoretical significance of some aspect of their work, *if* it were to be taken as the basis for a (psychological/linguistic) theory. "Theorem envy" is just as real in Cognitive Science as it was/is in Social Science.

On the other hand we have those who say they *are* doing (psychology/ linguistics) — it's just their theoretical framework is computational. There are fewer of these than formerly. Furthermore they tend to be young. Those of us in the university world are all too familiar with the new postgraduate who is eager to unlock the mysteries of language with his/her shiny new computer. And it is not too far-fetched I think to describe what eventually follows on as a loss of innocence.

If this innocence which is lost is in their case typically a naivety as to the complexity of human language, then there is a parallel case on the other side — that of the mature linguistic/psychologist who discovers computers and latches on to the promise of rigour and power they appear to hold out. Their naivety is computational, and although perhaps rarer, is equally frustrating.

What are we to make of our schizogenic past? For of course this dichotomy is not new: it has its roots in the old "cognitive simulation vs. abstract theory of intelligence" debate. Nor has it been completely ignored more recently: the opposition of the "neats" and the "scruffies" (IJCAI '81) is just the same debate under another name. The problem lies in people's failure to recognise the relevance *for them* of this debate. A clear understanding of what the watershed issues are and where one stands with respect to them is a prerequisite to non-schizoid research. Altogether too few of us seem to have taken the time to arrive at such an understanding.

By making explicit the distinctions I have implicitly been appealing to above, I hope to provide some impetus towards the necessary self-examination. Whether this impetus comes from recognition of the accuracy of the picture I paint, or from disagreement with it, is of less concern to me than that a motivation to confront these issues is generated.

II. NLP: ITS CONFUSED PRESENT

We can distinguish two broad categories of endeavour involving computational processing of natural language, which I will call Computational Linguistics proper and Computational Psycholinguistics. I will reserve Computational Linguistics for a superordinate term, covering these two as well as some others which will come up later.

Cross-cutting this distinction is another, teleological, one, which distinguishes applied from theoretical goals.

I do not mean at the applied end of this scale to include the instrumental use of computation in the pursuit of linguistic or psychological goals — for this I will use the terms Computation in service to Linguistics and Computation in service to Psychology. Computation in service to Linguistics covers on the one hand much of 'traditional' Computational Linguistics — concordance and usage count tabulation, aids to the lexicographer, etc.; and on the other the more recent applications of computational techniques to assist the theoretical linguist, for example by providing digital speech labs for phoneticians and phonologists, e.g. at the UCLA and Edinburgh phonetics labs, and by providing grammarians with generators and parsers, e.g. the work of Friedman with respect to transformational grammar (Zwicky *et al.*, 1965) and more recently Montague grammar (Friedman and Warren, 1978), and my own work with respect to GPSG (Thompson, 1981b). Computation in service to Psychology, although little discussed in the literature, encompasses a considerable amount of work, focussing on the integration of the computer into the experimental laboratory, both for administering experiments and for collecting and analysing the results.

Rather what I mean by Applied Computational Linguistics is the instrumental use of language processing, typically as a part of a larger system with some practical goal, such as accessing a database or helping to solve a problem. The natural language components of LIFER and MYCIN (Hendrix, 1977; Shortliffe, 1976) are paradigm cases.

Much of what goes on in the field belongs in this category. The theoretical end of the scale is much less densely populated. At this end we must preserve the distinction between linguistics and psychology. After a period of what can only be called wishful thinking, both linguists and psychologists seem to be returning to the position that their goals and methodologies are independent. A recent expression of this consensus, arrived at on the basis of widely differing motivations, could be seen at the joint Royal Society/British Academy meeting on the Psychological Mechanisms of Language (The Royal Society, 1981; Thompson, 1981a).

Theoretical linguists (non-Chomskian) attempt to characterise the nature of an abstract object, either a language or Language. Theoretical linguists (Chomskian) attempt to characterise the nature of a "psychological" object, either a grammar or Grammar. But this is a distinction without a difference, as in both cases the methods by which the object is accessed are the same, and are not those of the psychologist.

Thus theoretical Computational Linguistics proper consists in attempting such a characterisation *computationally*. I know of only one thoroughgoing example of this — Martin Kay's Functional Grammar (Kay, 1979). Cognitive Grammar (Lakoff and Thompson, 1975a; Lakoff and Thompson, 1975b), Lexical—Functional Grammar (Kaplan and Bresnan, 1982), the work of Ritchie (Ritchie, 1980) and of Steedman and Ades (Ades and Steedman, 1982) are other contenders for the label, but they are not unalloyed examples: Cognitive Grammar because it was insufficiently specified, LFG and Steedman and Ades's work because they are not in fact essentially computational, and Ritchie's work because it has not altogether escaped its Applied Computational Linguistics origins.

On the other hand psycholinguists are concerned with the cognitive structures and processes which are involved in human beings' linguistic behaviour. Nowadays any respectable practitioner in the field presents his/her theories in a quasi-computational fashion, as the dichotomy of "structures and processes" suggests. Again I know of only one occasion on which working *psychologists* have ever put forward a *computer program* as a way of presenting their psycholinguistic theories, namely Kaplan and Wanner's work on relative clauses (Kaplan, 1972; Wanner *et al.*, 1975; Wanner and Maratsos, 1978). The force of this statement is reduced somewhat by the fact that Alan Newell and his coworkers in the US and Richard Young among others in the UK have presented production systems as theories of some *non*-linguistic cognitive phenomena, but even they have not confronted fully one of the major stumbling blocks in the way of genuine Computational Psychology: the realisation question. This is the question of what counts as what − that is, what aspects of the computer program are considered fair game for comparison with what aspects of human behaviour. Barton (Barton, 1980) presents a telling analysis of the weakness of most attempts at Computational Psycholinguistics in this respect. Again Wanner and Kaplan are the only case I know of where this problem had been confronted at all.

If the psycholinguistics cannot be said to have been doing Computational Psycholinguistics, what about the many AI researchers who have claimed psychological plausiuility for their programs, or have even gone so far as to call them embodiments of explanatory psycholinguistic theories? It is they who have most thoroughly mistaken their place in the map I am constructing. Without making explicit the realisation hypotheses they assume, and without doing the experiments on human subjects necessary to test the conjunction of their theory and their realization hypotheses, they cannot claim any relationship with psychology, and hence whatever they are doing it is not Computational Psycholinguistics.

In general if AI researchers wish to legitimate their claim to be doing Computational Psycholinguistics, they must take their psychology a great deal more seriously than they have heretofore. The attractiveness of vaguely psychological posturing is easy to understand − we all share a tendency in that direction. But the time has come to put up or shut up: either put in the time and effort to provide hypotheses with explicit psycholinguistic content and go on to test them (or have them tested), or else eschew claims of psychological significance.

On the other hand, Computational Linguistics proper as described above doesn't seem to cover much of what we think of as theoretical in the field of natural language processing. But I do not mean to relegate everything else into the Applied Computational Linguistics category. It has given rise to its own independent meta-discipline, which in a spirit of aggrandisement I will call the Theory of Linguistic Computation.

That is to say that when people are considering deterministic versus non-deterministic parsing, or "syntactic" versus "non-syntactic" language processing, or the role of planning in dialogue models, they are engaging in a computational sort of theorising about language processing in the abstract. The object of concern is not language itself, which is the domain of linguistics proper, computational or otherwise. Nor is it the human language processing faculty, which is the domain of (computational) psycholinguistics. Rather it is the communicative process in the abstract, which is not an object at all. Just as philosophy of language is independent of linguistics and psycholinguistics, but frequently draws ideas and terminology from them, so I think this newly named but previously existing field should have independent status.

The important point here is that although they may draw on linguistics and psychology, philosophers of language do not claim to be *doing* linguistics or psychology, and neither should we.

My proliferation of terminology is now at an end, and Figure 1 lays out the relationships I have been discussing.

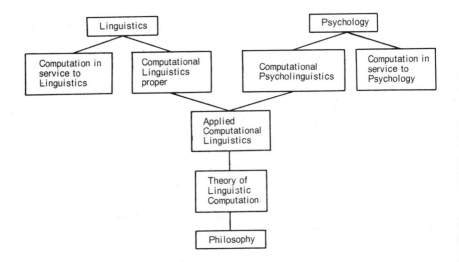

Fig. 1 – The structure of Computational Linguistics.

III. NLP: ITS UNCERTAIN FUTURE

In considering where we may go from here, the above analysis can be useful. Computation in service to Linguistics and Computation in service to Psychology will grow in importance as the availability of computational resources to working linguists and psychologists increases. Computational Linguistics proper may well prove viable, although so far only in the area of morphology has there been any sign of interest from the linguistics side (Kaplan and Kay, 1981; Kaplan and

Kay 1982; Sagvall, 1978). I am sceptical about the short-term future of Computational Psycholinguistics, but as the computational literacy of psychologists
increases, we may see some progress here. To the extent which Applied Computational Linguistics draws on linguistics, Computational Linguistics proper and
Theory of Linguistic Computation, as opposed to psychology and Computational Psycholinguistics, progress can be expected here as well. This amounts
to saying that such progress will be confined to areas of Applied Computational
Linguistics which do not involve natural language understanding. This somewhat
contentious assertion is based on the belief that to the extent that NLP depends
on NLU, it depends on (Computational) Psycholinguistics. An adequate (Computational) Psycholinguistics, however, depends on major breakthroughs in our
ability to "put the world in the machine", breakthroughs which do not appear
imminent. Such a breakthrough in computational ontology/philosophy of mind
is necessary to (Computational) Psycholinguistics and NLU because NLU, like
most human processes, is dominated by prejudice/pre-understanding/expectation,
and is thus crucially dependent on a detailed and extensive model of the world.

Thus, while we can expect large vocabulary word and phrase recognition
systems, man—machine interactions with respect to limited domains in restricted
subsets of English and other languages, extensive machine assistance for trans-
lators, and reasonable quality text-to-speech systems, we will not have unrestricted continuous speech recognition, unrestricted text understanding, or
fully automatic high-quality unrestricted machine translation in the foreseeable
future.

IV. SOME IMPLICATIONS FOR PARSING

What are the practical, which is to say methodological, consequences of taking
the above seriously with respect to parsing? I will consider each of the six
constituents of Computational Linguistics from Fig. 1 above in turn.

IV.1 Computation in service to Linguistics

For non-transformational grammatical formalisms, which I suppose will domi-
nate the field for the next little while, chart parsing technology seems hard to
beat. Admittedly I have a stake in this being true. I will be in a position to
distribute a well-documented, clean, flexible chart parsing framework in the
very near future, and I modestly suppose that anyone setting out to provide a
research tool for linguists developing grammars within a particular formalism
would do well to start from that as a base.

It is important to note the distinction between developing grammars within
a specified formalism, and developing the formalism, as Joyce Friedman pointed
out to me recently. The former can be done with machine assistance *without*
either computational sophistication on the part of the linguist, or the active
participation of a programmer, provided a sufficient initial investment in system

documentation and bomb-proofing is made. The latter cannot, and it is important that potential client linguists understand the distinction and what follows from it.

IV. 2 Computation in service to Psychology
I don't see any interaction with parsing here.

IV.3 Computational Linguistics proper
There is not really much to be said here. The interpretation of (morpho)phonemic rules as finite state transducers will I think prove very productive, but I don't have any insight as to what successful theories which are essentially computational may emerge at the syntactic level. Interestingly enough at the semantic level I think one can see much of the current excitement about discourse models as involving an essentially computational approach, but this has little to do with parsing.

IV.4 Computational Psycholinguistics
I am not really in a position to speak here. To my (very limited) knowledge, Kaplan, Janet Fodor, Marslen-Wilson and Steedman have all got some sort of commitment in this direction, but they do not so far seem to have made any progress towards discharging it. I know of no non-psychologists who are even trying.

IV.5 Theory of Linguistic Computation
I put this ahead of Applied Computational Linguistics as I will depend in my discussion of that on some things said in this section. It seems to me that there are two crucial questions here, one of which does not really involve parsing. This is the one about "putting the world in the machine". The millennial language processing system will be expectation-driven in a very rich sense, and will need to "know what's going on" ahead of time in a pretty profound way. How we move forward from our current almost total incapacity in this area I don't know.

Assuming no radical insights in the near future on that point, the question that remains to us is whether or not we can cash in that most frequently uttered of pious platitides, with which virtually every debate on "syntactic" versus "semantic" language processing always ends: "But of course we all agree that the ideal processor would use both syntactic AND semantic knowledge on an equal footing." – frequently assented to, but rarely if ever tackled.

It seems to me that even in the absence of large amounts of world knowledge, this avenue needs to be explored. The crucial questions seem to me to be: How can we use low-level e.g. constituent structure syntactic knowledge without being led down the slippery slope to massively recursive syntactic structures? How can we integrate lexically based functional expectations with the above? What is the 'output' of the analysis process?

The last of these is crucial, and I think that by and large we have been giving the wrong answer for a long time. If we set our sights on understanding, rather than e.g. question answering, then any answer of the form: the 'meaning' of the utterance, expressed as LISP expression/intensional logic formula/preference tree/CD net, makes little sense, because if carried to its logical conclusion this suggests that the result of reading, say this article, should be a vast collection of such 'meanings', and this seems untenable to me.

Thus the parsing question in this context leads inescapably for me to the knowledge representation question, and I think interesting work in this area will no longer be able to proceed in isolation from much deeper questions.

IV.6 Applied Computational Linguistics

I am of two minds here. There is a tension between the demands of economy and flexibility. Systems which include a purely syntactic phase are easy to construct, and I don't think it too far-fetched to see in the near future, e.g. a chart parser for GPSG on a chip, which you could buy together with a reasonably extensive grammar to plug into your expert system product. The problem with such an approach is that it is fragile and inflexible. It is not easily adaptable to quasi-grammatical or abbreviated utterances. It is also unclear whether a satisfactory domain-independent semantics can be supplied. On the other hand semantic grammars and their ilk are much less fragile, much more flexible. But they are much more expensive to produce and use, requiring as they do a programmer with linguistic sophistication to be involved throughout. And they must to a greater or lesser extent be recreated for each new domain.

I can think of four database access projects which sort of spread out along an axis from pure syntax to almost pure semantics, and perhaps in a year or so a comparative evaluation will help clarify which approach is most appropriate: Hewlett Packard's GPSG based system, Karen Sparck Jones's relatively domain independent syntactico-semantic project, SRI's customisable LADDER systems and the CD based JETS work at Illinois, which started out with ATNs but gave up on them because of fragility problems.

On a related point I should say that I am somewhat sceptical that natural language is the vehicle of choice for computationally naive access to databases. My suspicion is that a well-designed interactive system based on a high-resolution display, menus, and a pointing device would out-perform a natural language interface for most applications. John Brown at Xerox may be doing something in the way of controlled experiment to test this, but somewhat to my surprise I know of no other comparisons along these lines.

CONCLUSION

In closing, the obligatory pious hope: in looking ahead and planning parsing work to come, I hope some thought will be given to where the intended system fails in the structure laid out above, and that this may provide some useful guidelines as to how to proceed.

REFERENCES

Ades, A. and Steedman, M. (1982) On the order of words. *Linguistics and Philosophy* **4**, 517–558.

Barton, E. (1980) Psychological Reality and the Propriety of Abstraction. Ms. Artificial Intelligence Laboratory, M.I.T.

Dresher, E. and Hornstein, N. (1976) On some supposed contributions of Artificial Intelligence to the scientific study of language. *Cognition* **4**, 321–398.

Dresher, E. and Hornstein, N. (1977a) Reply to Schank and Wilensky.

Dresher, E. and Hornstein, N. (1977b) Reply to Winograd. *Cognition* **5**, 377–392.

Friedman, J. and Warren, D. S. (1978) A parsing method for Montague Grammars. *Linguistics and Philosophy* **2**, 347–372.

Hendrix, G. G. (1977) The LIFER Manual: A Guide to Building Practical Natural Language Interfaces. Technical Note 138, SRI International.

Kaplan, R. M. (1972) Augmented transition networks as psychological models of sentence comprehension. *Artificial Intelligence* **3**, 77–100.

Kaplan, R. M. and Bresnan, J. (1982) Lexical–functional grammar: A formal system of grammatical representation. In J. Bresnan (ed.) *The Mental Representation of Grammatical Relations*. Cambridge, Mass: MIT Press.

Kaplan, R. M. and Kay, M. Phonological rules as finite state transducers. Presented at the Winter Meeting of the Linguistic Society of America, New York.

Kaplan, R. M. and Kay, M. (1982) Word Recognition. Technical Report, Xerox PARC, Palo Alto, California. To appear.

Kay, M. (1979) Functional Grammar. In *Proceedings of the Fifth Annual Meeting of the Berkeley Linguistics Society*. Berkeley Linguistics Society.

Lakoff, G. and Thompson H. S. (1975a) Introducing Cognitive Grammar. In *Proceedings of the First Annual Meeting of the Berkeley Linguistics Society*. Berkeley Linguistics Society.

Lakoff, G. and Thompson, H. S. (1975b) Dative questions and Cognitive Grammar. In *Papers from the Parasession on Functionalism*. Chicago Linguistic Society.

Ritchie, G. (1980) *Computational grammar — an artificial intelligence approach to linguistic description*. Hassocks, Sussex: Harvester Press.

The Royal Society (1981) *The Psychological Mechanisms of Language. Philosophical Transactions of the Royal Society. Series B,* 295. London: The Royal Society.

Sagvall Hein, A.-L. (1978) Finnish morphological analysis in the Reversible Grammar System. In *Proceedings of the 7th International Conference on Computational Linguistics.* COLING, Bergen.

Schank, R. C. and Wilensky, R. (1977) Response to Dresher and Hornstein. *Cognition* **5**, 133–145.

Shortliffe, E. (1976) *Computer-Based Medical Consultations: MYCIN.* New York: Elsevier.

Thompson, H. S. (1981a) Joint Royal Society/British Academy Meeting on the Psychological Mechanisms of Language: A critical report. *AISB Quarterly* **40–41**, 16–19.

Thompson, H. S. (1981b) Chart parsing and rule schemata in GPSG. In *Proceedings of the Nineteenth Meeting of the Association for Computational Linguistics.* ACL, Stanford, California.

Wanner, E. R. and Maratsos, M. (1978) An ATN approach to comprehension. In M. Halle, J. Bresnan, and G. A. Miller (eds.) *Linguistic Theory and Psychological Reality.* Cambridge, Mass., MIT Press.

Wanner, E. R., Kaplan, R. M., and Shiner, S. (1975) Garden Paths in Relative Clauses. Ms. Harvard University.

Winograd, T. (1977) On some contested suppositions of Generative Linguistics about the scientific study of language. *Cognition* **5**, 151–197.

Zwicky, A., Friedman, J., Hall, B. and Walker, D. (1965) The Mitre syntactic analysis procedure for Transformational Grammar. *Proceedings of the Fall Joint Computer Conference, AFIPS Conference Proceedings* **27**, 317–326.

Parsing — an MT perspective

R. L. Johnson, University of Manchester Institute for Science and Technology

This paper is a statement of position on parsing from the point of view of some-one involved in fully automatic machine translation (MT), that is the kind of MT in which human intervention is limited to text preparation and post-editing. This kind of MT program is intended to run unsupervised in batch mode rather than in real time under user control, and so cannot transfer responsibility for its linguistic decisions to a human operator. In the MT systems I am interested in the function of the parser is to convert source language text input to an abstract structure, called the Intermediate Representation (IR). The IR, after some manipulation to adjust for structural idiosyncrasies in the target language and to substitute target language lexical items, is then used as input to a target synthe-siser. It is intended that synthesis should be deterministic, and that non-deter-minism in the interlingual phase should be limited to decisions about lexical items which are unambiguous with respect to the source language but have multiple translation equivalents in the target language (cf. 'wall' in English vs. 'muro' and 'parete' in Italian). The parser should therefore be capable ideally of yielding for a given source language text a single IR which is unambiguous up to the choice of lexical items in the target language.

Design of an effective parser for this kind of application raises preoccupa-tions which are rather different from those likely to be expressed by other participants in this workshop. In particular, the criteria for deciding on the ideal form of an MT parser are typically engineering criteria, as I shall try to illustrate in the rest of this paper.

PARSERS AS TRANSDUCERS

I propose to use as a basis for discussion a simple characterisation of a parser expressed in the block diagram (Fig. 1), where the circles represent data and the rectangle marked P is the parser. T and R represent respectively a class of texts and a class of representations derived from those texts by the parsing process. In this view, a parser is a transducer which converts texts into some kind of 'abstract' structure. The characterisation is meant to be uncontentious — although Steven Small at least would disagree, claiming (personal communication) that his parser produces no tangible output but merely, as it were, exhibits behaviour appropriate to given inputs. In engineering terms, it is rather important to know the properties of T and R *a priori*, since the ultimate success of an applications parser depends on its ability to get the mappings from T to R right. In any case, it seems to me that any discussion of the internal working of a parser depends on a clear answer to the logically prior question of what the parser is intended to produce and what inputs it is designed to handle. It seems somewhat gratuitous to enter into debate on the plausibility/efficiency of a *parsing* — as opposed to recognition — strategy without reference to the credibility/usefulness of the idealised artefact which the parser is intended to build.

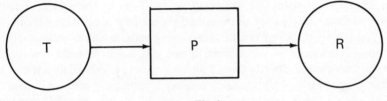

Fig. 1.

WHAT A PARSER NEEDS TO KNOW

Another way of looking at a parser is as an implementation of a theory about the relationships between a class of texts T and a class of representations R. Given some text, the parser applies the theory to a member of T, and if the implementation is correct the result should be the corresponding member(s) of R. This kind of theory implies a number of different kinds of knowledge about language and linguistic processes, all of which are somehow embodied in the parser. For MT purposes, it is useful to distinguish four types of knowledge which need to be present.

(a) Well-formedness conditions
These are the conditions which determine the class of inputs which the parser is equipped to handle, or, equivalently, define the language which can be parsed. They may be explicitly expressed as rules, or they may be embedded in procedures, or a mixture of both. In an ATN, for example, the basic conditions on well-formedness are expressed in the context-free grammar which underlies the RTN, supplemented by ad hoc procedural manipulations on registers. In some situations the input language is relatively easy to define *a priori*, much as a compiler specifies the well-formed constructs of a programming language. The situation in general purpose MT is rather more complicated: what is well-formed has to be assumed to be determined by the input rather than the parser. The consequence is that the parser must be able to make some useful decision on

unrecognised input *at execution time*; and the parser will probably need subsequently to be modified to take account of the new class of inputs. There are some important implications for system design here, having to do with the need for flexibility both at run time and in the facility to accept constant modification.

(b) Structure-building rules

Although it seems to me difficult to imagine a parser — as distinct from a recogniser — which does not produce output, many discussions of parsing strategies turn out to be essentially about recognition procedures which incidentally yield output somewhere along the way. As I have already pointed out, an MT parser is judged primarily on its output, in the form of some kind of intermediate structure. The nature of the structure–building component depends, of course, on the properties of the structures being built, as well as on interactions with other knowledge in the system. If our aim is just to build constituent structure trees derived directly from a phrase structure grammar, then it may be that the only structure-building rule necessary is simply a global instruction to turn the rewrite arrow through $90°$. Alternatively, if we have to build some kind of canonical structure which involves rearranging the order of constituents, then the rules for building structure are likely to be more complicated. Note that in a syntax-oriented MT system like TAUM METEO, which is designed around a production system architecture (cf. Colmerauer, 1970), the same productions serve both as well-formedness rules and as transduction rules — a relatively common arrangement.

(c) Knowledge about control

It is not sufficient to have access to rules which define what strings are well-formed and what structures can be built; a parser also needs to have knowledge of how to apply them. The third kind of knowledge, variously called control information, scheduling or metaknowledge, is frequently implicit — as in production system parsers — or bound up with other types of knowledge — as in ATNs. It is important to distinguish between control decisions which are taken simply to increase efficiency — like keeping a WFST to save recomputation — and those which affect the nature of the result — like rule-ordering in a top-down, depth-first parser which halts as soon as it finds a solution. In MT, while it is desirable that the first type of control should be built into the system, it is desirable that the second type should be external and user-definable. Unfortunately, many parsers do not distinguish between the two kinds of control information or between control information and other forms of knowledge. While this may be a useful attribute in systems where fine tuning is of the essence or where theoretical aims dictate a blurring of such distinctions, failure to differentiate can be disastrous in large MT systems where debugging and updating are constant priorities.

(d) Appropriateness criteria
In the general case, a good MT parser will deliver just one result, so the later
stages in the translation process can operate without having to deal with ambiguities which are characteristic of the source language. Boolean criteria of
well-formedness, used alone, tend either to be too weak, so you get

```
 [ [   Money] [ markets] [   [   close] [ down]]]
  S NP         V          NP Adj        N
```

as well as

```
 [ [   [ Money] [ markets]] [ close down]],
  S NP N         N           V
```

or too strong, so that you get nothing at all for

```
 ![ [   Money] [ promises] [   power]].
   S NP         V           NP
```

In cases like these, the parser needs to have access to some heuristic for choosing
the 'best' among available candidates, if more than one is available. The procedure may be explicit, for example some variant of preference semantics based
on computation of relative 'semantic density' of candidate structures (Wilks,
1973), or it may be implicit in some control decision like taking the first solution constructed from an ordered set of rules. In MT the most attractive course
seems to be the preference approach, operating with fairly weak co-occurrence
restrictions and using general criteria of 'felicitousness' to rank conflicting
solutions where they occur.

Again, one can imagine many parsing environments where this kind of conflict rarely occurs or is considered irrelevant: for example in 'semantic ATNs'
(Burton, 1976), where the universe of discourse is so tightly constrained that
co-occurrence restrictions can be assumed to hold consistently; in real time
systems generally, when ill-formed or ambiguous inputs can be referred back for
clarification; and in linguistic or psychological investigations where such phenomena are just not interesting in terms of the theory under examination.

DESIGNING MT PARSERS

The main problem with full-scale MT is *size* – size of the input language and size
of the team of people responsible for system development and maintenance.

Although the class of outputs from an MT parser is fairly well defined – or
should be – the class of possible inputs is so enormous as to be practically
impossible to predict when the system is designed. Consequently, linguistic
generalisations which appeared to hold when the system was first built tend to
become invalid rather quickly as the parser is exposed to a greater range of input
texts. MT systems are thus naturally prone to a fundamental instability which

has to be countered from the start by an intrinsic robustness in the system design. In the nature of things, the instability is almost certain to persist beyond the point when a system becomes operational and goes into service. If the system is to run — as is likely — unsupervised in batch mode, probably overnight, a failure in the parser which causes the system to hang up perhaps after the first sentence is quite unacceptable. Suppose, to take a banal example, that an English–Italian system finds in its input

> The president concluded that S.

The parser has 'conclude' in its dictionary, but does not have the information that 'conclude' can take a sentential complement. It therefore rejects the input and stops. This behaviour is clearly unfortunate. The least we can expect is that, like any good compiler, the parser will look for the next piece of input which it considers well-formed, insert a few asterisks in the place of the offending sentence, and carry on translating. A more useful strategy still would be, on discovering that a piece of the input is apparently ill-formed, to relax some of the constraints on well-formedness and try again. The result in this case could be something like

> ?Il presidente conclude che S

which is not particularly good Italian but certainly more intelligible than a string of spaces or asterisks.

The example is somewhat simplistic, but I believe the basic point is sound. The principle is really just an extension of the notion of preference to what appear to the parser to be syntactic as well as semantic anomalies — building into the parser an ability to do what it can with the information it has. The result looks something like a hierarchy of parsers, each requiring a weaker set of well-formedness conditions than the next, right down in the limit to the simple string substitution transducers of the 1950s. (A precondition for the functioning of the whole thing is of course that each process in the hierarchy should actually terminate in reasonable time, a condition which is not necessarily trivially simple to impose).

The other aspect of the size of an MT system is the number of individuals who at some time or other will contribute to it. Most of these contributions will be in the form of knowledge about language, ranging from many thousands of lexical entries to — one hopes — a fairly small amount of procedural or scheduling information. As the system becomes larger, it becomes increasingly important to maintain modularity, with defined interfaces between modules, so as to minimise the unintentional introduction of spurious interactions between system components. Moreover, since the majority of contributors are likely to be linguists, many of them computationally naive, it is desirable to provide a declarative formalism which maximises the separation between different types of knowledge.

The sort of system architecture which seems to me to respond best to these requirements is one which is basically declarative but without the massive homogeneity which characterises typical production systems. The ideal organisation requires a high level of modularity, with different types of rules and rule interpreters applicable to different types of task; for example: string manipulation rules for morphology/segmentation, phrase structure rules for determining well-formedness and building primitive constituent structure, explicit transduction rules for constructing canonical forms, and general criteria for ranking 'fuzzy' or partial matches to resolve multiple outputs. In addition, it is convenient to have some kind of declarative 'control language' (cf. Georgeff, 1979) for scheduling processes, so that the user can experiment with different control strategies without modifying the content of 'linguistic' rules. Finally, some kind of data structure like a chart, which preserves the history of a computation in an immediately accessible form, appears to offer the greatest flexibility as an aid both to debugging and to finding the best available parse for given input.

MT AND PSYCHOLOGICAL REALITY

Although I believe that designing and writing MT parsers is a worthy intellectual challenge, I imagine that many participants at this workshop will not consider parsing for MT a particularly interesting activity because it offers few insights into the way human beings actually understand language. I therefore offer some introspections about the way in which I myself as a human actually do translation. I discuss only translation of written text between Indo-European languages, which are the only ones I know. I also consider only translation of 'technical' or 'factual' texts, rather than recasting of literary works, of which I am incapable.

My introspection tells me that I do indeed translate from left to right, but that I tend to translate left to right by *sentence* rather than by *word* or *constituent*. However, my tendency is to follow as closely as possible the syntactic organisation of the original, making changes only when required by the rules of the target language or when I cannot find a lexical substitution with the appropriate category match. I also seem to detect the need for potential syntactic reorganisation *before* I produce any target language output, implying, I suppose, that I consider the entire syntactic structure of the sentence as a candidate for translation rather than producing my output piecemeal. Occasionally I find I need to go back and change something I have already written in a previous sentence, but these changes are usually occasioned by lexical rather than syntactic second thoughts. Most important of all, I am capable, so I am told, of producing quite adequate translations of texts which I do not actually understand – when the only information I have for key lexical items is a translation equivalent, without any semantic clues which I could use to impose a 'meaning'. Finally, if there are things I just cannot translate, I just leave them out – with a note – and carry on.

I am not for one moment suggesting that these anecdotal remarks should be taken seriously as a paradigm for MT, but I am trying to make a point. The technique which introspection suggests to me that I use to translate does not bear a great resemblance to the sort of mental activities generally assumed in the standard AI parsing model. I would speculate that this is probably because the activity of translating involves quite a different kind of understanding, and a conscious and deliberate application of linguistic knowledge which is altogether distinct from ordinary linguistic behaviour. Until we have a useful model of translation, there seems little point in confusing MT with issues of psychological reality.

REFERENCES

Burton, R. R. (1976). Semantic grammar: an engineering technique for constructing natural language understanding systems. BBN Report #3453, Bolt, Beranek and Newman Inc., Cambridge, Mass.

Colmerauer, A. (1970). Les Systèmes-Q ou un formalisme pour analyser et synthétiser les phrases sur ordinateur. Internal publication #43, Projet de Traduction Automatique, University of Montreal.

Georgeff, M. (1979). A framework for control in production systems. Memo #AIM-322, Artificial Intelligence Laboratory, Stanford University.

Wilks, Y. A. (1973). An artificial intelligence approach to machine translation. In R. C. Schank and K. M. Colby (eds.), *Computer Models of Thought and Language*. San Francisco: Freeman.

PART II

ATN parsing

Recognising conjunctions within the ATN framework

B. K. Boguraev, University of Cambridge

1. ABSTRACT

ATN grammars have been widely used for natural language parsing. However, providing a wide and comprehensive coverage of the varying conjunction constructions only through the grammar specification imposes a heavy burden on the grammar writer and produces an extremely bulky grammar. More importantly, attempts to provide a comprehensive set of rules for recognising coordinate constructions using the ATN formalism are destined to fail because of the constraints it places on moving between levels of computation during parsing. The paper presents an alternative approach to the conjunction problem: this is to extend the specification of the ATN interpreter by setting up a set of demons which take over control on encountering a conjunction and interleave their operation with the normal ATN state transition sequence.

This paper presents some ideas about extending the ATN mechanism to begin to deal with conjunctions. The emphasis is on *recognising* coordinate constructions keyed by "and" only (the assumption being that other conjoined constructs will lend themselves to similar analysis); no attempt will be made to discuss representation problems or the possible structure of a "Conj" semantic specialist. As a result the proposed mechanism will be as happy with the straightforward "hungry cats and dogs", as with the semantically different cases of symmetrical predicates, as in "Bill and John look alike", or asymmetric "and", as in "The Lone Ranger mounted his horse and rode into the sunset", etc.

2. CONJUNCTION AND ATNs

The ATN formalism, as presented in Woods (1970), although quite powerful in expressive power with regard to natural language grammars, faces serious problems when it comes to capturing the various coordinate constructions. To see why this is so, consider the (sketchy) ATN grammar for very simple noun phrases shown in Fig. 1.

$$Np \Rightarrow (det)\,(adj)^*\,noun\,(pp)^*$$

```
(Np/
        (Cat det . . . (to Np/det))
        (Jump Np/det . . .))
(Np/det
        (Cat adj . . . (to Np/det))
        (Cat noun . . . (to Np/Pop)))
(Np/Pop
        (Push pp/ . . . (to Np/Pop))
        (Pop (Npbuild) . . .))
```

Fig. 1

In order to make explicit all the coordinate Np/ constructions which can be derived from this simple Np/ specification, we will need to add five new arcs to the network (see Fig. 2).

```
(Np/ . . .)
(Np/det
        (Cat adj . . .)
        (Cat noun . . .)
        (Wrd and (to Np/))           : "the hungry and the lazy cats"
        (Wrd and (to Np/det)))       : "the hungry and lazy cats"
(Np/Pop
        (Push pp/ . . .)
        (Wrd and (to Np/))           : "the cats and the dogs"
        (Wrd and (to Np/det))        : "the hungry cats and dogs"
        (Wrd and (to Np/Pop))        : "the cats with whiskers and with long tails"
        (Pop (Npbuild) . . .))
```

Fig. 2

Generally, one will need *Wrd and* arcs to take the ATN interpreter from just about every state in the network back to almost each preceding state on the same level, thus introducing large overheads in terms of additional arcs and complicated tests. This is clearly an undesirable state of affairs. To make things worse, even an explicit extension of the grammar along the lines just indicated will not in fact handle certain types of coordinate construction: *gapping*, i.e. certain cases of verb or object deletion, as in "Bill designed and Joe wrote the program", or *reduced conjunctions* where the conjoined fragments are not constituents of the grammar, as in "I bumped into and injured a friend".

3. RECOGNISING COORDINATE CONSTRUCTIONS BY EXTENDING THE ATN GRAMMAR SPECIFICATION

It is possible to adopt an alternative approach to extending the grammar: Blackwell proposes a single *Wrd and* arc taking the interpreter from the final to the initial state of computation, ready to analyse the second argument of a coordinate construction on a second pass through the network (Blackwell, 1981). Clearly this is not a straightforward process, since it may require that a computation be pended and holes be filled. The processing at any level may be interrupted by "and", and after the coordinate structure has been analysed, the deletions in either of the conjoined constituents will have to be undone. Blackwell's approach is based on implementing two constraints in the ATN formalism: the Directionality constraint and the Peripherality constraint (van Oirsouw, 1980).

The former states that, under the assumption of Coordination Reduction (i.e. deletion in conjoined constituents is done only under identity in the coordinated structures), elements on right branches are deleted backwards, and elements on left branches are deleted forwards. The latter states that coordinate reduction optionally deletes constituents from under one immediately dominating node at the time, in one direction, only if the deletion target is peripheral to the immediately dominating node (i.e. a noun cannot be deleted if it is sandwiched between two other constituents — "adj" and "nppmods" for example — unless one of those accompanies it).

These constraints help to decide when, which registers, and in which direction to copy, depending on whether the coordinate construction has been derived through forward or backward deletion in the following way. Different sets of registers are associated with the different constituents. Whenever "and" is encountered from a final (Pop) state, the system may expect to have to fill in gaps caused by deletion. The Directionality constraint makes it possible to predict which registers relating to the first consituent may need to be copied over and vice versa. Furthermore, under the Peripherality constraint, if the registers corresponding to the elements on either side of a given constituent have been filled, then the constituent cannot have suffered deletion, and must not be supplied from any other register if it has not been set in its expected place in the network ("the new books and the journals" is not reduced from "the new books and the new journals").

Blackwell's proposal is more elegant than the brute force one; but it pays the price of substantial overheads in duplicating almost all registers in all network levels. It also requires the introduction of unnatural *Jump arcs* in order to impose the Directionality constraint for backward deletion: consider the analysis of "the syntactic and semantic processing". This, in effect, pends the processing of a constituent and starts a parallel computation for a similar phrase. Blackwell's approach, in other words, bends the ATN formalism to cope with procedural programming constraints, which is, to say the least, an unnatural application for a grammar-writing tool of its kind.

Even so, Blackwell's strategy cannot be extended to cope with reduced conjunctions. Indeed, it seems that this class of coordinate structure simply cannot be represented by the ATN formalism, however bent. This is because an ATN provides only limited cross-level process communication provided by the *Sendr/Liftr* actions, and the constraint that the only exit from a current computation level is through the *Pop* arc. The problem here is that the recognition of conjoined fragments of different type requires pending the current level computation, and initiating or restarting another one through a different subnetwork, on a different level! There are no such facilities in the ATN formalism.

4. RECOGNISING COORDINATE CONSTRUCTIONS BY EXTENDING THE ATN INTERPRETER SPECIFICATION

All this suggests that what may instead be required is some extension of the way the ATN interpreter works. This is very much what Woods did in implementing his SYSCONJ facility for conjunctions (Woods, 1973). On encountering "and", the interpreter starts working in special mode. It pends its current processing and tries to branch from some non-deterministically selected preceding point of the computation, to parse the text following the "and". This text is parsed until a point in the input string is reached from which both the resumed and the suspended computations can share the subsequent text. Woods's approach is specially designed to analyse reduced conjunctions, where identical substrings on the left and the right of two conjoined constituents have been factored out, to leave reduced constructs as the two text arguments of "and": e.g. "(I) bumped into (a friend) and (I) injured (a friend)" has the text form "I bumped into and injured a friend".

Analysing reduced conjunctions is the distinctive advantage of this method, but as a general approach it is very costly, because treating all coordinate structures (apart from gapping ones which are not dealt with at all) as special cases within the reduced conjunction model makes for nasty combinatorial explosions. These are compounded from the alternative choices of past computation to resume, of point at which to resume it, and of time at which to restart the suspended process. Woods is presumably forced to sacrifice processing efficiency because the environment in which his LUNAR parser operates requires a deep transformational analysis of coordinate constructions in order to reconstruct the deletion process which has operated on the conjoined underlying sentences. However, it has been argued elsewhere (Boguraev, 1979) that if ATN syntactic constituent analysis is coupled with semantic constituent assembly within the framework of a passive parser, we can leave it to the later semantic specialist routines to construct a meaning representation from the analysed syntactic components. Specifically if we do not expect the syntactic ATN to deliver a complete explicit (Conj S1 S2) analysis after undoing all the deletions, reductions and transformations, and are willing instead to accept conjoined constituents of any type at any level, because we assume that the system's semantic component will know what to do with an Np with (Conj adj1 adj2), or a Vp with (conj Np1 Np2), we can avoid many of the overheads and problems discussed.

5. DYNAMIC ARC CONSTRUCTION AND EVALUATION

My approach is based on the principle that only categorially identical constituents can be conjoined (Radford, 1981). (The term *category* here covers both lexical and phrasal categories.) One of the basic problems with coding conjunctions into an ATN is that the ATN is a top-down expectational device, whereas "and" is a bottom-up marker, i.e. predicting where "and" might occur in the input string is a lost cause, because it may occur just about anywhere (see Fig. 2). However, once it has been detected, we can set up some expectations as to what might follow it. In fact, what could follow it is a constituent categorially identical to the one currently being processed, or just recognised. Indeed, if we look back at Fig. 2, we will notice that the common feature of the explicit *Wrd and* arcs is that within a level, all of them return to the beginning of a constituent categorially identical to the one just analysed. Thus, assuming that our interpreter is capable of keeping a history of the parsing process,[†] we can create a demon to be woken up when "and" is encountered. This demon will suspend normal processing, inspect the current context (the local registers which hold constituents recognised at this level) and recent history, and use the information these supply to dynamically construct a new ATN arc which seeks to recognise a constituent categorially similar to the one just completed or being currently processed. This of course means that we need either to construct and attempt the transition of a *Cat* arc looking for a word belonging to a specific lexical category, or, failing that, to construct and evaluate a *Push* arc, whose argument can be deduced from the history of the analysis process so far. Clearly, if this fails, we will need to construct another arc, pushing again to a constituent from which the current level of computation was initiated, and so on.

For example, suppose the ATN interpreter encounters "and" when it is in a state of the Np/ network having just recognised an "adj". Further, suppose it is trying to recognise a noun phrase while looking for a prepositional phrase while looking for a verb phrase while looking for a sentence: "He inquired about the recent and (relevant updates)". The search for another "adj" in this position will be satisfied and after conflating "recent and relevant" into one, the analysis may continue normally. If the text is "He inquired about the recent news and relevant updates", the search for another "adj" will fail, and a *Push Np/* arc will be constructed (Np being the label of the constituent currently being processed). If this fails as well, as in "He saw in the park and with the telescope ...", the

---

[†]In terms of the chain levels of computations (processes) currently active, chains of state transitions through a level, and the actions associated with some important transitions.

label of an embedding constituent (still being processed in a sense) will be retrieved from the stack, and a *Push pp/* arc constructed and evaluated, and so on.

The demon which constructs the arc searching for the conjoined constituent embodies the two constraints mentioned above, namely Directionality and Peripherality, i.e. decides which registers to initiate by copying existing structures, and which structures to duplicate at the end of a successful dynamic arc transition, at the same time making sure that only well-formed partial structures are copied across. This mechanism is capable óf dealing both with forward and backward deletion in coordinate constructions, as well as combinations of these:

* forward deletion:

  "the tall houses with spires and + + + with gables"
  "the tall houses with spires and + + buildings with gables"

* backward deletion:

  "tall + + and austere houses with spires"
  "the tall + + and the austere houses with spires"

* forward and backward deletion:

  "the tall + + and + austere houses down the road".

Note that the dynamic arc construction is carried out until a successful transition of the arc occurs. Thus for the phrase "spaghetti with red sauce and wine", the extended interpreter on its single scan through the network will identify only "sauce and wine" as a conjoined group; the subsequently invoked semantic specialist(s) have to be relied on to get all the semantically alternative readings for the whole phrase. Thus, although the semantic components may have a lot of work to do, we have only a single pass through the text to do the syntactic work.

Reduced conjunctions can be dealt with by an extension of this strategy through the provision of a second demon: this waits for the computation initiated by the dynamic arc evaluation to initiate a search for the constituent expected at the point of the first demon activation (which is easy, because the ATN is a powerful predictive mechanism). On activation the second demon merges and builds a (Conj const1 const2) structure, and normal ATN processing is then resumed. Finally, *gapping*, which is a very different phenomenon, has to be considered separately, but it can be dealt with very easily by hard-wiring into the grammar.

6. CONCLUSIONS

The paper presents a hybrid method for recognition of coordinate constructions by an ATN parser, based both on (internally) extending the ATN interpreter specification and (externally) extending the ATN grammar. This approach seems to be superior to others proposed in several respects:

(1) It allows for more natural extension, compared with Woods (1973), of the way the ATN interpreter works in that there is no essential change of its specified mode of behaviour; only a slight interrupt to construct a new data structure, which is external to the grammar, but still totally compatible with the interpreter's view of the world.

(2) The decision about which arc to construct for searching for the second component of the coordinate structure is well defined in terms of the processing history of the interpreter. This means that, unlike Woods, the selection of a past parser configuration to resume is not a non-deterministic process, which reduces the danger of combinatorial explosion. The desired symmetry between the two constituents can moreover be imposed quite naturally by the actions on the arc.

(3) Since any formal grammar of English, together with the Directionality and Peripherality constraints, implicitly describes the classes of co-ordinate structures acceptable to the grammar, there is no need for the grammar writer to worry at all about explicitly specifying the syntax of conjunctions. This, in contrast to Blackwell's approach, clearly saves both man and machine effort.

7. REFERENCES

Blackwell, S, A. (1981) Processing conjunctions in an ATN parser. Unpublished M.Phil. Dissertation, University of Cambridge.

Boguraev, B. K. (1979) Automatic resolution of linguistic ambiguities. Technical Report No. 11, University of Cambridge Computer Laboratory, Cambridge.

Radford, A. (1981) *Transformational Syntax*. Cambridge: Cambridge University Press.

van Oirsouw, R. R. (1980) Deletion processes in coordinate structures in English. Ph.D. Thesis, University of Cambridge.

Woods, W. A. (1970) Transition network grammars for natural language analysis. *Communications of the ACM* **13**, 591–606.

Woods, W. A. (1973) An experimental parsing system for transition network grammars. In *Natural Language Processing*, Rustin, R. (ed.), New York: Algorithmics Press.

Parsing interactions and a multi-level parser formalism based on cascaded ATNs

Thomas Christaller and **Dieter Metzing**, University of Hamburg; University of Bielefeld

1. LINGUISTIC MOTIVATION

The parsing formalism to be introduced in the next section has been developed in order to analyse pragmatic properties of a certain type of discourse in a certain domain. Though this formalism may usefully be evaluated on different grounds, the requirements of a context of application will generally be an important challenge to a parser being developed.

Some dialogue-specific requirements:

(1) Special recognition devices applicable to pragmatic categories are needed.

We are interested in the process during which speakers recognise step by step which kind of verbal act appeared at which part of a dialogue. The kinds of dialogues considered are task-oriented dialogues, more specifically: naturally occurring direction givings.

(2) Representations for sequential and hierarchical properties of verbal acts are needed.

We are interested in the 'syntactic' structure of verbal acts occurring in routinised task-oriented dialogues. These acts may be either speech acts or units larger/smaller than speech acts. We suppose that a certain kind of ATN is a useful tool in order to recognise these units.

(3) A belief component and operations modifying speakers' beliefs are needed.

The parser should interact with a component of speakers' beliefs (e.g. general knowledge, current belief contexts), for the production/recognition of verbal acts presupposes certain states of speakers' beliefs will be modified in the course of the dialogue.

(4) A framework for different interacting modules is needed.

For reasons of generality we are interested in modules (e.g. several ATNs or 'subparsers') specifying general syntactic, semantic and interactional information on the one hand and special task-oriented or special linguistic information on the other hand.

(5) An organisational framework for modules analysing dialogue utterances incrementally is needed.

There are several empirical investigations studying structural as well as process-oriented properties of the type of interaction considered here (direction givings; cf. Klein, 1979; Metzing, 1982; Psathas and Kozloff, 1976; Riesbeck, 1980; Stenning, 1977; Wunderlich, 1978). But although an incremental analysis seems to be especially appropriate in the case at hand (e.g. the next speaker may (dis-)confirm pragmatic assumptions made by the first speaker), this analysis has not yet been attempted in this domain. Which kind of information appearing at which position in the input stream induces a hearer to assign which verbal act category? We are running a psycholinguistic experiment in order to get some more information about processing units and the communication between processing components (cf. Marslen-Wilson and Tyler, 1980).

(6) Though a Cascaded ATN is a good candidate to be tested when the above requirements are to be met, it will have to be modified for at least the following reasons:

- sequential ('ATN-style') orderings, useful for the syntactic, interactional and task-specific component, do not seem useful for a semantic (case frame) component;
- input not relevant for a certain component should be sent to the next one in a hierarchy of components;
- special components (e.g. a task-specific one) should be inserted in the course of processing if necessary.

Since there is not enough space to describe our dialogue model in any detail, an essential part of it, a generalised version of a Cascaded ATN, will be presented in the next section. In parsing verbal interactions we became especially interested in parsing interactions, and we hope to learn more about both. Furthermore, we think that experiments with more complex parsers will redefine the role of parsers as well as the role of inferencers.

2. A MULTI-LEVEL PARSING FORMALISM

What follows are more technical aspects of a formalism developed on these basic assumptions with respect to a set of transcribed natural dialogues (Klein, 1979). The concrete knowledge sources, their representation and interdependencies are presented in Metzing (1982). The starting point is the well-known ATN formalism (Woods, 1970). It is well-suited for specific kinds of sequential pattern matching of (syntactic) structures as described in (Ritchie, 1978). Some work has been done to allow a feedback communication with the semantic interpretation process (Woods, 1980) which leads to the theoretical formulation of cascaded ATNs. Briefly it is a way to define separate ATN grammars which can communicate with each other in a well-defined way.

2.1 A transducer vector

Figure 1 makes this more precise. There is a fixed(!) number of ATNs connected via a buffer. The input is 'floating' from left to right through this vector of machines. The output buffer of one machine is the input buffer of the right neighbour. A new action TRANSMIT is defined for the ATN-formalism. Its semantics says write the argument as a new token into the output buffer of the actual machine and transfer the control to the right neighbour.

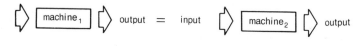

Fig. 1 – A cascade vector.

On the other hand each time when the input buffer of the actual machine is empty but it hasn't reached a final state the left machine is reactivated to produce a new token. The whole process ends successfully iff each machine is in a final state and all tokens in the appropriate input buffers are accepted.

2.2 Introducing process instances for ATN states

In principle you have to take into account the non-determinism in each ATN and its context-sensitivity. Our interpreter implementation can handle these features in a very efficient way. The processing overhead is the same as for interpreting a single ATN. Only the number of the date structures for representing a snapshot of a machine is enlarged to hold two additional pointers.

The concept of cascaded ATNs will serve as a starting point for a more flexible type of parser. Normally a state in an ATN grammar serves for two purposes. First there is a declarative one, i.e. it defines a portion of a formal grammar. The second one is that during the parsing process a state is viewed as a procedure (this is made explicit, e.g. in some ATN-compilers (Finin, 1977; Jameson, 1980; Christaller, 1982).

For reasons which will become obvious later on we transfer the latter purpose to a new kind of object. We will call them 'process instances for ATN states'. Such a process instance will be created every time when the transition function goes to a new state in an ATN grammar. Each process instance is a snapshot of an ATN, i.e. it holds the ACF used by normal ATN-interpreters (Bates, 1978).

The generic concept of all process instances is defined as an object as in SMALLTALK (Kay and Goldstein, 1974). Therefore it has a message protocol which defines how process instances can communicate with themselves and the rest of the world. They are realised as flavours and flavour instances (Moon and Weinreb, 1981) (see Fig. 2).

```
(DEFFLAVOR ATN-PROCESS
    (OUTPUTBUFFER
     INPUTBUFFER
     LOWERMACHINE; this is the next lower stage in the cascade
     UPPERMACHINE ; this is the next higher stage
     PROGENITOR   ;
     OFFSPRING       ; is the set of tried alternatives
     STATE            ; the name in the ATN grammar
     ARCS             ; is the set of untried alternatives
     REG-STACK        ; accumulated registers along the parsing path
     ATN-CL))         ; depth of recursion
```

Fig, 2 – Definition of ATN-PROCESS.

An ATN-process has four pointers which will connect a process instance with other instances. Their names are PROGENITOR, OFFSPRING, UPPER-MACHINE and LOWERMACHINE. The first two pointers will normally hold instances of the same ATN-grammar while the latter ones hold instances of the left and right ATN in the cascade respectively.

Only the transition function creates new process instances. This is achieved by sending the message

Create   <name of new state>

to the actual process instance.

```
(DEFMETHOD (ATN-PROCESS CREATE) (ASTATE)
    (LET [NEWPROCESS (MAKE-INSTANCE 'ATN-PROCESS
                                    'STATE ASTATE 'PROGENITOR SELF)]
        (PUSH OFFSPRING NEWPROCESS) ; remember it as tried alternative
        NEWPROCESS))
```

Fig. 3 – The CREATE-method.

The CREATE-method (Fig. 3) is associated with the generic class ATN process with this message pattern. It sets up the PROGENITOR pointer in the new instance and updates the OFFSPRING pointer in the actual one. It is not shown in the definition of ATN-process (Fig. 2) that most of the instance variables have default values, e.g. ARCS will be bound to the leaving arcs of a state.

2.3 A simple example

The following example (Fig. 4) is a two-stage cascade from Woods (1980). It represents a grammar for the context-sensitive language $a^n b^n c^n$ with $n > 1$.

When the parsing process starts a process instance for the initial states X1 and Y1 are created which are connected with each other via LOWER-

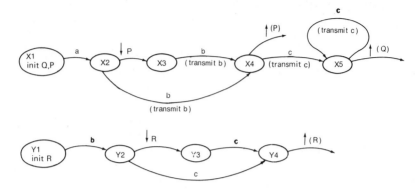

Fig. 4 – A simple example.

MACHINE and UPPERMACHINE respectively. The grammar doesn't tell you how to get a token into the buffer of the first stage in the cascade. Therefore we have to define an appropriate machine which is in our case the terminal. It is also defined as a flavour with specific methods (Fig. 5).

(DEFFLAVOR TERMINAL ((READ-FUNCTION 'READ)))
(DEFMETHOD (TERMINAL READ) (APROCESS ABUFFER)
    (ABUFFER 'WRITE (READ-FUNCTION))
    (APPROCESS 'EVAL SELF))

Fig. 5 – The TERMINAL-front end.

To provide an output medium we take an additional terminal, i.e. we have a four-stage cascade in our case. They are connected by pointers with each other and with buffers. These pointers are meanwhile used as message paths, i.e. paths along which messages are sent (Fig. 6).

Because the input buffer of M1 is empty the message

Read Self Inputbuffer

is sent to TERMINAL$_1$. Which in turn will first send the message

Write <value of the function call (Read-Function)>

to the input buffer mentioned in the received Read-message, i.e. the input buffer of M1. Then the terminal$_1$ sends

Eval Self

to the requesting process instance of M1. Where the Eval-method for ATN-process is defined as shown in Fig. 7.

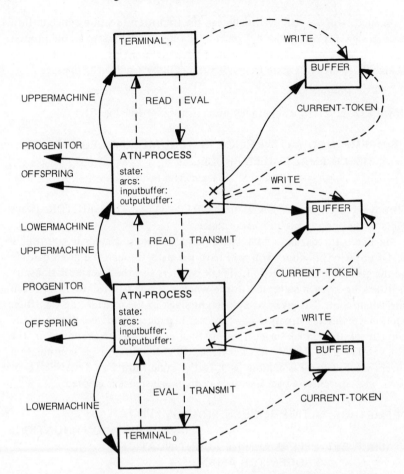

Fig. 6 – Pointer structure and message paths in a cascade with two stages.

- - - - ▷   a message path

───────▶   a pointer between two objects primarily used to define message path

The boxes represent instances of flavours. The flavour name is written in capital letters. Some of the instance variables are omitted. The names of the instance variables UPPERMACHINE, LOWERMACHINE, PROGENITOR, and OFF-SPRING are written as labels of the appropriate pointers. The keywords of the messages are also written as labels for some message paths.

```
(DEFMETHOD (ATN-PROCESS EVAL) (APROCESS)
    (LOOP   [WHILE ARCS]
            [DO (EVAL-ARC (POP ARCS))]
            [RESULT (PROGENITOR 'RESUME SELF)]]))
```

Fig. 7 – The EVAL-method.

A successful arc will eventually call the transition function which in turn creates a new process instance. Control will only come back to an old process instance in case of backtracking. The EVAL-method (Fig. 7) initiates backtracking iff all arcs of a state were not successful by sending the message

Resume Self

to the PROGENITOR of the failed process instance (see Fig. 8).

(DEFMETHOD (ATN-PROCESS RESUME) (FAILED-PROCESS)
    (SELF 'EVAL FAILED-PROCESS))

Fig. 8 – The RESUME-method for backtracking.

It is obvious from the CREATE-method (Fig. 3) that PROGENITOR always points to the appropriate process instance.

In Fig. 9 the parsing of the string "abc" is demonstrated. If you follow the OFFSPRING-pointers you will have the path through the given cascade and the given input. The PROGENITOR-pointers give the inverse relationship. Backtracking in each stage and in the whole cascade will follow them. Each time when control is given to a different stage in the cascade the transition function creates (as usual) a new process instance for the next state in the grammar of the actual stage. This instance is given as an argument in the TRANSMIT- and READ-messages (Fig. 10). It serves as a continuation process when control is coming back to the same stage via a TRANSMIT- or READ-message. In case backtracking occurs this instance is ignored.

(DEFMETHOD (ATN-PROCESS TRANSMIT)
                                (APROCESS ACONTINUATION)
    (SELF 'SET 'UPPERMACHINE ACONTINUATION
        'PROGENITOR APROCESS)
    (SELF 'EVAL SELF))
(DEFMETHOD (ATN-PROCESS READ)
                                (APROCESS ACONTINUATION)
    (SELF 'SET 'LOWERMACHINE ACONTINUATION
        'PROGENITOR APROCESS)
    (SELF 'EVAL SELF))

Fig. 10 – Inter-stage communication.

The TRANSMIT- and READ-methods are very similar. They update two pointers in the receiving process and send the message

Eval Self

to itself. (At the moment the argument in the EVAL-method is ignored.) From the above discussion it is obvious that the transition function has to decide what message should be sent to which process. The algorithm used by it is shown in Fig. 11.

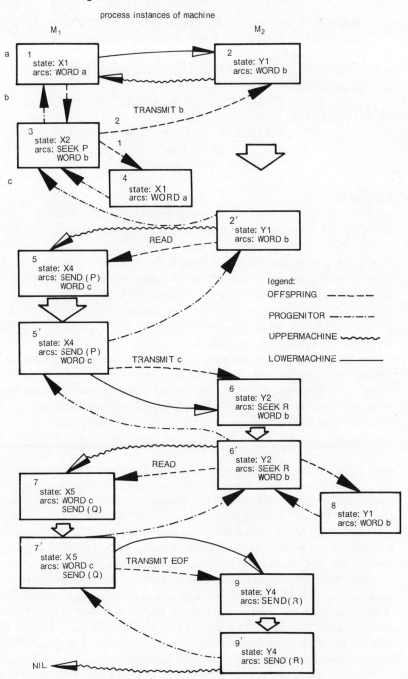

Fig. 9 – The creation of process instances during the parse of the string "abc".

1. TRANSMIT-ACTION EVALUATED ON A SUCCESSFUL ARC
        SEND TRANSMIT MESSAGE TO LOWERMACHINE
2. NON-CONSUMING ARC
        SEND EVAL MESSAGE TO THE NEW PROCESS
3. ALL TOKENS PARSED
        SEND READ MESSAGE TO UPPERMACHINE
4. OTHERWISE
        ADVANCE THE POINTER INTO INPUTBUFFER
            SEND EVAL MESSAGE TO NEW PROCESS

Fig. 11 – The transition function.

2.4 The flexibility

For the first time a parser formalism is presented which reads the input and processes this input over more than one processing stage in an incremental way. Parsing starts as soon as the first token is typed in by the user and read by TERMINAL. What a token is, is defined in the first stage of the cascade. (In our actual implementation a space serves as token delimiter.) One of the consequences is e.g. if an unknown word is encountered (unknown to morphology, syntax or lexicon) the parser may interrupt the user before s/he has finished the complete utterance. While this alone gives us by no means real-time processing behaviour it is a necessary prerequisite.

In the example given above it may not be very obvious which parsing strategy was used for the whole cascade. This might be due to the abstract character of the given grammar. But assume that we have a natural language processing cascade consisting of a morphological, syntactic and semantic stage. When the first word of the first sentence is uttered it will be sent to the morphological stage. This will try to analyse it in a top-down manner. At a point where a hypothesis is well supported it may transmit its results to the syntactic stage. Only now will the latter try to do its job (again using a top-down strategy). If the morphological results are acceptable to the syntax, i.e. its input buffer is empty and it needs a new token, it will reactivate the morphology. Eventually the syntax has accumulated enough information to transmit it to the semantic stage which can try to analyse it is a top-down manner. In this way expectations are only set up when there is a token in the input buffer which may confirm them or not. In the latter case backtracking will occur.

This bottom-up strategy is achieved purely by the organisation of the cascade and our definition of the hierarchy of the participated processes. The top-down strategy is one used inside a single stage, i.e. one is free to choose any strategy inside one stage. As it is shown to normal ATNs in Christaller (1982) this can be done dynamically using so-called meta arcs. E.g. The GROUP-arc mentioned by Burton (1976) defines local determinism.

Because inter-stage communication is done by message-passing it isn't really necessary that each stage be based on an ATN-grammar. That is to say the messages TRANSMIT and READ can be used without knowing that the receiving processes are process instances of ATN states. They could be very different processes, e.g. an interpreter for a semantic case grammar or a process working on a morphological discrimination net. That is we define processes in an object-oriented style using messages where the arguments are pointers to the appropriate sender. Therefore we can define a cascaded parsing algorithm where each stage can be internally different from each other.

With this notation it is possible to use the ATN-formalism only at stages where it seems appropriate. But to demonstrate difficulties when using a 'parsing cascade' for dialogues we will refer again to the simple ATN-formalism.

The third consequence of this approach is that blind (chronological) backtracking might be avoided. In the definition of the RESUME-method (Fig. 8) the failed process is returned as its argument. Because it is a process instance of an ATN state it holds e.g. all register binding done before backtracking occurred. The process which receives a RESUME-message is therefore able to inspect these registers trying to find out what was going wrong. Relaxation in the sense of Kwasny (1980) should be relatively simple to implement.

The concept of process instances described so far is only another implementation of an interpreter evaluating an ATN-grammar. But it is possible to view an ATN-grammar as a default description for analysing utterances. A process instance might have the possibility to modify dynamically let's say the order in which arcs of a state are evaluated.

There are three different cases where a process instance can modify the sequence of arcs (Fig. 12).

ARCSETS MAY BE MODIFIED

ONLY FOR A DETERMINED TIME OR NUMBER OF INSTANCES

FOR EACH INSTANCE OF A SPECIFIC STATE FOR THE REST OF THE DISCOURSE

FOR A SPECIFIC STATE

Fig. 12 – Modification of arcsets.

3. APPLICATION TO DIALOGUES

In the following we discuss some problems which occur when one tries to design a multi-stage parser which should handle real dialogues. We have contributed ourselves to a set of 40 transcribed dialogues (Klein, 1979). Figs. 13 and 14 present the setting for the task and one of the dialogues.

X: could you please tell me, how I can come to the old opera?
Y: what?
X: to the old opera
Y: to the old opera; straight forward, yes. come on I show
X: yes yes
Y: it to you.   (10 sec pause) ahead to Kaufhof. on the right side there
X: yes
Y: is Kaufhof, isn't it?   and there you stay on the right hand side
X: yes, the eh   eh
Y: straight on through the Fressgass   it is new   that is, it's just in
X: mhm
Y: a new shape. the Fressgass, yes   then you will reach directly the opera
X: thank you very much   square
Y: that is the opera ruin.

Fig. 13 – Translation of a sample dialogue.

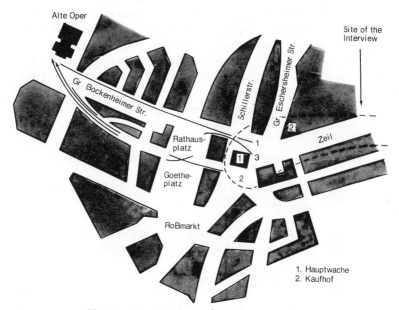

Fig. 14 – Simplified map of the city of Frankfurt.

The list of problems is:

— what processing stages are necessary?
— how can we represent generating and parsing together?
— how can we bypass or insert processing stages?
— is it possible to have a look ahead facility?

To keep things simple enough we assume three processing stages. A syntax stage written as an ATN-grammar, a semantic stage written as a production system, and a discourse stage written as an ATN-grammer.

The discourse stage defines the structure of verbal act patterns for both partners. Therefore it is necessary to 'colour' the sequences of arcs which represent a verbal act which can be uttered by one of them. Colour boundaries are possible turn-taking positions. The usage of these patterns for generating and parsing alternates through a dialogue. For example, an information-inquiry act is followed by an information-giving act and which is used for generating or parsing is determined by the different roles of the partners. On the other hand there are some very frequently used patterns, e.g. for questions and answers, which might be used by both partners, i.e. their colouring must be done dynamically.

The semantic stage uses case frames connected to verbs while the syntax stage uses a simple set of phrase structure rules for German sentences. It is obvious that these two stages are working on different units of a dialogue than the discourse stage. But remember the stop condition mentioned above for cascaded ATNs.

This will not work in our case. Therefore we have defined a new type of arc in the ATN-formalism called RESTART. It will restart the given ATN-grammar in its initial state with cleared registers. The difference between an 'initial' start and a restart is that in the latter case a PROGENITOR pointer exists to allow in principle backtracking into the parsing path of the previous unit (i.e. word or sentence). When introducing this arc the stop condition has to be redefined. We have formulated it as follows: a cascade of parsing processes stops, iff the lowest one in the cascade (the rightmost in the machine vector) is in a final state and its inputbuffer is empty, i.e. completely processed.

In such a situation one or other stage may be (via a RESTART-arc) in an initial state but hasn't produced a new token for its LOWERMACHINE. This condition is coupled to the parsing strategy in the cascade. It must be changed when the strategy is different.

There is another problem when using a cascade for analysing dialogues. One quite often finds one-word utterances like 'mhm', 'yes', 'oh', etc. They should be processed by a morphological stage and the discourse stage but it is by no means clear what syntax or semantics should do with them. Furthermore the proposed formalism has a fixed number of stages. Control can't bypass one of them. In Fig. 15 it is shown that it is possible to define such a bypassing. If to take an example 'mhm' is analysed by morphology and it knows somehow that its result should be transmitted to the discourse stage, at once the following algorithm could be used. Look up via the LOWERMACHINE pointers what the last process instance at the discourse stage is. This is an instance, say D_1, to which the semantic stage will transmit the next token produced by it. Transmit the result from morphology to this instance bypassing all intermediate stages.

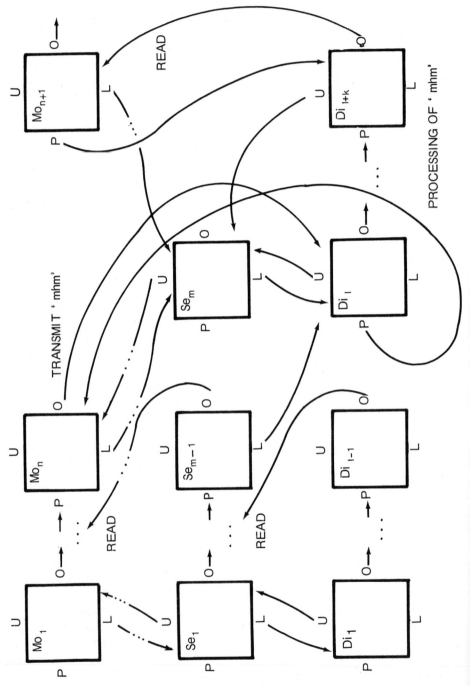

Fig. 15 – General scheme for bypassing stages in a cascade.

The PROGENITOR pointer in D_1 will be set to the transmitting instance to ensure a correct backtracking.

4. CONCLUSIONS

We have introduced a parser formalism based on cascaded ATNs. This formalism allows us to write dialogue grammars where each stage in the cascade might differ from others. Therefore it is possible to use the most appropriate knowledge representations and processes for specific tasks in the dialogue grammar. The basic control structure between different stages can be seen as bottom-up with backtracking. We have furthermore shown how to define a bypassing mechanism to allow a more appropriate processing of units in the discourse which have meaning only for some of the involved stages. The implementation is done by means of flavours in MacLISP and UCI-LISP.

ACKNOWLEDGEMENTS

We would like to thank J. Goodwin and U. Hein at Linköping University for many helpful discussions and the chance to implement a first version of CATN interpreter there (Christaller, 1981). This work wouldn't be possible without our co-workers M. Gehrke and B. Terway in the project 'Procedural dialogue grammars' funded by the Deutsche Forschunsgemeinschaft.

REFERENCES

Bates, M. (1978) The theory and practice of augmented transition network grammars'. In L. Bolc (ed.) *Natural Language Communication with Computers,* Berlin: Springer Verlag.

Burton, R. R. (1976) Semantic grammar. Report no. 3453, Bolt Beranek and Newman Inc., Cambridge, Mass.

Christaller, T. (1981) Cascaded ATNs and their implementation. Unpublished memo, Research Center for Software, Linköping.

Christaller, T. (1982) An ATN programming environment. In L. Bolc (ed.) *ATN Interpreters, Compilers and Editors,* Heidelberg: Springer.

Finin, T. W. (1977) An interpreter and compiler for augmented transition networks. Report T-48, Coordinated Science Laboratory, University of Illinois.

Jameson, A. (1980) Ein Compiler für einen rekursiven ATN-Interpreter. In J. Petöfi and D. Metzing (eds) *Jährlicher Bericht zum Projekt Textverarbeitung,* University of Bielefeld.

Kay, A. and Goldstein, A. (1974) SMALLTALK. Xerox PARC, Palo Alto, California.

Klein, W. (1979) Wegauskünfte, *Zeitschrift für Linguistik und Literaturwissenschaft* **9**, 9–57.

Kwasny, S. C. (1980) Treatment of ungrammatical and extra-grammatical phenomena in natural language understanding systems. Indiana University Linguistics Club.

Marslen-Wilson, W. and Tyler, L. K. (1980) The temporal structure of spoken language understanding, *Cognition,* 8, 1–71.

Metzing, D. (1982) Dialogue interaction in a task domain: model and some problems of application. In: U. Hein and S. Hägglund (eds) *Models of Dialogue,* München: Hauser-MacMillan. To appear.

Moon, D. and Weinreb, D. (1981) Lispmachine Lisp manual. Symbolics Inc., Cambridge Mass.

Psathas, G. and Kozloff, M. (1976) The structure of directions, *Semiotica* 17, 111–130.

Riesbeck, Ch. (1980) 'You can't miss it', judging the clarity of directions. *Cognitive Science* 4, 285–303.

Ritchie, G. (1978) Augmented transition network grammars and semantic processing, Report CSR-20-78, University of Edinburgh.

Stenning, K. (1977) On remembering how to get there: how we might want something like a map. In: A. M. Lesgold, J. W. Pellegrino, S. D. Fokkera and R. Glasser (eds) *Cognition and Instruction.* New York.

Woods, W. A. (1970) Transition networks for natural language analysis. *Communications of the ACM* 13, 591–606.

Woods, W. A. (1980) Cascaded ATN grammars, *American Journal of Computational Linguistics* 6, 1–12.

Wunderlich, D. (1978) 'Wie analysiert man Gespräche? Beispiel Wegauskünfte', *Linguistiche Berichte* 58, 41–76.

PART III

Marcus parsing

Determinism and its implementation in PARSIFAL

E. J. Briscoe, University of Cambridge

A major goal of a psychological model of sentence processing must be to explain the relative complexity of sentences. Much psycholinguistic experimentation is designed to reveal this relative complexity; to take just one example, Hakes *et al.* (1976) report that in English, relative clauses that modify the subject of a main clause are easier to process than those modifying the object. Similarly relative clauses whose head functions as subject within the relative are easier to process than relatives whose head functions as object. Those specifically psychological models of processing that have been proposed (Kimball, 1973; Fodor *et al.*, 1974; Frazier and Fodor, 1980; amongst others) have attempted to incorporate results of this kind. By contrast no computational parser has been developed that has provided a satisfactory correlation between complexity and the number of steps taken by the device to analyse the input. Recently, however, Marcus (1980) has designed a parser which 'allow[s] left-to-right deterministic parsing of those sentences *which a native speaker can analyse without conscious effort*' (1980: 204). Marcus defines a deterministic parser as one which constructs just one correct representation of the structure of an input sentence. His parser − PARSIFAL − only fails, he claims, in cases of obvious psychological complexity, namely so-called garden path sentences.[†]

 If Marcus's claims for PARSIFAL were correct then we would be considerably closer to obtaining a precise computational model of processing;

[†] It also fails to provide both readings of an ambiguous sentence, since this would be non-deterministic. However, this is not a serious weakness in Marcus's approach as he could quite plausibly argue that the decision about which reading to adopt needs to be made at a higher level. Once this decision was made PARSIFAL would then be able to construct the desired interpretation deterministically.

unfortunately they are incorrect. In what follows I demonstrate that PARSIFAL fails to accurately delimit the class of garden path sentences and conflicts with important experimental results.

The basic insight into language which emerges from the computational study of sentence processing is the notion of temporary ambiguity. To the grammarian there is no ambiguity in (1)

(1) Who has John married?

Since he analyses the relations that hold in the complete sentence. By contrast processing occurs from left-to-right and relations must be analysed dynamically. To the processor that has just "seen" *who has* (1) is ambiguous since it might continue as in (2).

(2) Who has married John?

At a certain point in the analysis *who* could be functioning as subject or direct object. A parser can behave in two ways, faced with this type of ambiguity: the first is to guess the role of *who* and reanalyse it if necessary, the second is to delay the decision until the information which resolves the ambiguity is available. The guessing technique is employed by most ATN parsers, but the immediate problem with such an approach (from the point of view of psychological processing) is to explain the intuitively large difference in complexity between (1), (2) and (3).

(3) The horse raced past the barn fell.

In (3) as well, there is a temporary ambiguity between *raced* as main verb or reduced relative, yet this sentence is virtually uninterpretable whilst (1) and (2) are simple. The approach taken by Marcus to delay the crucial decision for some period can, he claims, explain why (3), but not (1) and (2), is a garden path. PARSIFAL is designed so its grammar rules are allowed to "look ahead" into the sentence far enough to resolve all temporary ambiguities except those which are garden paths. So PARSIFAL contains a buffer which allows the parser to examine the next three words and/or NPs in the input; for example when analysing (1) and (2) the buffer will look like this:

(1) [NP]   [AUX]   [V]
   Who   has   married . . .

(2) [NP]   [AUX]   [NP]
   Who   has   John . . . .

In this case PARSIFAL's buffer is sufficient to resolve the ambiguity over the role of *who* before any decision is made, but this manouevre does not extend to (3). If we imagine the parser has already analysed the subject, *the horse,* the buffer will contain:

(3) [V]   [PREP]   [NP]
   raced   past   the barn . . .

The crucial item *fell*, that would tell PARSIFAL that it is processing a reduced relative is beyond the range of its buffer, and thus the psychological complexity of (3) is predicted.

Immediately several problems with this approach come to mind; Church (1980) notes that if the buffer contained preprocessed PPs as well as NPs, PARSIFAL would no longer predict the complexity of (3) because the buffer would now contain *fell* at the point when *raced* was analysed. Marcus justifies processing NPs in the buffer on the basis that their "leading edges" are clearcut (1980; 177); thus a determiner signals the beginning of an NP. But by this argument the leading edges of PPs are as clearcut; prepositions introduce PPs at least as frequently as words such as *his* and *that* turn out to be functioning as determiners. It seems then, that the decision to only process NPs in the buffer is motivated by the garden path effects themselves.

Secondly, allowing this preprocessing of NPs gives PARSIFAL infinite lookahead at the word level, since well-formed NPs can consist in principle of arbitrarily many words. In practice this translates into very delayed processing: many of PARSIFAL's rules need to examine items on the "far side" of an NP before making a decision. However, this is psychologically implausible; there is good evidence that we process language with virtually no delay (Marslen-Wilson and Welsh, 1978; Marslen-Wilson and Tyler, 1980).

Nevertheless PARSIFAL does make specific and testable predictions about the nature of the sentences it cannot process deterministically and therefore the set which Marcus claims will be psychologically complex. Marcus claims that these predictions are borne out, that garden paths are "the exception that proves the rule" (1980: 202), lending PARSIFAL psychological plausibility. However, the following sentences are all garden paths,[†] yet in each case the temporary ambiguity falls within the range of PARSIFAL's buffer:

(4) I gave the boy the dog bit a bandage.
(5) I told the girl the boy seduced the story.
(6) The granite rocks during earthquakes.
(7) The old train the young.
(8) Without her contributions to the fund would be inadequate.
(9) Whilst Mary was mending the sock fell off her lap.
(10) I gave the boy who you wanted to give the books to three books.
(11) Sue wouldn't give the man who was reading the book.

In (4) and (5) the object relatives *the dog bit* and *the boy seduced* are consistently misanalysed as part of a sentential complement, but in both cases

---

[†]Each one has been taken from the literature so that the intuition that they are garden paths is not originally my own; although in each case I concur. In addition I have further tested these intuitions by presenting them to naive readers.

PARSIFAL, after analysing the initial SVO sequence would have the rest of the sentence in its buffer:

[NP]   [V]   [NP]
the dog   bit   a bandage.

the boy seduced   the story.

So, Marcus's parser fails to predict the psychological complexity of these sentences. Similarly in (6) and (7) the lexical ambiguity of *rocks* and *train* seems to lead readers down the garden path about 50% of the time, but both these ambiguities are resolved by the next item in the sentences and thus would fall well within buffer range. The remaining examples all present PARSIFAL with similar problems, as the reader is welcome to verify.

In addition there are sentences that are clearly not garden paths but which contain temporary ambiguities beyond the range of PARSIFAL's buffer:

(12) Cars raced at Silverstone are now collector's items.
(13) The tenants constantly delivered letters threw them away unopened.
(14) That man is a biped is obvious.
(15) That man is tall.

PARSIFAL predicts that (12) and (13) are garden paths since they are structurally identical to (3), but in these there seems to be little tendency to interpret the reduced relatives as part of the main clause. Similarly, when analysing (14) and (15), PARSIFAL's buffer will initially contain the same sequence:

[THAT]   [MAN]   [V]
                 N or NP?   is . . . .

Therefore there can be no principled way for the parser to assess the role of *that* in either sentence. Marcus (1980: 291) provides a diagnostic rule to solve this problem which will treat *that* as a determiner if the following word allows this interpretation. This predicts that (14) should be a garden path.[†]

It should be clear from the evidence of examples (3) and (12) and (13) that it is not possible in principle to provide a structural definition of garden paths, as Marcus has attempted to do. Steedman (this volume) and Steedman and Crain (forthcoming) suggest that garden path effects are largely pragmatically induced. They demonstrate that by varying the linguistic context in which utterances containing reduced relatives are embedded, subjects can be made to garden path or not garden path on identical sentences. Since the semantic function of restrictive relatives is to select a referent for the head, a context which has already provided a definite referent will not support a reduced relative

---

[†]In this connection it is interesting to note that complementiser *that* is nearly always realised in speech in a phonetically reduced form —/ðət/; effectively distinguishing it from demonstrative and pronomial *that*.

interpretation. By the same argument a definite noun phrase, such as *the horse* is less likely to support a reduced relative interpretation, unless it is embedded in a context where its reference is made ambiguous, than an indefinite noun phrase such as *cars*. These pragmatic effects are powerful, but not the only non-syntactic factors which influence garden paths; Crain and Steedman (1982) also mention semantic plausibility.

(16)   The postman constantly delivered letters threw them away unopened.

It seems clear that knowledge of the world can influence syntactic decisions, for example we are likely to find (16) more complex than (13) since we know that postmen are normally the active agents in the delivery of letters and are therefore more inclined to select the active main clause interpretation.

Marcus does allow semantic information to interact with syntactic processing, to a limited extent, but in general his research strategy is rather different. For instance he recognises that garden paths rarely occur in speech since prosodic information normally blocks the unwanted interpretation, but goes on to suggest:

> The phenomenon [garden paths] discussed here is thus artificial by necessity; by throwing away prosodic information, the performance of the syntactic analysis mechanism degrades, and some of its internal characteristics may be deduced from the form of this degradation. The garden path phenomenon might be largely artifact but I believe it is an artifact that yields important clues about the real nature of the process of syntactic recognition (1980: 218)

In fact Marcus has offered a structural substitute for semantic pragmatic and prosodic information and thus distorted, rather than revealed, the nature of syntactic processing. Once we accepted that there are prosodic, pragmatic and semantic effects in garden paths the question we must ask is whether delayed processing is relevant to any form of temporary ambiguity. That is, the original justification for suggesting delayed processing was to circumvent temporary ambiguities by syntactic means, but since we can find no support for this approach from garden paths we must ask whether non-syntactic information might not be sufficient for the resolution of other temporary ambiguities?

We have seen that non-syntactic information can intervene during processing to effect essentially syntactic decisions, such as whether to interpret a verb as part of a main clause or relative, in (3), (12) and (13). This kind of observation supports a model of processing in which the different components analyse an input in parallel and are able to dynamically constrain choices as they arise within other components. Such a model is also supported by the work of Marslen-Wilson and his colleagues. However, parallel interaction does not of itself rule out the possibility that delayed processing may be essential to deterministic parsing.

I suspect that delayed processing will turn out to be unnecessary to the resolution of virtually all temporary ambiguities. However, our present understanding of temporary ambiguity, and the nature of the interaction of the various types of information in processing, do not permit any positive demonstration of this point. Rather I shall argue against delayed processing on the basis of certain features of English grammar which would be redundant if this type of processing were a reality.

English *that* functions as a complementizer, as in (17)

(17) I believe that Mary is pregnant.

In this environment it can be deleted, as in (18).

(18) I believe Mary is pregnant.

However, there is psycholinguistic evidence that this deletion results in greater psychological complexity (Hakes, 1972). One explanation for this result is that deleting *that* introduces a temporary ambiguity about the function of the subject of the embedded complement. In (19) for example *Mary* is functioning as direct object of *believe*.

(19) I believe Mary
     I believe Mary to be pregnant.

Further support for this explanation comes from the fact that *that* can never occur when *Mary* is functioning as direct object: consider (20).

(20) * I believe that Mary.

     * I believe that Mary to be pregnant.

Similar experimental results hold for the use of *that* as a relative marker (Hakes *et al.*, 1976). PARSIFAL, however, predicts no difference in complexity between examples like (17) and (18), or indeed in general for deleted grammatical markers. In the case of (18) PARSIFAL would not be tempted to view *Mary* as the direct object of *believe* since at the point when *Mary* is analysed the rest of the sentential complement would be in the buffer.

In fact PARSIFAL predicts the exact opposite of these psycholinguistic results; since *that*, when it is present occupies one buffer cell it tends to hinder rather than assist processing. For example if we return to the garden path (4), PARSIFAL predicts that this is not psychologically complex but that (21) its counterpart containing *that* is:

(21) I gave the boy that the dog bit a bandage.

since at the point when the parser must decide whether it is processing a relative or complement the buffer will contain:

| [THAT] | [NP] | [V] |
| that | the dog | bit . . . |

The same point can be made with non-garden paths: PARSIFAL predicts that (23) but not (22) should be a garden path since *that* blocks the parser's view of the final NP. However, on the basis of both intuition and the experiments cited above, we know that (23) is the simpler.

(22) I gave the girl I loved a diamond ring.
(23) I gave the girl that I loved a diamond ring.

Of course these latter criticisms of PARSIFAL could be rectified by ensuring, in some way, that grammatical markers were cleared from the buffer before crucial decisions were made.[†] However, PARSIFAL, modified in this way, would still not predict the complexity results reported in the above experiments. More seriously such a move would miss the fundamental point that grammatical markers of this kind exist universally in languages, yet a parser using lookahead suggests that they are totally redundant and even that languages would be more efficient without them.

In conclusion then, I would claim that what Marcus calls deterministic parsing is an essential goal for a psychologically interesting parser. However, the specific method used in PARSIFAL to achieve deterministic parsing is both psychologically and linguistically implausible.

ACKNOWLEDGEMENTS

I would like to thank Terry Moore for his many helpful comments on this paper.

REFERENCES

Church, K. W. (1980) On memory limitations in natural language processing. Report MIT/LCS/TR-245, Laboratory for Computer Science, MIT.

Crain, S. and Steedman, M. (1982) On not being led up the garden path: the use of context by the psychological parser. In D. Dowty, L. Kartunnen and A. Zwicky (eds). (Title to be announced). Cambridge: Cambridge University Press. To appear.

Fodor, J. A., Bever, T. and Garrett, M. (1974) *The Psychology of Language*. New York: McGraw-Hill.

Frazier, L. and Fodor, J. D. (1980) The sausage machine: a new two stage parser. *Cognition* **6**, 291–325.

Hakes, D., Evans, J. and Brannon, L. (1976) Understanding sentences with relative clauses. *Memory and Cognition* **4**, 283–290.

Hakes, D. (1972) Effects of reducing complement constructions on sentence comprehension. *Journal of Verbal Learning and Verbal Behaviour* **11**, 278–286.

---

†In much the same way perhaps, that NPs are reprocessed by means of "attention shifts" in the buffer before clause level rules are applied.

Kimball, J. (1973) Seven principles of surface structure parsing in natural language. *Cognition* **2**, 15–47.

Marcus, M. P. (1980) *A Theory of Syntactic Recognition for Natural Language.* Cambridge, Mass.: MIT Press.

Marslen-Wilson, W. and Tyler, L. (1980) The temporal structure of spoken language understanding: the perception of sentences and words in sentences. *Cognition* **8**, 1–74.

Marslen-Wilson, W. and Welsh, A. (1978) Processing interactions and lexical access during word recognition in continuous speech. *Cognitive Psychology* **10**, 29–63.

The implementation of a PIDGIN interpreter

G. D. Ritchie, Heriot-Watt University

1. MOTIVATION

The parser constructed a few years ago by Marcus (1980) has attracted some interest within the computational linguistics community (e.g. Sampson, 1983; Charniak, 1983; Church 1981), largely as a result of the theoretical claims which Marcus made for its relevance to various linguistic phenomena (see Briscoe, 1983; Steedman, 1983; Milne (in preparation) for some critical comments). In view of this, it is worthwhile looking more closely at the parsing mechanism proposed, and investigating its usefulness for the design of English language parsers.

Marcus's program (PARSIFAL) was in various components, with the syntactic parsing rules being written in a notation called "PIDGIN", which was a very high level language Marcus had designed for writing recognition grammars, and there was an interpreter (implemented in LISP) which executed these rules in the course of parsing a sentence. The abstract machine provided by the PIDGIN interpreter embodies Marcus's theory of sentence-processing, in that it defines the grammatical constructs which are available to the grammar-writer. Hence, to attempt to clarify or explore the details of Marcus's theory of parsing (as opposed to particular details of the grammar used in PARSIFAL), it is necessary to examine PIDGIN.

From a more practical point of view, PIDGIN also has a certain interest. In attempting to write parsers for English, it is useful to be able to write in a fairly high-level grammatical notation, rather than directly in (say) LISP. If one is interested in defining, as part of the grammatical description, *how* parsing is to occur, then a high-level formalism which states (or directly implies) something about the flow of operations during parsing is useful; the classic ATN (Woods, 1970) was one such system. For those who wish to follow this latter course, a language like PIDGIN is naturally of interest — is it a suitable general tool for writing parsers?

This article does not set out to answer such questions directly, but aims to clarify the details of PIDGIN so that further assessment is facilitated. It should provide some of the information that is necessary for those who wish to use

PIDGIN (or something like it) as a practical tool, and the clarified version should also be of interest to those concerned with PIDGIN as a theoretical model.

The detailed discussion here is based on a recent re-implementation of the PIDGIN interpreter in POP-2 on a DEC System 10. It is not always easy to re-implement a large program (or component of a large program), when the original version grew up gradually without a prior definition and is documented only in a doctoral thesis. Indeed, it is sometimes not easy to work out how such a program functioned, or even to define a clear specification of its functional behaviour. This obstacle can prove frustrating to those who wish to build on existing work, and is a recurring problem in artificial intelligence (cf. McDermott, 1976; Ritchie and Hanna, 1982). Fortunately, Marcus published an unusually full description of PIDGIN, so it is possible to sketch out a rough specification from the published information. (All page references will be to Marcus (1980).) There are one or two problems of detail which arise when trying to make this specification fully comprehensive, and any reader who wishes to implement the PIDGIN language (as a practical tool) should find the discussion presented below helpful.

2. A BRIEF OVERVIEW

It is not feasible to provide a full introduction to Marcus's proposals (see Sampson (1983)), or Thompson and Ritchie (1983) for a fuller description), but the following is a summary of the basic mechanisms.

A PIDGIN parser uses two temporary stores to hold words, phrases, and partially-built constituents. The *buffer* is a list of 5 items, accessed in an approximately first-in-first-out basis, of which only 3 (what will be called here the "window") may be accessed at once. Input words enter the buffer at the right-hand end and progress towards the left, and phrases (once built) reside in the buffer until they can be attached to the syntax tree. There is also a *stack* of partially-built syntactic subtrees (nodes), to which items from the buffer may be attached.

Each grammatical rule has a set of *patterns*, which describe what syntactic items will cause that rule to be applicable, and a set of *actions* which are structure-building operations to be performed when the rule does apply. The range of items which rules can describe in their patterns are the 3 items in the current window, and the item at the top of the stack (the "current node"). Rules are grouped into *packets* and the parser maintains a list of "currently active" packets throughout the parsing of a sentence. Only rules which are in "active packets" can be used at any given instant.

As well as the syntactic parsing, PARSIFAL carried out a limited amount of semantic processing during sentence analysis, using a "case-frame interpreter". These semantic rules performed certain checks relating to the placement of subject and objects around the main verb. As the published summary of this component (Appendix E) is not as full as that provided for the main PIDGIN interpreter, it is quite difficult to draw up a detailed specification for that module. The remainder of this paper is concerned only with the syntactic component, which is the component to which most of Marcus's theoretical claims relate.

The original rules given by Marcus are in a sophisticated English-like notation which is supposed to make them easily comprehensible, but this is not essential — the rules could be written in a simpler function-argument notation (cf. Thompson and Ritchie, 1983) without affecting the central ideas. The discussion in Section 3 is not concerned with the particular concrete syntax of that notation, but with the abstract operations involved. That is, what has been re-implemented, and is discussed here, is the abstract machine underlying PIDGIN — the same set of functions, commands, etc., but a different concrete syntax (notation).

Marcus allows syntactic nodes to have "registers" attached to them, containing data items (e.g. pointers to other nodes). Marcus comments (p. 144) that these are used only for semantic information, but there seems to be some confusion between registers, types, and daughters, since the "type" of a node seems to be similar to a register-name for accessing the node (see 3.1 below), and (p. 286) there is a "special wh register" on some S nodes. The re-implementation simply allows the existence of these named slots on a node — their intended usage is left open.

In PIDGIN, there are special nodes called "traces", which look like NP (noun phrase) nodes in many respects, but which have a "register" pointing to another NP node (the "binding" of the trace). This idea (which originates in Chomsky's "Extended Standard Theory" — see Radford (1981)) is used to give a structure for clauses (e.g. relative clauses) where there appears to be a "gap" caused by a missing NP. The "trace" node is marked as being both an NP and a TRACE, and rules may treat it as an ordinary NP in some respects. Although PIDGIN includes certain commands for manipulating traces, it has not been possible to explore the precise way in which these constructs are used, in the absence of a full case-frame interpreter. The re-implementation has therefore not exercised this facility to its limit, and there may be residual undocumented difficulties there.

3. CLARIFYING THE SPECIFICATION

3.1 Node Types
Each node in the syntax tree has a "type", and there are PIDGIN commands to manipulate these markings. It is not clear what the difference is between a "type" and a "feature", and what linguistic information the "type" is supposed to convey.

Marcus mentions (p. 42) that the type is "also one of its features", but in the description of PIDGIN (and the example rules) there are commands which refer to the type of a node rather than mentioning its features (e.g. "the NP above C" means the nearest type NP node on the stack; "the NP of C" means the rightmost type NP node among C's daughters).

Despite the possibility of referring in PIDGIN to "the NP of C", a node can have more than one daughter with the same type. The main unresolved issue is whether or not the type of a node refers to its grammatical role with respect to its parent constituent. Marcus's sample rules in the main text contain no examples of role-like types such as "OBJECT" or "HEAD" (only concrete syntactic categories like "NP")' but the rule "TWO-HUNDRED" (p. 298) uses types "num1", "num2" and "quant" with the command:

> Set the quant of c to
> times (the quant register of 1st, the quant register of 2nd)

It may be that Marcus's implementation stored registers and daughter nodes in the same way, so that "the quant of c" could refer to a daughter or a register. However, the definitions given of the PIDGIN commands, and the illustrative examples, suggest that (formally) a type is one feature which can be referred to specifically. This is the way the PIDGIN interpreter treats the "type" entry – any interpretation as a "role" seems to be in the mind of the reader.

This leaves open the question of whether a node can have its type changed from its initial value. Marcus's philosophy was that structure must not be discarded once built, which suggests that types should not be altered. However, there is at least one rule cited by Marcus (PREDP, p. 283) which seems to require a type-change, since it attaches a "pp" item (i.e. a phrase with type "pp") as type "predp".

In the POP-2 re-implementation, the system kept track of which particular feature had been attached to the node as its "type". All feature-checking tests included this feature in their computations, so it had full status as a feature, but all the operations which referred to the "type" of a node checked just this item (rather than scanning all the feature-list). The only advantage of this was efficiency in type-checking, and clarity of printing – it had no theoretical status. Types of nodes could not be altered once defined.

3.2 Attachment Commands

Marcus's sample rules contain commands such as:

> "Attach 1st to C as NP"
> "Attach a new NP node to C as NP"

These are in fact different abstract operations, even although they are expressed in very similar English-like notation (see pp. 80–81 and 264). The first is an example of an "attach" operation which takes three arguments – an arbitrary node (to become the daughter), a node (to become the parent) and a node type (see 3.1 above). The second example can be regarded as a different operation which takes only one argument – a node type. The extra description "to C as NP" is redundant – this command always attaches to C (the current node), and the daughter (which is newly created by this attachment command) always retains the type that it had when created; this operation could be called "cattach". Moreover, "cattach" has the side-effect of pushing the new node on to the stack after attachment, thus making it the new current node; "attach" has no such effect. Close examination of the sample grammar shows commands such as (p. 288):

"Attach a new S node labelled sec, relative to C as S"

Hence, it appears that "cattach" takes another argument – a list of features to be placed on the new node – with the proviso that this argument may be null (as in the example above).

Marcus's description of the attachment commands (p. 264) does not state that attached nodes should be removed from the buffer, but on p. 103:

"After AUX-INVERSION has been executed, the grammar interpreter notices that NP43 is attached and *it therefore removes NP43 from the buffer*". (Marcus's emphasis)

It appears that attachment of a buffered node should cause its removal from the buffer, although the above quotation implies that this should not happen as part of the execution of "attach", but should be delayed until the entire set of rule-actions have been performed. It is possible that this delay has no theoretical consequence, and is only an implementation detail to simplify the way in which Marcus's program referred to the 1st, 2nd and 3rd items in the buffer; immediate removal might have disrupted these bindings. Hence, if the interpreter makes a note of which items are 1st, 2nd and 3rd at the time of the pattern-match, then the node can be removed immediately. This is the policy adopted in the re-implication.

3.3 Maintenance of Active Packets
The published accounts give a fairly clear outline of the way in which the active-packet-list grows and shrinks during parsing, but there is a little confusion regarding the temporary suspension of the list in association with nesting on the node-stack.

It is commonplace in parsing mechanisms for the system to maintain a set of current grammatical predictions, and for these to be temporarily suspended while some internal constituent (phrase or clause) is built; on the completion of the constituent, the parser reinstates the set of shelved expectations, and resumes parsing using this information (cf. PUSH in an ATN (Woods, 1970)). Marcus includes such a mechanism, by linking the set of currently active packets to the node-stack. When nodes are pushed on to or popped off the stack, a similar last-in-first-out storage happens for the entire list of current packets; when a node is popped off the stack (i.e. "dropped" into the buffer), the active-list of packets is restored to the state it had when that node first went on to the stack.

However, there is one small detail of this process which is not fully specified — what does a newly pushed node (usually newly created) acquire as an associated list of packets? If this were a blank list of packets, then no packets would be active until explicitly activated by the currently executing rule (i.e. the rule creating and pushing the node on to the stack); if this rule failed to activate any, the parse would grind to a halt for lack of available rules (this is one of the many points that a grammar-writer must in general keep in mind — the active-list must not accidentally become empty). Alternatively, it may be that a new node acquires a copy of the currently active packets, which remain available (active) during the parsing of the new constituent, together with any new packets which become active during that parsing. What would then happen at the end of the constituent would not be that *hidden* rules emerge, but that the active-list resumes the exact form that it had on entering the constituent (which might well be shorter than the length it acquired during the parsing of the constituent). This second arrangement might not interact so well with "attention-shift" rules — see Section 3.4 below. One other possibility (see Thompson and Ritchie, 1983) is to allow the grammar writer to define a set of packets which are always activated when a new node is created.

The compromise adopted in the re-implementation is as follows. There is, in the PIDGIN interpreter, a global list called "alwaysact" which is initially empty, but which the grammar writer may set to contain any list of packet-names. When a node is pushed on to the stack, it is associated with a new active-list containing only those packets named in "alwaysact"; all other active packets are temporarily suspended. (So far, no need has been found for this facility, and the list is empty in all the test grammars.) When a node is popped, the previous active-list re-emerges. Hence, the grammar-writer has the choice of how the parser acquires new active packets when commencing a new constituent — the rule which pushes on the new root node may explicitly activate packets, or the device of defining packets to be activated automatically may be used (or both).

This is related to the issue of how the parse commences. Marcus uses the trick of having a special "INITIAL-RULE" (p. 280), which is in a non-existent packet ("NOWHERE") and which contains LISP code to set up one of the global variables ("s", conventionally the root of the parse tree).

This is rather inelegant — the INITIAL-RULE is a mixture of interpreter and grammar. In the re-implementation, the interpreter, to initiate a parse, creates a completely unlabelled, untyped node on the stack, and then activates all the packets in a global list called "initpacks". The list "initpacks" is under the control of the user (grammar-writer), so the grammar may include a definition of what packets are on this list. Any other initialisation actions have to occur in the rules in these packets (e.g labelling the root node). There is a variable "ROOT" which refers to the bottom node on the stack (i.e. the first pushed on to the stack); if the stack is empty, it has the value NIL, and the interpreter maintains this binding automatically.

3.4 Attention-shifts

One of the main facilities discussed by Marcus in the "attention-shift". An "attention-shift" rule has a single pattern which can be matched against any position in the window, and a successful match of such a rule causes the "window" to move to the right so that the matched item is then in position 1 (left end) of the window. However, it is not clear exactly how this was implemented, or how much it was exercised on demanding examples. Marcus discusses one method of implementation (pp. 180–184), but comments (fn. 3, p. 181) that his actual program did not work in exactly this way, although he regards his implementation as "equivalent in behaviour". The main question that faces a programmer setting out to implement this mechanism is – when and how do attention-shift rules get matched against the input buffer?

An AS-rule can match against any position in the current window, and Marcus observes (p. 184) a shift may be only a logical shift, if a rule triggers on the first buffer position. He also states that AS-rules are checked on every cycle of the pattern-matcher (i.e. before every test of a possible ordinary rule against the window). Hence, once an AS-rule has matched and caused a shift, there seems to be nothing to prevent that rule triggering again on the same item (which will now be in position 1 of the window). This could lead to an endless series of vacuous attention-shifts, as the same AS-rule is triggered without an ordinary (non-AS) rule ever having a chance to alter the state of the buffer.

It might appear that this could be avoided by stipulating that AS-rules are checked only when an item is first read into the buffer from the input-list, but this then raises the issue of the relationship between the set of currently active AS-rules and the moment at which an item becomes available for triggering a shift (as Marcus comments on p. 183). Since AS-rules are in packets, they are not all globally available all the time (that is their whole purpose – to organise the flow of processing). The relevant packet for detecting the necessary attention-shift might not be active at the moment when an item enters the window. Even if we test AS rules at every cycle of the pattern matcher, there is still a slightly worrying arbitrariness about the set of rules available at any given time. The juncture at which an item "appears" in the current window is somewhat random, in the following sense. Any attempt by the system to match a pattern against the buffer will cause items to be read in, if there are not sufficient items present. Even if the overall match of a rule fails, it may have caused an item to be read into the window, and hence to become available. This is the case even if the item thus brought in is actually irrelevant to the (failed) match, since rules may contain the "true" pattern (Marcus's [t]), which matches any item — but which forces the system to read something into the buffer. Hence, the point at which an item makes its presence felt may be determined by the presence of completely irrelevant rules which have failed to match, even rules which do not take account of what might be in that position (since they have "true" patterns).

The following arrangement has been used in the re-implementation. A distinction is introduced between items being available for matching (i.e. within the lookahead window), and having actually participated in the processing (which is relevant to the theoretical issue of how much lookahead is needed). Items in the buffer which have actually taken part in a successful rule-match are marked as "used", and the system maintains a table of the status of each item (not just in the current "window" of matchable items), updating this whenever the buffer changes. The entire buffer is kept constantly filled from the input-list, and every time in the buffer is regarded as "present" (i.e. available for rule-matching if within the current window). However, an item is not marked as "used" until it has participated in successful rule match. The aim of this is to allow AS-rules (or ordinary rules) to detect any "present" item within the current window (i.e. the criterion for triggering a rule is simply that the item lies within the 3-item look-ahead scope), but the set of such items is not affected by unsuccessful rule-matches. The set of "used" items does not correspond to Marcus's notion of items actually in the buffer, but the idea is that if the number of adjacent "used" items exceeds 3 (or the current window length, if experimenting with this parameter), then the strict hypothesis on limited lookahead is being violated. Such a violation could occur in various ways; for example, the PIDGIN system allows rules to insert material into the buffer, and to "drop" items off the stack (into the front of the current window). These operations could cause a "used" item to be pushed rightwards, perhaps even out of the window. If this occurred, then subsequent matching of grammar rules would be relying on the 3 items in the current window, *and* there would also be a "used" item further to the right. Similarly, a "restore" command could move the window back to the left (at the end of an attention-shift), leaving a total of more than 3 items which have participated in processing. The re-implementation does not prevent the movement of a "used" item off the right of the buffer (since this seems to be a necessary facility), but such events are detected and a warning is printed on these occasions.

The distinction between "present" and "used" is the distinction between what items are available for matching (i.e. lie within the window) and what items are actually required by any particular grammar or set of rules. The former information is essential to making the system of rule-matching work; the latter is relevant if some investigation of the restricted lookahead hypothesis is being undertaken.

The problem of avoiding infinite loops of AS-rules is passed on to the grammar-writer, rather than being built into the interpreter, in the following way. An AS-rule can have, like any other rule, a body (i.e. a list of actions to be performed). It is up to the grammar-writer to ensure that the actions in an AS-rule deactivate the packet containing the rule (e.g. by pushing a new node on to the stack — see Section 3.3. above), so that the item now in position 1 cannot trigger the rule again. Incidentally, this suggests that creating a new code on the stack should "hide" the current active list, rather than inheriting a copy of it, since this would give a natural way of achieving the deactivation in most cases (cf. Marcus's sample AS-rule on p. 179).

3.5 Stacked nodes and termination conditions

One issue which is not fully explained by Marcus is the condition under which a parse terminates successfully, and what constitutes the result of the parse. In PIDGIN, there is a command which states that the parse is finished — this can be used in any rule under any conditions. In the PARSIFAL grammar, the end is announced when there is a final punctuation mark in position 1 of the window. (The same grammar rule attaches the final punctuation symbol to the syntax tree, so that the buffer is then empty at the end of the parse.) Also, the parse tree is the contents of the variable "s", set up at the start of the parse to be the first node on the stack. That is, parse termination can depend on an arbitrary condition, and there is no necessity to finish with one node (the result) on the stack.

The re-implementation follows this (rather untidy) scheme, but it would appear to be cleaner to define some general termination condition (e.g. an empty buffer and one node on the stack), on the assumption that the current node and the root node should coincide in a properly organised parse.

This raises the question of whether nodes go on and off the stack in an orderly fashion. In Marcus's outline, there seems to be only one way to remove a node from the stack, namely to drop it into the front of the buffer. Also, one of the attachment commands (see section 3.2 above) creates a new node *and* attaches it to the parse tree.

This leads to the problem of removing such nodes from the stack, when they are already attached. If a node is both current (top of stack) and attached, then "dropping" it into the buffer will cause there to be an attached node in the buffer, and the "dropped" node will become eligible to match further rules, which may try to attach it. (There are no commands for deleting items from the buffer or detaching nodes from trees.) One possibility might be to eliminate "cattach" from the language altogether, and adopt a style of grammar-writing in which a new unattached current node is created at the beginning of each constituent, this node is "dropped" on completion of the constituent, and some rule (describing the environment of that constituent) attaches the node. Alternatively, one could include a command "popstack" which simply removes the current node from the stack. This should be used only if the node is attached, and a check to that effect should be built into the "popstack" operation. The "popstack" command has been included in the re-implementation.

Marcus is not entirely clear about what items on the stack can be accessed by grammar rules. Sometimes it seems to be just the topmost node C, sometimes it is C and the current S node (p. 145) and sometimes (p.146) it is the nearest "cyclic" node, with the question of whether NP is "cyclic" being left open (pp. 162–163). The re-implementation includes the constructs "currentNP" and "currentS" – no concept of "cyclic" is used.

4 EVALUATING THE MODEL

The PIDGIN parsing mechanism is still partly ill-defined. Although the exercise of re-implementation has been instructive, there is still the problem mentioned in Section 1 above – a semi-formal description of a complex, organically-grown program leaves areas of doubt. The re-implementation resolves most of the issues in an internally consistent manner – what is not clear is how well it reflects what Marcus did, or what he would wish to have done.

As a result of these ambiguities, most of the work carried out on the re-implemented interpreter was spent on developing the specification, and it has not (at present) been tested with a very large grammar. Therefore, there is not yet an independent verification of Marcus's claims. Marcus's own test grammar relies heavily on the semantic component and case-frame handler to make decisions, and it is not possible to assess the syntactic component in isolation (despite the fact that PARSIFAL is normally discussed in those terms). At present, all that can be said is that Marcus's claims are not proven. The performance of the particular grammar in PARSIFAL (which includes one or two ad hoc rules to make it work) on a relatively restricted set of test sentences, certainly does not substantiate Marcus's "Determinism Hypothesis".

From the point of view of using PIDGIN as a useful practical tool, some enhancements are certainly needed. One improvement which has been suggested (Marcus, 1980, p. 60; Church, 1981; Charniak, 1983) is to connect the flow of processing directly to phrase structure rules of some kind, so that there is less need for explicit activation and deactivation of packets, and certain routine structure-building can be handled automatically. Experience with small test grammars supports this suggestion – in PIDGIN, the user is forced to write similar sets of commands in several places which in fact reflect the basic hierarchical arrangement of surface constituents.

The use of "features" to annotate nodes is excessively crude, since it does not allow for the notion of "properties" which have specific values (as in Ritchie, 1980). For example, it is often useful to specify in a rule that some aspect of a daughter node is to be passed to the parent node (or vice versa). In PIDGIN, this results in commands such as "transfer vspl, vis, v1 + 3s, vpl + 2s, v − 3s, v3s from 1st to C", where what is actually meant is "transfer the verb-agreement marking from 1st to C". Possibly "registers" could be adapted for

this. A related problem is the need for some uniform approach to the percola-
tion or inheritance of features between nodes. At present this has to be done
explicitly, using the "transfer" command. Some rules specifically for feature (or
property) passing might be better or a general convention (e.g. the "Head
feature convention" of Gazdar (1981)).

Some mechanism is needed to cope with multiple lexical entries (which
Marcus largely ignores). Milne (in preparation) has observed that an adaptation
of the attachment mechanism mentioned by Winograd (1972, p. 89–90) would
be an improvement. In this, a successful rule-match defines which of several
possible feature-markings are being used for a word, and this particular version is
the only one attached to the syntax tree by the rule.

However, the main drawback of PIDGIN from a practical point of view is
its dependence on deterministic parsing. Whereas in a more conventional system
(e.g. an ATN grammar), the user can try to be as careful ("deterministic") as
possible, it is not a disaster if he fails, as long as his grammar does cater for the
different options. A non-deterministic interpreter will handle temporary ambiguities automatically. Hence, it is relatively straightforward to write an ATN
grammar which covers the constructions desired – what varies is the extent to
which the parser behaves "non-deterministically".

With PIDGIN, the converse is the case – the interpreter *cannot* behave
"non-deterministically", but what varies is the extent to which the grammar-
writer can cover the data. There is a heavy responsibility on the grammar-writer
to find a way of writing his grammar (with the limited set of PIDGIN commands)
so that the parser will find exactly the right option without any backtracking
or pseudo-parallelism. This is actually very difficult for non-trivial examples, so
the tendency is to write clever grammars with rather narrow coverage, which
may be interesting theoretically but which may not always be very useful
practically. This leads to the slightly paradoxical conclusion (given the origins
of PIDGIN) that the most urgent requirement if PIDGIN is to be useful as a
general grammar-writing tool is the introduction of some form of non-determinism. This could be overt (controlled explicitly by the grammar rules) or covert
(handled automatically by the interpreter as in an ATN system). With all of
these enhancements, a much-revised PIDGIN could be a useful tool for linguistics;
otherwise, it is merely an interesting curiosity.

ACKNOWLEDGEMENTS
This work was carried out with the support of SERC grant GR/B9874.6. I would
like to thank Henry Thompson and Robert Inder for useful discussions and
suggestions.

REFERENCES
Briscoe, E. J. (1983) Determinism and its implementation in PARSIFAL. In
this volume.

Charniak, E. (1983) A parser with something for everyone. In King (1983).

Church, K. M. (1981) On memory limitations in natural language processing. Report MIT/LCS/TR-245, Laboratory for Computer Science, MIT.

Gazdar, G. (1981) Phrase structure grammar. In Jackson, P. and Pullum, G. K. (eds.) *The Nature of Syntactic Representation.* Dordrecht: Reidel, 131–186.

King, M. ed. (1983) *Parsing Natural Language.* New York: Academic Press.

Marcus, M. P. (1980) *A Theory of Syntactic Recognition for Natural Language.* Cambridge, Mass: MIT Press.

McDermott, D. V. (1976) Artificial intelligence meets natural stupidity. *SIGART Newsletter* **57**, 4–9.

Milne, R. W. (in preparation) Resolving lexical ambiguity in a deterministic parser. Ph.D. Thesis, Department of Artificial Intelligence, University of Edinburgh.

Radford, A. (1981) *Transformational Syntax.* Cambridge: Cambridge University Press.

Ritchie, G. D. (1980) *Computational Grammar.* Hassocks, Sussex: Harvester Press.

Ritchie, G. D. and Hanna, F. K. (1982) AM: A case study in AI methodology. Technical Report 18, Department of Computer Science, Heriot-Watt University, Edinburgh.

Sampson, G. R. (1983) Deterministic parsing. In King (1983).

Steedman, M. J. (1983) Natural and unnatural language processing. In this volume.

Thompson, H. S. and Ritchie, G. D. (1983) Implementing a natural language parser: two techniques. In Eisenstadt, M. and O'Shea, T. (eds) *Artificial Intelligence Skills.* New York: Harper and Row.

Winograd, T. (1972) *Understanding Natural Language.* Edinburgh: Edinburgh University Press.

Woods, W. A. (1970) Transition network grammars for natural language analysis. *Communications of the ACM* **13**, 591–606.

PART IV

Context-free parsing

NLs, CFLs and CF–PSGs

G. Gazdar, University of Sussex

0. INTRODUCTION

Consider the following quotations:

> As already mentioned, a context-free phrase structure grammar is not suffi-
> cient to describe or analyze the whole range of syntactic constructions
> which occur in natural language texts (cf. Chomsky, 1957). Even if one
> disregards the theoretical linguist's demand for satisfactory descriptions of
> the syntactic structure of sentences, there are strong reasons to design a
> more powerful parser than the one described above. ... Cases in point are
> the phonomenon of agreement within noun phrases, the correspondence in
> the verb phrase between the form of the main verb and the type of the
> auxiliary, and subject verb agreement. The argument structure of predicates,
> that is, their various types of objects and complements, represents another
> kind of context-sensitivity in natural language. ... The best strategy seems
> to be to take care of the particular types of context-sensitivity recognized
> by linguistic theory by means of special procedures which act as a super-
> structure of the algorithm for context-free analysis. ... In addition to the
> above-mentioned drawbacks of context-free phrase structure grammar has
> difficulty handling word order variation in a natural way. (Welin, 1979:
> 62–63).

> One significant use of the general context-free methods is as part of a
> system of processing natural languages such as English. We are not sugges-
> ting that there is a context-free grammar for English. It is probably more
> appropriate to view the grammar/parser as a convenient control structure
> for directing the analysis of the input string. The overall analysis is moti-
> vated by a linguistic model which is not context-free, but which can fre-
> quently make use of structures determined by the context-free grammar.
> (Graham, Harrison and Ruzzo, 1980: 415–416).

This research was supported by grant HR 7829/1 from the SSRC (UK). I am also grateful to
Ewan Klein, Geoff Pullum, Ivan Sag, and Henry Thompson, for interactions relevant to
this paper.

These two passages have a number of things in common, of which three are relevant here. Firstly, the issue of whether natural languages (NLs) are context-free languages (CFLs) and are susceptible to analysis by context-free phrase structure grammars (CF-PSGs) is one the authors take to be relevant to parsing. Secondly, both passages assume that this issue has already been resolved, and resolved in the negative. Thirdly, I did not have to look for them, I merely bumped into them, as it were, in the course of recent reading. However, I am sure that if I had been in the business of finding passages with this kind of flavour in the parsing literature of the past twenty years, then I could have found dozens, probably hundreds.

The purpose of the present paper is simply to draw the attention of computational linguists to the fact that the issue of the status of NLs with respects to the CFLs and CF-PSGs is not resolved, and to the fact that all the published arguments seeking to establish that NLs are not CFLs, or that CF-PSGs are not adequate for the analysis of NLs, are completely without force. Of course, this does not entail that NLs are CFLs or that CF-PSGs constitute the appropriate formal theory of NL grammars. But it does have as a consequence that computational linguists should not just give up on CF-PSGs on the grounds that theoretical linguistics has demonstrated their inadequacy. No such demonstration exists.

In assessing whether some formal theory of grammar is an adequate theory for NLs, at least the following three criteria are relevant, and have been historically. (i) Does it permit NLs qua sets of strings to be generated? (ii) Does it permit significant generalisations to be expressed? (iii) Does it support semantics, that is, does it provide a basis on which meanings can be assigned to NL expressions in a satisfactory manner?

In the remainder of this paper, I shall consider these three criteria in turn with reference to the adequacy of CF-PSGs as grammars for NLs. The issues are large, and space is limited, so my discussion will take the form, for the most part, of annotated references to the literature where the various issues are properly dealt with.

1. GENERATING NL STRING SETS

The belief that CF-PSGs cannot cope with synthetic concord and long-distance dependencies, and hence that NLs are not CFLs, but, say, properly context-sensitive languages, is well-entrenched. One textbook goes so far as to assert that 'the grammatical phenomenon of Subject Predicate Agreement is sufficient to guarantee the accuracy of [the statement that] English is not a CF-PSG language' (Grinder and Elgin, 1973: 59). The phenomenon guarantees no such thing, of course. Nor is the character of the problem changed when agreement is manifested across unbounded distances in strings (*pace* Bach, 1974: 77; Bresnan, 1978: 38). Indeed, finite state languages can exhibit such dependencies (see Pullum and Gazdar, 1982).

The introductory texts and similar expository works in the field of generative grammar offer nothing that could be taken seriously as an argument that NLs are not CFLs. However, five putatively non-specious arguments to this effect are to be found in the more technical literature. These are based on the following phenomena:

(a) English comparative clauses (Chomsky, 1963: 378–379),
(b) the decimal expansion of pi (Elster, 1978: 43–44),
(c) 'respectively' (Bar-Hillel and Shamir, 1960: 96; Langendoen, 1977: 4–5),
(d) Dutch subordinate clauses (Huybregts, 1976),
(e) Mohawk noun incorporation (Postal, 1964).

Pullum and Gazdar (1982) show that (a) is based on a false empirical claim and a false claim about formal languages, (b) has no bearing on English or any other natural language since it depends on a confusion between grammar and arithmetic, (c) is based on a false empirical claim, and the facts such as they are, are relevant to semantics rather than syntax in any case, (d) provides no basis for any string set argument[1], and (e) Postal crucially failed to take account of one class of permissible incorporations — once these are recognised, the formal basis of his argument collapses.

Thus, Pullum and Gazdar (1982) demonstrate that every published argument purporting to show that one or another NL is not a CFL is invalid, either formally, or empirically, or both. Whether any NL, construed as a string set, falls outside the class of CFLs remains an open question, just as it was twenty-five years ago.

2. CAPTURING SIGNIFICANT GENERALISATIONS

Argumentation purporting to show that CF-PSGs will miss significant generalisations about some NL phenomenon has been woefully inadequate. Typically it consists simply of providing or alluding to some CF-PSG which obviously misses the generalisation in question. But, clearly, nothing whatever follows from such an exhibition. *Any* framework capable of handling some phenomenon at all will typically make available indefinitely many ugly analyses of the phenomenon. But this fact is neither surprising nor interesting. What is surprising, and rather disturbing, is that arguments of this kind (beginning, classically, in Chapter 5 of Chomsky (1957)) have been taken so seriously for so long.

Capturing significant generalizations is largely a matter of notation. But CF-PSGs, taken as a class of mathematical objects, have properties which are theirs independently of the notations that might be used to define them. Thus they determine a certain set of string sets, they determine a certain set of tree sets, they stand in particular equivalence relations, and so on. An analogy from logic is pertinent here: the truth function material implication just is material implication whether you notate it with an arrow, or a hook, or the third letter of the alphabet, and whether you use prefix, infix, or postfix positioning of the symbol.

Over its twenty-five year history, transformational grammar developed a whole armoury of linguistically useful notations, and many of these can just as well be used in characterising CF-PSGs. Three such notational devices merit individual mention: (a) complex symbols, (b) rule schemata, and (c) mappings from one set of rules into another (metarules).

Harman (1963) deserves the credit for first seeing the potential of PSGs incorporating complex symbols. The use of a finite set of complex symbols, in place of the traditional finite set of monadic symbols, leaves the mathematical properties of CF-PSGs unchanged. Every CF-PSG employing complex symbols generates a tree set that is isomorphic to the tree set generated by some CF-PSG not employing complex symbols. However, complex symbols including features, "X-bar conventions", and "slash categories", etc., allow numerous significant syntactic generalizations to be captured rather straightforwardly.

For example, in Gazdar (1981a, 1981b) and Sag (1982a, 1982b) complex symbols called "slash categories" are shown to be able to capture the generalisations underlying the class of unbounded dependency constructions in English (e.g. relative clauses, wh-questions, topicalisation, etc.) including a generalisation about the interaction of such constructions with coordination that was never satisfactorily captured in transformational analyses (see Gazdar, Pullum, Sag and Wasow 1982). And Gazdar and Pullum (1981) show how the use of complex symbols for subcategorisation in a CF-PSG can capture generalisations that had had to be stipulated in the standard transformational account employing context-sensitive lexical insertion.

Rule schemata allow generalisations to be captured by collapsing sets of rules with some common property into a single statement. In a CF-PSG, one can capture the familiar generalisation that only like-constituents conjoin with a schema along the following lines:

$$\chi \to \chi \ and \ \chi$$

where χ is any category.

The generalisation that this captures was not captured in classical TG: part of it was expressed in the base rules, and the rest was intendedly expressed in the formulation of a transformation called "Coordination Reduction".

Another example of the power of rule schemata (applied to complex symbols) involves agreement phenomena:

$$S \to NP[\alpha] \ VP[\alpha]$$

where α ranges over permissible combinations of agreement features.

This schema, taken together with a widely assumed, and putatively univeral, convention of feature transfer, suffices to capture all the straightforward facts about subject verb agreement in English (see Gazdar, 1982).

A metarule is a grammar characterisation device (i.e. a clause in the definition of the grammar) which enables one to define one set of rules in terms of another set, antecedently given. Generalisations which would be lost if the two sets of rules were merely listed are captured by the metarule[2]. Note that transformations were mappings from sets of structures to sets of structures, whereas metarules are mappings from sets of rules to sets of rules. Gazdar and Sag (1981) show how metarules can capture the active-passive and reflexive pronoun generalisations in the definition of a PSG for English, and Gazdar, Pullum and Sag (1982) use metarules to provide accurate and non-redundant analyses for "Subject–auxiliary inversion", adverb placement, and VP ellipsis in a grammar of the English auxiliary system.

There is, thus, at the present time, no reason whatsoever to think that the goal of capturing linguistically significant generalisations is in any way inconsistent with the use of CF-PSGs[3].

3. SUPPORT OF A SEMANTICS

In asking whether some theory of syntax "supports a semantics", we are asking whether there exists some semantic theory which will interpret the structures provided by the syntax in a manner consistent with our judgments concerning ambiguity, synonymy, entailment, etc. Within linguistics, the key semantic development of the 1970s was the appearance of a model theory for natural languages originating in the work of Montague (see Montague, 1974; Dowty *et al.* 1981). Before Montague, linguists had been disposed either to do their semantics in the syntax, a practice that reached its apogee in the work of the Generative Semanticists, or not at all, as in Chomsky's oeuvre. But the sophisticated machinery (including lambda abstraction, meaning postulates, higher order quantification, intension and extension operators, etc.) which Montague had made available meant that semantics could now be done as such. This had all kinds of implications for syntax.

Here are some examples. (i) Heny (1970) and Cooper (1975) showed that quantifier scope ambiguities could be handled entirely in the semantics, without the need for quantifier movement in the syntax. (ii) Dowty (1978) showed that the semantic properties of dative, passive, unspecified object, "Raising" and "Equi" constructions could all be provided for directly, without corresponding syntactic operations that moved or deleted NPs. (iii) Also in 1978, three sets of authors independently proposed closely related cross-categorial semantic theories for coordination (Cooper, 1979; Gazdar, 1980a; Keenan and Faltz 1978). This work, which is further advanced in Partee and Rooth (1982), completely undercuts all semantic motivation for "Coordination Reduction" transformations or equivalent operations in the syntax. (iv) McCloskey (1979) was able to show that the deep structure/surface structure distinction was irrelevant to giving a semantics for relative clauses and wh-questions: structures of either kind provide a suitable locus for semantic interpretation. (v) And recent work by Klein (1980, 1981a, 1981b, 1982) has demonstrated that the meaning of all the various comparative constructions found in English can be derived directly from their surface syntactic forms as given by a CF-PSG along the lines of Gazdar (1980b).

Thus there is every reason to believe that CF-PSGs can support appropriate semantic theories for NLs at least as well as multilevel syntactic frameworks[4,5]. Indeed, there is an *ad hominem* argument which suggests that they may be preferable. It is noteworthy that almost all the linguists currently working out the implications of Montague's semantic legacy have gravitated towards essentially monostratal syntactic theories[6], although this concreteness is not obviously presaged in Montague's own, rather abstract, approach to syntax.

4. CONCLUSIONS

In brief, I have tried to make plausible the following three claims. (1) There is no reason, at the present time, to think that NLs are not CFLs. (ii) There are good reasons for thinking that the notations we need to capture significant syntactic generalisations will characterise CF-PSGs, or some minor generalisations of them, such as Indexed Grammars. (iii) There are very good reasons for believing that such grammars, and the monostratal representations they induce, provide the necessary basis for the semantic interpretation of NLs. And that, concomitantly, there is no semantic motivation for syntactic operations that move, delete, permute, copy or substitute constituents. The relevance, if any, of these claims to computational linguistics and the parsing of NLs is something that, in the present context, I am content to leave to others[7].

NOTES

1. Whether or not a CF-PSG can generate the correct structural descriptions for the relevant set of Dutch sentences is an intriguing open question. *If* the structural descriptions are what Bresnan, Kaplan, Peters and Zaenen (1982) assume them to be, then, as they show, the answer is no.

2. The idea of using one grammar to generate another originates in computer science with the work of van Wijngaarden (1969), who used the technique to give a perspicuous syntax for ALGOL 68. A good introduction to his work can be found in Cleaveland and Uzgalis (1975). Janssen (1980) employs a van Wijngaarden-style two-level grammar to define a generalisation of Montague's PTQ syntax.

3. So-called "free word order" languages have sometimes been alleged to pose a problem in principle for the generalisation-capturing powers of CF-PSGs. That they do not is amply demonstrated in Pullum (1982) and Stucky (1981).

4. This is not to suggest, of course, that all significant semantic problems are solved by the shift to surface structure syntax. One currently interesting puzzle concerns how one binds pronouns that appear in "dislocated" constituents (Cooper, in press; Dahl, 1981, 1982; Engdahl, 1982a, 1982b). Another concerns the possibility of multiple wh-type dependencies in Scandinavian languages, and the variable-binding issue that this gives rise to (see Engdahl, 1980; Maling and Zaenen, 1982). One promising strategy for getting a solution to both these problems entails grounding the semantics on an indexed grammar (Aho, 1968; Hopcroft and Ullman, 1979, pp. 389–390) rather than on a CF-PSG. Indexed grammars are similar to CF-PSGs which employ complex symbols, except that there is no finite limit on the number of distinct complex symbols that can be used. This generalisation of CF-PSG is potentially relevant to the issue mentioned in note 1, above, and to the nesting of equative and comparative clauses (see Klein, 1981b). Cf., also, the tree adjunction defined MSCLs of Joshi (1982) (the MSCLs properly include the CFLs but are properly included by the indexed languages).

5. I assume that this conclusion would carry over to non-Montague approaches to semantics. However, I have restricted myself here to the Montague paradigm since it is by far and away the most detailed and extensive framework for NL semantics available at the present time. That Montague's ideas are compatible with a computational orientation to language is evidenced or argued in a sizable body of recent work: e.g. Bronnenberg *et al.* (1980), Friedman (1978, 1981), Friedman, Moran and Warren (1978), Friedman and Warren (1978), Fuchi (1981), Gunji and Sondheimer (1980), Hobbs and Rosenchein (1978), Ishimoto (1982), Janssen (1976, 1977), Landsbergen (1981), Matsumoto (1981, 1982), Moran (1980), Nishida *et al.* (1981), Nishida and Doshita (1982), Root (1981), Saheki (1982), Sawamura (1981), Sondheimer and Gunji (1978), and Warren (1979). See also Gunji (1981) for a description of the programming language EIL – Extended Intensional Lisp.

6. E.g. Bach, Cooper, Dahl, Dowty, Karttunen, Keenan, Klein, Partee, Peters, and Sag, to name but ten.

7. E.g. Bear and Karttunen (1979), Ejerhed (1980), Fodor (1982a, 1982b), Gawron *et al.* (1982), Joshi and Levy (1980), Kay (1983), Konolige (1980), Pulman (1983), Robinson (1980, 1982), Ross (1981), Schubert and Pelletier (1982), and Thompson (1981, 1982). And see Berwick and Weinberg (1982) for a rather extended metatheoretical disquisition.

REFERENCES

Aho, A. (1968) Indexed grammars – an extension of context-free grammars. *Journal of the ACM* 15, 647–671.
Bach, E. (1974) *Syntactic Theory*. New York: Holt, Rinehart and Winston.

Bar-Hillel, Y. and Shamir, E. (1960) Finite state languages: formal representations and adequacy problems. Reprinted in Y. Bar-Hillel (1964) *Language and Information.* Reading Mass.: Addison-Wesley, 87–98.

Bear, J. and Karttunen (1979) PSG: a simple phrase structure parser. *Texas Linguistic Forum* **15**, 1–46.

Berwick, R. and Weinberg, A. (1982) Parsing efficiency, computational complexity, and the evaluation of grammatical theories. *Linguistic Inquiry* **13**, 165–191.

Bresnan, J. (1978) A realistic transformational grammar. In M. Halle, J. W. Bresnan and G. A. Miller (eds) *Linguistic Theory and Psychological Reality.* Cambridge, Mass.: MIT Press.

Bresnan, J., Kaplan, R., Peters, S. and Zaenen, A. (1982) Cross-serial dependencies in Dutch. *Linguistic Inquiry* **13**, 613–635.

Bronnenberg, W. J. H. C., Bunt, H. C., Landsbergen, S. P. J., Scha, R. J. H., Schoenmakers, W. J. and van Utteren, E. P. C. (1980) The question-answering system PHLIQA 1. In L. Bolc (ed.) *Natural Language Question-Answering Systems.* Munich: Carl Hanser Verlag.

Chomsky, N. (1957) *Syntactic Structures.* The Hague: Mouton.

Chomsky, N. (1963) Formal properties of grammars. In R. D. Luce, R. R. Bush and E. Galanter (eds) *Handbook of Mathematical Psychology,* Volume II. New York: Wiley.

Cleaveland, J. and Uzgalis, R. (1975) *Grammars for Programming Languages: What Every Programmer Should Know About Grammar.* New York: Elsevier.

Cooper, R. (1975) Montague's semantic theory and transformational syntax. Ph.D. dissertation, University of Massachusetts at Amherst.

Cooper, R. (1979) Model theory for a fragment of English. MS., University of Wisconsin at Madison.

Dahl, Ö. (1981) Bound pronouns in dislocated constituents – the case for contextually interpreted variables. Mimeo, University of Stockholm.

Dahl, Ö. (1982) Converting in bound pronouns: the problem and its solution. Mimeo, University of Stockholm.

Dowty, D. (1978) Governed transformations as lexical rules in a Montague Grammar. *Linguistic Inquiry* **9**, 393–426.

Dowty, D., Wall, R. and Peters, S. (1981) *Introduction to Montague Semantics.* Dordrecht: Reidel.

Ejerhed, E. (1980) A context-free phrase-structure parser for English auxiliaries. Paper presented to the Fourth Groningen Round Table Conference on Auxiliaries, Groningen, Holland, July 1980.

Elster, J. (1978) *Logic and Society: Contradictions and Possible Worlds.* New York: Wiley.

Engdahl, E. (1980) The syntax and semantics of questions in Swedish. Ph.D. dissertation, University of Massachusetts at Amherst.

Engdahl, E. (1982a) Constituent questions, topicalization, and surface structure interpretation. In D. Flickenger, M. Macken and N. Wiegand (eds) *Proceedings from the First Annual West Coast Conference on Formal Linguistics*, 256–267.

Engdahl, E. (1982b) A note on the use of lambda-conversion in generalized phrase structure grammars. *Linguistics and Philosophy* **4**, 505–515.

Fodor, J. (1982a) Phrase structure parsing and the island constraints. *Linguistics and Philosophy*. To appear.

Fodor, J. (1982b) How can grammars help parsers? Paper presented at the Conference on Syntactic Theory and How People Parse Sentences, Ohio State University, May 14–15, 1982.

Friedman, J. (1978) Computational and theoretical studies in Montague Grammar at the University of Michigan. *SISTM Quarterly* **1**, 62–66.

Friedman, J. (1981) Expressing logical formulas in natural language. In J. Groenendijk, T. Janssen and M. Stokhof (eds) *Formal Methods in the Study of Language*. Mathematical Centre Tracts, Amsterdam, 113–130.

Friedman, J., Moran, D. and Warren, D. (1978) An interpretation system for Montague Grammar. *American Journal of Computational Linguistics* microfiche 74, 23–96.

Friedman, J. and Warren, D. (1978) A parsing method for Montague Grammars. *Linguistics and Philosophy* **2**, 347–372.

Fuchi, K. (1981) Natural language and its formal representation: a case study of translation in Montague style from a programmer's point of view. Paper presented to the first Colloquium on Montague Grammar and Related Topics, Kyoto, February 1981.

Gawron, J. M., King, J., Lamping, J., Loebner, E., Paulson, A., Pullum. G., Sag, I. and Wasow, T. (1982) The GPSG linguistics system. *Proceedings of the 20th Annual Meeting of the Association for Computational Lingusitics*, 74–81. Also distributed as Hewlett Packard Computer Science Technical Note CSL-82-5.

Gazdar, G. (1980a) A cross-categorial semantics for coordination. *Linguistics and Philosophy* **3**, 407–409.

Gazdar, G. (1980b) A phrase structure syntax for comparative clauses. In T. Hoekstra, H.v.d. Hulst and M. Moortgat (eds) *Lexical Grammar*. Dordrecht: Foris Publications, 165–179.

Gazdar, G. (1981a) Unbounded dependencies and coordinate structure. *Linguistic Inquiry* **12**, 155–184.

Gazdar, G. (1981b) On syntactic categories. *Philosophical Transactions of the Royal Society* Series B **295**, 267–283.

Gazdar, G. (1982) Phrase structure grammar. In P. Jacobson and G. Pullum (eds) *The Nature of Syntactic Representation*. Dorsdrecht: D. Reidel, 131–186.

Gazdar, G. and Pullum, G. (1981) Subcategorization, constituent order and notion "head". In M. Moortgat, H.v.d. Hulst and T. Hoekstra (eds) *The Scope of lexical Rules*. Dordrecht: Foris Publications, 107–123.

Gazdar, G. and Sag, I. (1981) Passive and reflexives in phrase structure grammar. In J. Groenendijk, T. Hanssen and M. Stikhof (eds) *Formal Methods in the Study of Language.* Mathematical Centre Tracts, Amsterdam, 131–152.

Gazdar, G., Pullum, G. and Sag, I. (1982) Auxiliaries and related phenomena in a restrictive theory of grammar. *Language* **58**, 591–638.

Gazdar, G., Pullum, G., Sag, I. and Wasow, T. (1982) Coordination and transformational grammar. *Linguistic Inquiry* **13**, 663–676.

Graham, S., Harrison, M. and Ruzzo, W. (1980) An improved context-free recognizer. *ACM Transactions on Programming Languages and Systems* **2**, 415–462.

Grinder, J. and Elgin, S. (1973) *Guide to Transformational Grammar.* New York: Holt, Rinehart and Winston.

Gunji, T. (1981) Toward a computational theory of pragmatics – discourse, presupposition, and implicature. Ph.D. dissertation, Ohio State University.

Gunji, T. and Sondheimer, N. (1980) The mutual relevance of model-theoretic semantics and artificial intelligence. *SMIL: Journal of Linguistic Calculus* **3**, 5–42.

Harman, G. (1963) Generative grammars without transformation rules: a defense of phrase structure. *Language* **39**, 597–616.

Heny, F. (1970) Semantic operations on base structures. Ph.D. dissertation, University of California at Los Angeles.

Hobbs, J. and Rosenschein, S. (1978) Making computational sense of Montague's intensional logic. *Artificial Intelligence,* **9**, 287–306.

Hopcroft, J. and Ullman, J. (1979) *Introduction to Automata Theory, Languages, and Computation.* Reading, Mass.: Addison-Wesley.

Huybregts, M. A. C. (1976) Overlapping dependencies in Dutch. *Utrecht Working Papers in Linguistics* **1**, 24–65.

Ishimoto, I. (1982) A Lesniewskian version of Montague grammar and its application to computational linguistics. In J. Horecký (ed.) *Proceedings of the Ninth International Conference on Computational Linguistics.* Amsterdam: North-Holland. To appear.

Janssen, T. (1976) A computer program for Montague Grammar: theoretical aspects and proofs for the reduction rules. *Amsterdam Papers in Formal Grammar* **I**, 154–176.

Janssen, T. (1977) Simulation of a Montague Grammar. *Annals of System Research* **6**, 127–140.

Janssen, T. (1980) On problems concerning the quantification rules in Montague grammar. In C. Rohrer (ed.) *Time, Tense, and Quantifiers.* Tübingen: Max Niemeyer, 113–134.

Joshi, A. (1982) How much context-sensitivity is required, if any, for assigning reasonable structural descriptions? Paper presented at the Conference on Syntactic Theory and How People Parse Sentences, Ohio State University, May 14–15, 1982.

Joshi, A. and Levy, L. (1980) Phrase structure trees bear more fruit than you would have thought. Revised and expanded version of a paper presented at the 18th Annual Meeting of the Association for Computational Linguistics, University of Pennsylvania, Philadelphia, June 1980.

Kay, M. (1983) When meta-rules are not meta-rules. In this volume

Keenan, E. and Faltz, L. (1978) Logical types for natural language. *UCLA Occasional Papers in Linguistics 3*.

Klein, E. (1980) A semantics for positive and comparative adjectives. *Linguistics and Philosophy* **4**, 1–45.

Klein, E. (1981a) The interpretation of adjectival, nominal, and adverbial comparatives. In J. Groenendijk, T. Janssen and M. Stokhof (eds) *Formal Methods in the Study of Language*. Mathematical Centre Tracts, Amsterdam, 381–398.

Klein, E. (1981b) The syntax and semantics of nominal comparatives. In M. Moneglia (ed.) *Atti de Seminario su Tempo e Verbale Strutture Quantificate in Forma Logica*. Florence: Presso L'Accademia della Crusca, 223–253.

Klein, E. (1982) The interpretation of adjectival comparatives *Journal of Linguistics* **18**, 113–136.

Konolige, K. (1980) Capturing linguistic generalizations with metarules in an annotated phrase-structure grammar. *Proceedings of the 18th Annual Meeting of the Association for Computational Linguistics*, 43–48.

Landsbergen, J. (1981) Adaptation of Montague grammar to the requirements of parsing. In J. Groenendijk, T. Janssen and M. Stokhof (eds) *Formal Methods in the Study of Language*. Mathematical Centre Tracts, Amsterdam, 399–419.

Langendoen, D. T. (1977) On the inadequacy of type-2 and type-3 grammars for human languages. In P. J. Hopper (ed.) *Studies in Descriptive and Historical Linguistics*. Amsterdam: John Benjamin, 159–171.

Maling, J. and Zaenen, A. (1982) A phrase structure account of Scandinavian extraction phenomena. In P. Jacobson and G. Pullum (eds) *The Nature of Syntactic Representation*. Dordrecht: D. Reidel, 229–282.

Matsumoto, Y. (1981) Software implementation of Montague grammar and related problems. In S. Iguchi (ed.) *Formal Approaches to Natural Language: Proceedings of the First Colloquium on Montague Grammar and Related Topics*. Kyoto: Kyoto Working Group of Montague Grammar, 148–158.

Matsumoto, Y. (1982) A Montague grammar of Japanese with special regard to meaning adjustment. Paper presented to the Second Colloquim on Montague Grammar and Related Topics, Kyoto, March 1982.

McCloskey, J. (1979) *Transformational Syntax and Model Theoretic Semantics*. Dordrecht: Reidel.

Montague, R. (1974) *Formal Philosophy*. New Haven: Yale University Press.

Moran, D. B. (1980) Dynamic partial models. Ph.D. dissertation, University of Michigan.

Nishida, T.-A., Kiyono, M. and Doshita, S. (1981) An English–Japanese machine translation system based on formal semantics of natural language. In S. Iguchi (ed) *Formal Approaches to Natural Language: Proceedings of the First Colloquium on Montague Grammar and Related Topics.* Kyoto: Kyoto Working Group of Montague Grammar, 104–147.

Nishida, T.-A. and Doshita, S. (1982) An English–Japanese machine translation system based on formal semantics of natural language – a progress report. Paper presented to the Second Colloquium on Montague Grammar and Related Topics, Kyoto, March 1982.

Partee, B. and Rooth, M. (1982) Generalized conjunction and type ambiguity. In A. von Stechow *et al.* (eds) *Meaning, Use, and Interpretation.* Berlin: de Gruyter. To appear.

Postal, P. (1964) Limitations of phrase structure grammars. In J. A. Fodor and J. J. Katz (eds) *The Structure of Language: Readings in the Philosophy of language.* Englewood Cliffs: Prentice-Hall, 137–151.

Pullum, G. (1982) Free word order and phrase structure rules. In J. Pustejovsky and P. Sells (eds) *Proceedings of the Twelfth Annual Meeting of the North Eastern Linguistic Society.* Graduate Linguistics Student Association, University of Massachusetts, Amherst, Mass., 209–220.

Pullum, G. and Gazdar, G. (1982) Natural languages and context free languages. *Linguistics and Philosophy* **4**, 471–504.

Pulman, S. (1983) Generalised phrase structure grammar, Earley's algorithm, and the minimisation of recursion. In this volume.

Robinson, J. (1980) Computational aspects of the use of metarules in formal grammars. Research Proposal No. ECU 80–126, SRI International, Menlo Park, California.

Robinson, J. (1982) DIAGRAM: a grammar for dialogs. *Communications of the ACM* **25**, 27–47.

Root, R. (1981) SMX: a program for translating English into Montague's intensional logic. MS., Department of Linguistics, University of Texas at Austin.

Ross, K. (1981) Parsing English phrase structure. Ph.D. dissertation, University of Massachusetts at Amherst.

Sag, I. (1982a) Coordination, extraction, and generalized phrase structure. *Linguistic Inquiry* **13**, 329–336.

Sag, I. (1982b) On parasitic gaps. In D. Flickenger, M. Macken and N. Wiegand (eds) *Proceedings from the First Annual West Coast Conference on Formal Linguistics.* Stanford, 35–46. Also to appear in *Linguistics and Philosophy.*

Saheki, M. (1982) A software program for a language like natural language. Paper presented to the Second Colloquium on Montague Grammar and Related Topics, Kyoto, March 1982.

Sawamura, H. (1981) Intensional logic as a basis of algorithmic logic. Paper presented to the First Colloquium on Montague Grammar and Related Topics, Kyoto, February 1981.

Schubert, L. and Pelletier, J. (1982) From English to logic: context-free computation of "conventional" logical translations. In J. Horecký (ed) *Proceedings of the Ninth International Conference on Computational Linguistics*. Dordrecht: North Holland. To appear.

Sondheimer, N. and Gunji, T. (1978) Applying model-theoretic semantics to natural language understanding: representation and question-answering. *Proceedings of the Seventh International Conference on Computational Linguistics*, Bergen.

Stucky, S. (1981) Word order variation in Makua: a phrase structure grammar analysis. Ph.D. dissertation, University of Illinois at Urbana-Champaign.

Thompson, H. (1981) Chart parsing and rule schemata in PSG. *Proceedings of the 19th Annual Meeting of the Association for Computational Linguistics*, 167–172.

Thompson, H. (1982) Handling metarules in a parser for GPSG. Research Paper No. 175, Department of Artificial Intelligence, University of Edinburgh. To appear in J. Horecký (ed) *Proceedings of the Ninth International Conference on Computational Linguistics*. Dordrecht: North-Holland.

van Wijngaarden, A. (1969) Report on the algorithmic language ALGOL68. *Numerische Mathematik* **14**, 79–218.

Warren, D. (1979) Syntax and semantics in parsing: an application to Montague Grammar. Ph.D. dissertation, University of Michigan.

Welin, C. W. (1979) *Studies in Computational Text Comprehension*. Stockholm: Institute of Linguistics.

When meta-rules are not meta-rules

M. Kay, Xerox Palo Alto Research Center

INTRODUCTION

I want to exploit an analogy between phonological rules and meta-rules in Generalised Phrase Structure Grammar (GPSG) resulting in an alternative for the model usually presented of the role meta-rules play. It should have consequences for the way we assess grammars of that type as mental models and particularly for the kinds of parser that might be appropriate for them. In brief, I shall advocate a model in which meta-rules are viewed as constituting a transducer that intervenes between the ordinary rules and the strings of constituents they describe much as phonological rules intervene between the lexicon and the strings of phonetic matrices that make up an utterance.

Phonological[†] rules are usually stated from the speaker's point of view, that is, they are designed to take strings of canonical lexical headings as input and to deliver textual strings as output. The reasons for this are not clear, but they are probably related to the fact that, whereas utterances are primary data, lexical forms are under the linguist's control so that they can be manipulated to make the rules more convenient. It is therefore generally the case that, up to free variation, things can be arranged so that a string of lexical forms is unambiguously translatable into a textual string whereas a textual string may correspond to large numbers of lexical strings. It is not a trivial matter to find a hearer's equivalent for a set of phonological rules of this kind and, in its absence, the designer of a parser or recognition model has two alternatives: he can expand the lexicon to include all possible variants, or *allomorphs,* of each morpheme, annotating each with the characteristics of the environments in which it could legitimately be used. Alternatively, he can design a new set of rules from scratch, not systematically related to those assumed used by the speaker or included in the competence model.

---

†Computational linguistics have usually been more concerned with *graphological*, orthographic, or spelling, than with phonological rules. In this paper, I shall continue to use phonological terminology for the sake of the status it confers while taking examples mainly from orthography for the sake of their familiarity and ease of statement.

The usual descriptions of GPSG are based on a model in which meta-rules are used as much as in the allomorph approach to phonology, every possible variant of the basic set of rules being assembled in a *working* grammar before any processing is undertaken, whether by speaker or hearer. This is the obvious strategy to follow because it requires a very few new kinds of object to be posited – essentially only the meta-rules themselves. In addition, once the working grammar has been assembled, analysis is set on an equal footing with generation. This is important to the adherents of GPSG, who take seriously their commitment to treat the hearer as a first-class citizen.

Other approaches to the treatment of meta-rules would not have these advantages because the problem of reversing syntactic meta-rules is every bit as difficult as the parallel problem in phonology. The approach I shall advocate requires a considerable array of unfamiliar devices and kinds of objects. To that extent it is less appealing. However, the standard approach is also not without its disadvantages. The conceptual simplicity of the "allorule" approach is bought at some considerable expense to the language learner, who presumably must engage in a major processing effort when modifications are made to his grammar, especially if they affect the meta-rules. In fact, the more he knows about the language, the more and the faster the complexity of that processing step increases. From the learner's standpoint, simplicity comes with being able to treat rules and meta-rules as unit-cost items.

The cost incurred in theory by the language learner is paid in an obvious and straightforward way by the computational linguist who is using a generation or parsing program as a tool in perfecting a grammar, for he must presumably repeat the computation of a new working grammar after every change that he makes. Another potential disadvantage of the standard allorule approach is that the number of working rules required for a realistic grammar of a language may turn out to be unmanageably large. One of the most striking formal properties of GPSG is certainly the great combinatoric power of its meta-rules. Precise statements cannot be made about this power because it has yet to be decided how the ability of meta-rules to apply their own output, and that of other rules, should be limited. However, it is at least clear that meta-rules are interesting only to the extent that they retain a considerable amount of combinatoric power.

The alternative view of meta-rules that I propose in this paper does not avoid all the disadvantages of the standard theory. For efficient use, it also requires considerable preprocessing of the grammar, though differing amounts of this can be traded off against the efficiency of the generation and parsing processes. Certainly, it does not require the working grammar to be recomputed whenever a new meta-rule is proposed. Just what the relative costs of the two schemes will turn out to be is far from clear. For the moment I will be content to claim only that this scheme offers greater flexibility to infant and algorithm designer alike.

Limitations on the ordering of meta-rule applications is a topic that has received too little attention from the proponents of GPSG. It is a pressing issue if only because the claim that the grammars are in fact context free turns upon being able to show, at the very least, that the number of rules they contain is finite. Meta-rules have the form of general rewriting rules which, if allowed to apply without restraint, would not support this assumption. In the absence of guidance from the theoreticians, the writer of a computer program for generation or analysis is forced to take some sort of stand on the issue, and those with which I am familiar have imposed what seems to be the minimal restriction, namely that rules may apply each to the output of the one before and in any order, but that no meta-rule may be applied more than once to the same rule.

It is presumably appropriate for a technician to make only minimal assumptions while awaiting clarification from those endowed with theoretical insight. But the *use-once* proposal is flagrantly implausible. As far as I know, no such principle has been made in all the illustrious rule-making history of our subject. It requires more mechanism for its execution than any other proposal I have heard; in all but the simplest cases, it necessitates the use of a computer to determine just what working rules a given basic rule gives rise to; it is remarkably brittle in the sense of producing very sweeping changes in the working grammar as a result of apparently trivial changes in the basic grammar; in short, of all the proposals that might meet the basic theoretical requirement, it is the most powerful and the least manageable.

In the balance of this paper, I shall assume that meta-rules are simply ordered, just as the phonological rules of almost any theory are considered to be. This makes for a weaker device and therefore involves a much stronger empirical claim: on that basis alone, it would be regarded as superior in many quarters. This proposal has the practical advantage of making the outcome of applying a set of meta-rules to a given set of context-free rules a simple and intuitive matter, with the concomitant advantage for grammarian and infant alike that grammars become altogether less brittle. The proposals I have to make are much easier to carry through under this assumption about meta-rule application, though it turns out that they do not turn on it crucially. However, from my point of view, the use-once proposal is about as bad as any that could be readily imagined because it would give rise to data structures that would be unmanageably large and expensive to compute.

A STRAW MAN

Logically speaking, nothing turns on whether we think of the rules of the working grammar as being computed once for all before they are needed or as being worked out on demand in the course of sentence generation and analysis. The mechanism that is responsible for applying meta-rules can be thought of as a transducer interposed between that store of grammar rules and the generation or analysis device, from the point of view of which it is immaterial whether the computation is being repeated each time a rule is required, or has been done in advance and the results stored away.

There are also other logically possible ways of obtaining the effects for which meta-rules were devised. One possibility is to regard meta-rules as applying to strings of constituents in the course of parsing. The following example gives a rough sketch of how this might go. Consider the meta-rule[†]

$$VP \rightarrow V \ NP \ldots \ \Rightarrow \ VP \rightarrow V_{[form:\ passive]} \ \ldots (PP_{[case:\ by]}) \qquad (1)$$

which is normally described as taking as input a rule such as

$$VP \rightarrow V \ NP \ PP* \qquad (2)$$

and delivering as output

$$VP \rightarrow V_{[form:\ passive]} \ PP* \ (PP_{[case:\ by]}) \qquad (3)$$

Suppose that some form of chart parser is to be used and the sentence to be analysed is *the job could be done in a week by a good technician*. After some number of steps, we may assume that the chart contains among others, the edges shown in Fig. 1.

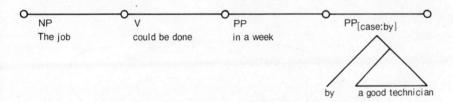

Fig. 1 – An early stage in the analysis of a sentence.

The rule needed to take the next step is clearly (3), the passive *VP* rule. But suppose that no working grammar has been constructed by applying meta-rules to rules so that no passive *VP* rule is available. Instead a minor variant, which we may write as (4), of the meta-rule (1) is applied directly to the chart, rewriting the sequence $V \, PP \, PP_{[case:\ by]}$ as $[_{VP} \ V \ NP \ PP]_{VP}$ as in Fig. 2.

$$V \ldots PP_{[case:\ by]} \rightarrow [_{VP} \ V \ NP \ PP*]_{VP} \qquad (4)$$

[†]Since I am not concerned with semantics, I am not adopting the notation for rules and meta-rules preferred by the proponents of GPSG, preferring one that follows more traditional lines.

The role of the subscripted brackets, which are entered in the chart explicitly, is to ensure that the sequence *V NP PP* that they enclose be incorporatable into the sentence structure only in a manner that the meta-rule sanctions. The subscript *inside* the first bracket states the requirement that the material matching the specification *inside* the brackets must be analysed as *VP*. The subscript *outside* the second bracket says that *VP* will be labelled as a *VP* when it is entered in the chart, rather than as some other non-terminal symbol specified in the meta-rule. In short, the sequence must be analysed as a *VP* and can function as a *VP* in larger structures. More generally, a meta-rule of the form (5) will allow any sequence of constituents in the chart that fits the pattern to be rewritten as (6).

$$\alpha \to \beta \Rightarrow \gamma \to \delta \tag{5}$$

$$[_\gamma \, \beta \,]_\alpha \tag{6}$$

If β is a single constituent of category γ, or can be reduced to one by the application of other rules, then it can be labelled as belonging to category α and incorporated into larger structures as such. In other words, for every pair of categories γ and α, there is a rewriting rule of the form

$$[_\gamma \, \gamma \,]_\alpha \to \alpha \tag{7}$$

The heavy loops labelled **VP** in Fig. 2 are active edges.[†] The one at the right-hand end of the $[_{VP}$ edge is introduced with the purpose of finding a *VP*-analysis of the bracketed material. A corresponding active edge would be introduced following any such open bracket according to this scheme. In the present case,

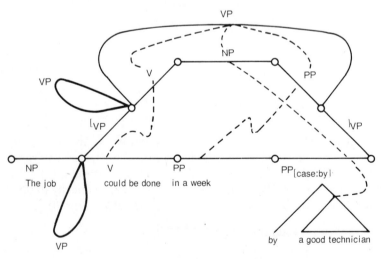

Fig. 2 – A later stage in the analysis of a sentence.

†For a discussion of this terminology, and of chart parsing in general, see Kay (1977).

it gives rise, in due course, to the *VP* edge shown at the top of the diagram. The other active **VP** edge is the one that would be introduced in the normal course of the parsing. The dotted lines represent associations between constituents that would be established by the semantic component of the rules and which are beyond our scope. Roughly, they represent either constituency or semantic identity.

The use that is being made of the chart here is unconventional in rewriting strings as other strings and not simply as single symbols. It was in fact just in order to permit such operations that charts were first proposed in Kay (1967). Meta-rules are placed on an even footing with context-free rules and made to look for all the world like the local transformations of yesteryear. However, by applying meta-rules without regard to which context-free rules will apply to their output, such a technique runs into serious difficulties that the above example does not bring out sharply enough. They are made immediately clear by a so-called *linking* meta-rule[†] that introduces "slashed" categories. I take this to be somewhat as follows:

$$X \to \ldots Y \ldots \Rightarrow X/Z \to \ldots Y/Z \ldots \qquad (8)$$

where X, Y and Z are variables ranging over suitable categories. In reading a rule like this, it is to be understood that the first and second set of dots, "...." that appear on the left side correspond to the first and second set on the right side. Situations in which such unspecified strings occurred in different orders in the two parts of the rule would require additional notational devices which we shall not need. The problem with this is that the unspecified strings occur at the ends of the pattern to be matched so that if the specified central element is found in the ith position of a string of n constituents, there are $i-1$ places before the ith position where the rule could begin matching and $n-i$ following the ith position where it could finish matching for a total of $(i-1)(n-i)$ times. Furthermore, a realistic grammar would doubtless contain many meta-rules that would provoke this kind of behaviour and, since many of them could be applied to the output of others, their explosive effects would be multiplied. If this is added to the already known sources of combinatory explosion that characterise the parsing process, the result will clearly be impracticable.

To one regularly involved with parsing techniques, the problem just identified has a familiar ring. It arises because a mechanism that converts one thing into another — a rewriting rule or transducer — is being used in an *undirected*[‡] manner, that is, without regard to whether the results will be useful in some other part of the process. In a later section, I shall show how a directed version of the technique just discussed can be made to work. By way of preparation. I now turn to the analogous problem in phonology.

† See Gazdar, Pullum and Sag (1981).

‡For a discussion of the notions of *directed* and *undirected* rule application in parsing, see Griffiths and Petrick (1965) and Kay (1980).

PHONOLOGICAL AND GRAPHOLOGICAL RULES

There is a large and interesting class of phonological rules that can be systematically restated in a way that not only permits them to be incorporated in a recognition model but allows for unexpectedly efficient processing by speaker
and hearer alike. The translation process produces a finite-state transducer,
similar to a finite-state machine except in that its transactions carry two labels
instead of one, each label referring to one of the two tapes to which the machine
is connected. A standard finite-state machine is said to *accept* a tape if the
characters on it match the labels on a sequence of transitions taken from its
state-transition diagram starting in the initial state and ending in one of a set of
designated *final* states. If no such sequence can be found, the tape is rejected.
A finite-state transducer, for us, is just like this except that it accepts or rejects
pairs of tapes. Accordingly, its transitions are labelled with pairs of symbols.
Provision is made for transitions in which the symbol to be matched against one
or other of the tapes is empty, in which case the corresponding tape is ignored
when the transition is taken. This provision is necessary if it is to be possible to
accept pairs of tapes of unequal length.

The transition diagram for a simple transducer is shown in Fig. 3. This
machine embodies a greatly simplified version of the rules governing the spelling

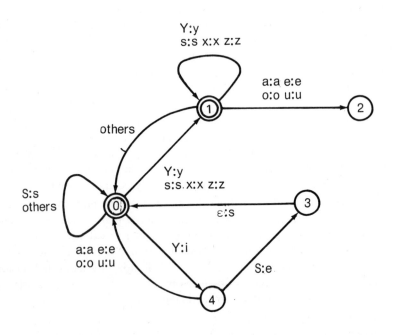

Fig. 3 – A transducer for morphographemic rules.

of the endings of regular plural nouns and third person singular verbs in English, and the changes in spelling that occur when certain endings are appended to a word that ends in "y". For the purpose of the example, I assume that lexical entries are written with a twenty-eight-letter alphabet consisting of the lower case letters plus two special characters, S and Y. The plural or 3rd-person ending is the only lexical entry spelled with the S, and the Y is used for the last letter of words like *flY* and *emptY*.

In the interests of simplicity, I have nowhere shown more than one transition between a given pair of states but have written all the labels on such a set of transitions against a single arc. The word *others* is used in the diagram as a short-hand for a list of up to 26 labels of the form *x:x* where x is a lower case letter that does not appear explicitly as the label on any other transition from that state. So, for example, the *others* label on the arc from and to state 0 stands for 23 transitions, *a:a . . . r:r, t:t, u:u, v:v, w:w, y:y*, whereas the one from state 1 to state 0 stands for 19 transitions, because *a:a, e:e, o:o,* and *u:u* are missing in addition as they label transitions from that state to state 2. State 0 is the initial state and double circles indicate final states.

The transducer works in an extremely simple way, which is illustrated in Fig. 4. The upper tape is assumed to contain a sequence of lexical items and the

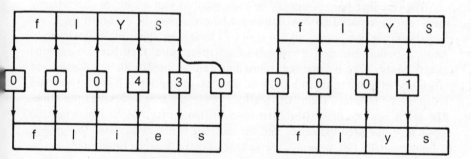

Fig. 4 – The operation of the morphographemic transducer.

lower a putative textual string. The diagram on the left shows the states that the machine would pass through in the course of accepting a pair of tapes with the string *flYs* on the first and *flies* on the second, namely 0, 0, 4, 3, 0. The boxes in the centre of the diagram show the state of the machine when it is in the position indicated by the upper and lower arrows. Notice that the last transition moves only the lower tape; the symbol ϵ in Fig. 3 is the *empty* symbol and causes the corresponding tape to be ignored. The diagram on the right demonstrates that the machine does *not* accept the pair *flYS* and *flys* because there is no transition from state 1 for the pair *S:s*.

A more traditional way to capture the facts enshrined in this transducer would be in a set of ordered rules such as the following:

1. S → es/**Sibilant**_
2. S → es/Y_
3. S → s
4. Y → y/_i
5. Y → i/_**Vowel**
6. Y → y

where **Sibilant** = {s, x, z}
and   **Vowel** = {a, e, i, o, u}

Kaplan and I designed an algorithm for deriving a transducer from such a set of rules. This algorithm operates in two stages. In the first, a transducer is built for each of the rules in the set. The details of this stage are not relevant to our present concerns. I shall describe a new one, designed for use with meta-rules in a later section. In the second stage, these machines are composed, two at a time, until only one remains. The composition operation is applicable to any pair of transducers and will also have a role to fill in the techniques to be proposed for handling meta-rules.

The fact that transducers can be composed, so that a cascade of arbitrarily many can be reduced to one simple machine that can be modelled by an extremely simple computer program is one of their most appealing characteristics. Another is that, unlike ordered sets of rewriting rules; they have no essential directionality, that is, that same machine can be used with equal ease and efficiency in generation and analysis. Instead of reading a pair of tapes and accepting or rejecting them, the machine reads one tape and writes the other. The result consists of whatever has been written on the output tape when the input tape has been exhausted and the machine is in a final state. The process is fundamentally non-deterministic so that, if more than one output tape can be set in correspondence with the given input tape, they can all be found. Those that fail to carry the machine into a final state are simply ignored.

I said in the introduction to this paper that lexical strings usually translate unambiguously into textual strings but the reverse does not hold. Notice that even the very simple transducer discussed above, and whose transition diagram is given in Fig. 3, allows the following correspondences:

> flYS   flies
> flYes   flies
> flies   flies

The strings on the left, viewed as canonical lexical forms, can each be paired with only one textual string, namely *flies*. However, this can be paired with three lexical strings. If more rules were added to the grammar, we should expect the number of lexical strings corresponding to a given textual string to increase. It should apparently follow from this that analysis would be a fundamentally less efficient process than generation, even if carried out with one and the same transducer, because a significant proportion of the intermediate results produced by the transducer would not match anything in the lexicon. But this depends, once again, on whether the analysis is done in a directed manner.

Let us make the reasonable assumption that the word analyser stores the canonical forms of lexical entries in the form of a tree. Such an arrangement, suitable for recognising just the words in the sentence "Fiction flies in the face of fact" is depicted in the upper left corner of Fig. 5. The point is that, whenever two entries share some initial characters, these are represented only once.

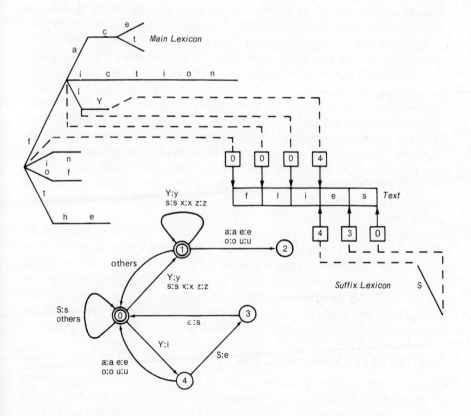

Fig. 5 – Word recognition.

Using such a tree, it is a straightforward matter to conduct an incremental search for lexical entries in parallel with the operation of the transducer, so that any non-deterministic path on which the latter embarks can be curtailed as soon as it requires a character in the lexicon that cannot be found there. The fundamental notion is to use the lexical tree in place of one of the transducer's tapes. An example will make this clear.

At the top of Fig. 5 is the main lexical tree. At the bottom right is a second lexicon containing the single entry "S". The bottom left of the figure is simply a reproduction of Fig. 3 and the figure as a whole shows how the tree-structured lexicon and the transducer conspire in the recognition of the word "flies" which is laid out on the tape represented in the centre of the figure. Just as in Fig. 4, little boxes with numbers in them are used to show the various states of the transducer. The transducer is in state 0 before reading the first character of the text and its other pointer is to the root node of the larger lexical tree. After reading f from the text tape, it remains in state 0 and its lexical pointer moves over the character f in the tree. The machine also remains in state 0 as both pointers move over the character l. From the current lexical node, the only possible move is over the character Y. The transducer can pair this with an i in the text by moving to state 4, as the figure shows. The entry flY in the lexicon has now been provisionally recognised. The recognition is only provisional because the transducer is not in a final state. Since flY is a word that allows, among others, the suffix S, we now replace the main lexicon with a suffix lexicon which, for the sake of simplicity, we assume to contain this suffix alone. The depictions of the transducer's states are now shown below that of the text tape. The transducer remains in state 4 while the lexicon change takes place. It then advances to state 3 over e on the text tape and S in the suffix lexicon. Finally, the transducer advances from state 3 to state 0, reading s from a text tape and ignoring the dictionary. The recognition of the word "flies" is thus completed.

The point of this somewhat protracted example has been to show how the dictionary, if made available in a suitable form, can be used to *direct* the operation of the transducer so that, instead of producing all candidate lexical strings that the spelling rules would allow and looking each of them up independently in the lexicon, it uses the transducer to evaluate a predicate on a pair of objects, one the text string, and the other a path through the dictionary trees. I shall now show how this same strategy can be applied to syntactic rules and meta-rules.

CONTEXT-FREE RULES AS TRANSITION NETWORKS

We saw in the last section how one of the transducer's tapes can be replaced with a tree-structured lexicon. Since the finite-state transducers are non-deterministic devices, nothing fundamental changes when a tape where every cell has a unique successor is replaced by a tree whose nodes may have more than one. If the tape and the transition diagram of the transducer permit more than one branch of the tree to be followed, the non-deterministic process simply splits and independent paths are followed for each possible branch of the tree.

In adapting this scheme to syntactic analysis, the first step we take is to replace the *other* tape – the text tape – with a branching data structure, namely the chart. The second is to replace the tree-structured lexicon with a tree-structured version of the basic grammar, that is the context-free rules of the grammar, untreated by meta-rules. Finally, we must convert the meta-rules into a transducer that can mediate between these two data structures. The first step need not detain us; the second will occupy us only briefly, and the third will require more discussion.

At the heart of almost any parser is a process in which rules are sought which could be applied to an initial subsequence of a particular string of constituents. In a directed parser, only a certain subset of the rules in the grammar is considered, typically those that expand a certain non-terminal symbol; in a non-directed parser, all rules are eligible. Suppose that there are n eligible rules, as follows:

$$1. \quad \alpha_1 \rightarrow \beta_1$$

$$n. \quad \alpha_n \rightarrow \beta_n$$

The object of the step, then, is to determine which members of the set $\{\beta_1 \ldots \beta_n\}$ are initial subsequences of the string at hand. This problem is logically indistinguishable from that of identifying the first word of a text in a lexicon, and the procedure can often be expedited by arranging the members of the set $\{\beta_1 \ldots \beta_n\}$ in just the kind of tree structure described in the last section. Such a representation is particularly appropriate if, as in the case of GPSG, the rules make use of the Kleene star and other devices borrowed from the formalism of regular expressions. Under these circumstances, the tree structures that figure in the above discussion become finite-state transition networks. This is a desirable move to make, independently of the considerations raised here, because finite-state machines are inherently more amenable to computational processes than regular expressions. If the following were the only eligible rules, the transition network might be as in Fig. 6.

1. S → NP VP
2. NP → DET ADJ* NP
3. NP → NP REL
4. NP → NP PP*
5. VP → V NP PP*

The heavier lines, whose labels end in an arrow, represent the symbols on the left-hand side of the rule; we shall take up the function of these shortly.

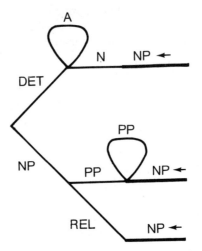

Fig. 6 – A transition network for grammar rules.

META-RULES AS TRANSDUCERS

Figure 7 is a transducer which embodies the information in the two meta-rules we have considered, namely (1) and (8). I shall make at least a *prima facie* case for this claim after first explaining the few additional notational devices in the diagram.

The symbol φ is simply a shorthand device. It matches any categorial symbol and it is to be understood that a transition over a pair $\varphi : \varphi$ is allowable only if the same unspecified category level appears both in the lexicon and in the chart; in other words, it is implicit that the symbols matched by such a pair are the same.

The labels in some transitions make use of subscripts. These constitute a fundamentally new device added to the structure of transducers to allow them to represent meta-rules. Towards the end of this paper, I shall propose a more general mechanism to replace subscripts; however, they will satisfy our present needs and their intuitive appeal is more immediate. The purpose of the subscripts is to coordinate unspecified substrings on the two tapes. If some number of symbols on the upper tape is matched by symbols in the transition diagram with a given subscript, say i, then that same number of symbols on the lower tape must also be matched by symbols with that subscript. Furthermore, if a symbol on the upper tape, say x, is matched by φ_i, and this is the kth symbol on the upper tape matched by a symbol with the subscript i, then the kth symbol on the lower tape that matches a symbol with subscript i must also be x. So, consider the paths that lead from the initial state $\langle 0, 0 \rangle$ to the final state $\langle 3, 2 \rangle$ in Fig. 7. These in fact correspond to the situations in which both the passive and linking meta-rules apply. The transitions from state $\langle 1, 0 \rangle$ are the

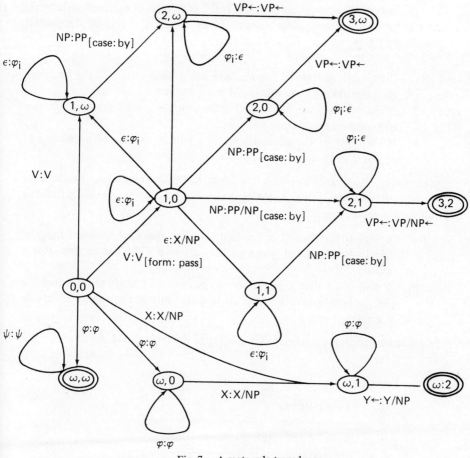

Fig. 7 – A meta-rule transducer.

ones that actually match slashed categories on the lower tape, the one incident to state $<2, 1>$ for the case where the NP gap will occur in the *by* prepositional phrase of the passive construction, the one incident to state $<1, 1>$ for all other cases. Three looping transitions are encountered along this path, two labelled $\epsilon : \varphi_i$ and one labelled $\varphi_i : \epsilon$. The convention governing subscripts requires that the number of times this last one is traversed be the same as the total number of times either of the other two is traversed. Furthermore, since the subscripted symbol is always φ, the symbols traversed on the upper tape by these loops must be the same symbols, and in the same order, as those traversed by loops on the lower tape. In particular, a string $V \; NP \; x \; y \; z \; VP \leftarrow$ on the upper tape will match $V \; x \; y \; z \; PP/NP_{[case:by]}$ on the lower tape, whereas the same upper tape would not match $V \; x \; y \; PP/NP_{[case:by]}$ or $V \; w \; x \; y \; z \; PP/ NP_{[case:by]}$.

The reason for naming the states of Fig. 7 with pairs of numbers rather than more simply will be made clear shortly. For the moment, it may be illuminating to note the following facts about these pairs.

1. If the current state of the machine has a label with ω in the first position, the linking meta-rule is not being applied.
2. If the current state has a label with ω in the second position, the passive meta-rule is not being applied.
3. If the label of the current state is a pair of digits, the possibility of applying neither meta-rule has been foreclosed.

Accordingly, the transducer has four final states corresponding to the four possible combinations of meta-rule applications. The state labels also permit the following generalizations:

4. A digit other than 0 in the first position of a label indicates that the current rule application can go through only if the linking meta-rule is applied.
5. A digit other than 0 in the second position of a label indicates that the current rule application can go through only if the passive meta-rule is applied.

Particular digits can be interpreted according to the table in Fig. 8.

First position	
State	Interpretation
0	Initial state
1	Last pair was $V{:}V$—committed to passive
2	Last pair was NP: *by*-phrase of passive
3	Passive completed

Second position	
State	Interpretation
0	No slashed category seen
1	One slashed category seen
2	Linking meta-rule complete

Fig. 8 – Key to the states of the meta-rule transducer.

Figure 9 is an example, parallel to the phonological one shown in Fig 5, of the transducer in operation. On the left of the figure is a simple grammar organised in the form of a tree. Dashed lines connect a sequence of nodes in this tree to depictions of the transducer as it moves through the states $<0, 0>$, $<1, 0>$, $<2,1>$, $<2, 1>$, $<3, 2>$. The sequence of constituents encountered in the chart is *V, PP/NP, PP*. The last transition, from state $<2, 1>$ to state $<3, 2>$, is treated somewhat specially; the second symbol named in the transition is not compared with the label on an edge in the chart, like the preceding ones, because the symbol ends with the character "←". All such symbols are interpreted by the parser as the labels of new edges to be inserted into the chart, that is as the output of successful rule applications. Accordingly, in making this last transition, the parser completes the analysis of the sequence *V PP/NP PP* as a constituent of category *VP/NP*.

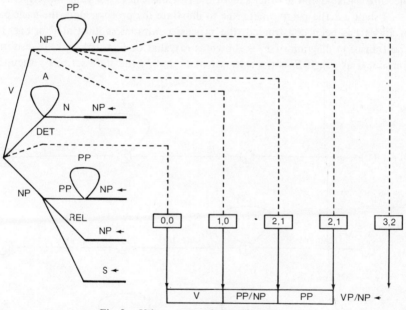

Fig. 9 – Using a meta-rule transducer.

CONSTRUCTING META-RULE TRANSDUCERS

It remains to explain how a transducer can be constructed for an individual meta-rule and how a set of these can then be combined into a single transducer. As I pointed out earlier, meta-rules have the structure.

$$\alpha \rightarrow \beta \Rightarrow \gamma \rightarrow \delta \tag{9}$$

and β and δ are regular expressions. By concatenating $\alpha{\leftarrow}$ and $\gamma{\leftarrow}$ (both single symbols) on the ends of β and δ respectively, we reduce the meta-rule to a simple pair of regular expressions. On the principle that computation is easier with finite-state machines (FSMs) than with regular expressions, and that the end result of the present computation will be a member of the same family of devices as FSMs, we next convert these regular expressions to a pair of FSMs, F_l and F_r, corresponding to the left and right sides of the meta-rule. An algorithm for doing this can be found in any elementary text on automata theory. The only modification required for the present purpose is to allow for subscripts. Whenever a variable is encountered in the course of carrying out the algorithm that is intended to match a substring of unspecified length, it will naturally be translated as though it were a simple variable covering a single symbol, but annotated with a Kleene star to show that it can be repeated any number of times. It must also receive a subscript, different from any used in any other rule or on the same side of the present rule. Any other occurrences of the same variable on the other side of the rule must have the same subscript.

I shall use the passive meta-rule to illustrate the process. Once the basic pair of FSMs has been constructed, the process continues as illustrated in Fig. 10. The transition diagram of F_l is shown as (a), that of F_r as (b), and the resulting transducer as (c). If S_l is the state set of F_l and S_r the state set of F_r, then the

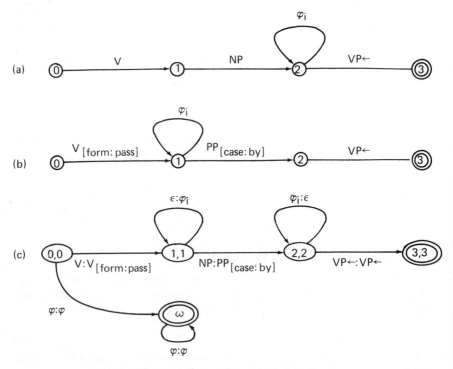

Fig. 10 – The construction of a meta-rule transducer.

transducer we shall construct will have states corresponding to a subset of $S_l \times S_r$. The problem of constructing the transducer therefore reduces to one of deciding, for a given state $<p, q> \in S_l \times S_r$, what transitions will be incident from it and at which states each of them will terminate. The obvious strategy is to start with the initial state, and then consider in turn hitherto untreated states at the end of which already constructed transitions terminate. We thus avoid constructing transitions for states that are not reachable, directly or indirectly, from the initial state.

Consider a state $<p, q>$. The transducer will be in this state when enough of the rule tree has been examined to carry F_l into state p and enough edges in the chart have been examined to carry F_r into state j. We therefore take each of the transitions t_l that can be made from state p in F_l in conjunction with each of the transitions t_r that can be made from state j in F_r. Suppose that t_l terminates at state m and t_r at state n, then the transducer must have a transition from $<p, q>$ over the symbol pair $t_l{:}t_r$ to the state $<m, n>$.

This procedure covers all but two kinds of circumstance. The first arises when one of the states is final even though further transitions are possible from the other. In other words, the left and right sides of the meta-rule can match strings of different lengths so that one reaches a final state before the other. What is required is a way of allowing the FSM that is scanning the shorter string to mark time while the other one catches up. This is easily done by providing every final state with one additional transition, labelled with the null symbol, ϵ, leaving and returning to the same state. The null symbols from the machine that reaches its final state first will be paired with enough symbols to carry the other machine into a final state. By convention, we abstain from adding transitions to the transducer that leave and enter the same state and are labelled $\epsilon{:}\epsilon$, for these clearly embody no information.

The other special circumstance that must be provided for arises when one of the transitions in the pair is a subscripted symbol. These are not paired with symbols from the other FSM in constructing the transducer; the other member is of the pair is always the null symbol, ϵ. Notice that these subscripted symbols always loop back to the same state from which they start. Thus, suppose that t_l is a transition to and from state p over φ_i. Regardless of t_r, the only transition to which it contributes will be from $<p, q>$ over $\varphi_i{:}\epsilon$ and back to $<p, q>$.

The final step in the construction process is to add a transition from the initial state of the transducer to a special final state labelled ω, and two transitions to and from that state, labelled $\omega{:}\omega$ and $\psi{:}\psi$. The ψ transitions match only the symbols that come from the left-hand sides of rules, that is symbols whose last character we have systematically written as "←". The effect of this addition is to allow a non-deterministic alternative at the initial state which, if taken, causes the transducer to carry any rule whatsoever into itself. When the transducers for the various rules are composed, this will cause a result to be produced in which each individual meta-rule is treated as optional. If it were omitted, a successful transduction would be possible only in the case where the rule applied in the chart came from applying *all* the meta-rules.

COMPOSING TRANSDUCERS

The final step in the process of creating a single transducer capable of mimicking an ordered set of meta-rules is to compose the individual transducers produced in the manner just outlined into a single machine. The algorithm I shall describe composes a pair of transducers. Its result can be characterised more specifically as follows. Suppose M_1 and M_2 are transducers and T_1, T_2 and T_3 are tapes such that M_1 accepts the pair $<T_1, T_2>$ and M_2 accepts the pair $<T_2, T_3>$, then M_3 accepts the pair $<T_1, T_3>$. Furthermore, the pairs of tapes that M_3 accepts are completely characterised in this way.

The procedure for composing transducers has a strong family resemblance to the one just described for obtaining a transducer from a pair of FSMs representing the two sides of a meta-rule. Once again, the state-set of the resulting machine will correspond to a subset of the Cartesian product of the state sets of the component machines. The principal step is therefore one of determining what transitions will leave a state $<p, q>$ in this set. Consider a pair of transitions, $a{:}b$ leaving state p and entering state x in the first machine and $c{:}d$ leaving state q and entering state y in the second, and assume temporarily that subscripts and instances of the variable φ are not involved. In order for the composed machine to make a transition corresponding to this pair, one of the following propositions must clearly be true:

(i) $b = c$
(ii) $b = \epsilon$
(iii) $c = \epsilon$

Condition (i) simply states that, if the two component machines are to make a move in parallel, and that move requires them both to examine their common tape, T_2, then they must both find the same symbol there. Conditions (ii) and (iii) state that one of the machines can read any symbol whatever on the shared tape if, in the same move of the transducer, the other machine ignores the shared tape.[†] If condition (i) obtains, a transition is introduced in the composed machine from $<p, q>$ over $a{:}d$ to $<x, y>$. Condition (ii) is one in which the first tape can move independently of the second tape; a transition is therefore introduced from $<p, q>$ over $a{:}\epsilon$ to $<x, q>$. Condition (iii) is the obverse of this; a transition is introduced from $<p, q>$ over $\epsilon{:}d$ to $<p, y>$.

The unsubscripted variable φ adds little complication to this basic scheme.

---

†It is, of course possible for all three conditions to obtain. For reasons too detailed to pursue here, the simplest machine is obtained when this is regarded as a situation in which condition (i) obtains, the other two being ignored.

Rather than discuss each case in detail, I provide a table in Fig. 11 of the ways in which some representative pairs of transitions compose.

Upper from p to x	Lower from q to y	Result	to
a:b	c:d		
a:b	b:d	a:d	$\langle x, y \rangle$
ϵ:b	b:c	a:ϵ	$\langle x, y \rangle$
a:ϵ	c:d	a:ϵ	$\langle x, q \rangle$
a:b	ϵ:d	ϵ:d	$\langle p, y \rangle$
a:b	c:ϵ	a:ϵ	$\langle x, y \rangle$
a:ϵ	ϵ:d	a:d	$\langle x, y \rangle$
φ:b	c:d	φ:d	$\langle x, y \rangle$
a:φ	c:d	a:d	$\langle x, y \rangle$
a:b	φ:d	a:d	$\langle x, y \rangle$
a:b	c:φ	a:φ	$\langle x, y \rangle$
φ:φ	c:d	c:d	$\langle x, y \rangle$
a:b	φ:φ	a:b	$\langle x, y \rangle$

Fig. 11 – Key to the states of the meta-rule transducer.

Finally we must consider the treatment of subscripts in the composition process. As I pointed out earlier, it is in respect of the subscripts that the formalism proposed here as a replacement for meta-rules differs from the one Kaplan and I proposed for phonology. Not surprisingly, it is also in respect of the subscripts that most of the subtlety in dealing with the formalism arises. It is for this reason that I announced the replacement of the original subscripts by a somewhat more general mechanism. The reason for deferring the introduction of that mechanism until now is that, while subscripts capture the information in a single meta-rule quite adequately, they are unable to represent one additional piece of information that must be included in the kind of composed machine we are about to consider. The point will be most readily made with an example.

Figure 12 shows the result of first composing two transducers (a) and (b) to form a single machine (c), and then of composing this with a third (d) to give a final result (e). Only when such a cascade of compositions is considered can the inadequacies of the basic scheme be revealed.

Notice that the subscripts in Fig. 12 take the form of expressions such as $[i \leftarrow D]$. For each symbol x in a subscript of the form $[x \leftarrow Y]$, we assume that the transduction mechanism is furnished with a *buffer* of symbols and the subscripts are each interpreted as operations on the buffer they name. The buffers obey a strict queue discipline, that is, the symbols are removed in the order in which they were inserted. Furthermore, it will invariably be the case that all the symbols in the buffer at any given time were put there under direction of subscripts associated with the same tape. A subscript $[x \leftarrow Y]$ is interpreted as follows:

1. If buffer i is empty or if the symbols it currently contains came from interpreting subscripts associated with the same tape as the current one, insert the symbol Y into it.
2. If the symbols in the buffer came from interpreting subscripts associated with the other tape, remove the next symbol from the buffer and allow the current transition to succeed just in case that symbol is Y.

All the buffers are required to be empty at the end for the pair of tapes to be accepted. The net effect is to require that each tape presents the same sequence of symbols to each buffer; however, those symbols are not read from the tapes themselves but are explicitly named in the label of the transition. This move is necessary because composition effectively removes intermediate tapes from the cascade, so that the symbols that would have been associated with subscripts in the original proposal may no longer be on any tape in the resulting machine. This modification preserves just the symbols required to make the subscripting scheme work as explicit parts of the structure of the transducer.

Let us examine Fig. 12 in somewhat greater detail. (a) is a machine that accepts a pair of tapes if the first consists of a string over $\{A, B\}$ terminated by P, and A on the first tape maps onto B on the second, C onto D, and P onto Q. (b) carries a tape containing any αQ onto one containing $R\alpha$, where α is an arbitrary string. The result of composing these, (c), carries a string over $\{A, B\}$ terminated by P onto a string consisting of R followed by Cs and Ds corresponding one for one with the As and Bs on the first tape. It would, for example, accept $AACAP$ and $RBBDB$. Composition with (d) simply replaces R with S, B with E, and D with F, so that (c) would accept $AACAP$ and $SEEFE$. Figure 13 shows this transduction with a diagram similar to the ones I have used previously, augmented to show the contents of the i-buffer between each pair of transitions. The final composite machine, (e), can therefore be characterised as carrying a string over $\{A, B\}$ terminated by P onto a string consisting of S followed by Es and Fs corresponding one for one with the As and Bs on the first tape.

Consider now how transducers (a) and (b) in Fig. 12 compose to give (c). In particular continue the move in which the transition $A : B$ in (a) combines with $\varphi : \epsilon$ to give $A_{[i \leftarrow B]} : \epsilon$. Except for the subscript, this is as prescribed by the table in Fig. 11, and the subscript comes from taking the subscript on φ_i and combining it with the symbol B that the first machine of the pair would have matched against its lower tape in this transition. Instead, this symbol is stored in a buffer to be matched against a symbol at some other position in the lower tape of the composed machine. This is just the kind of movement operation for which subscripts were devised.

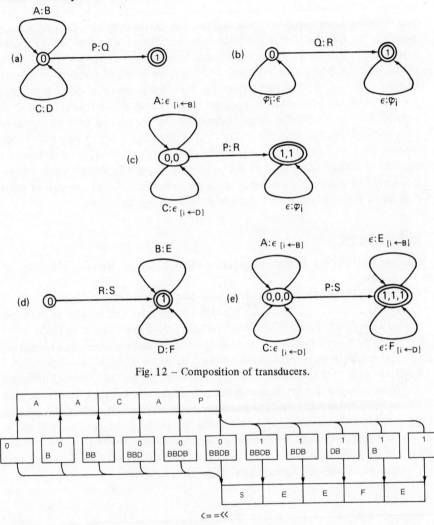

Fig. 12 – Composition of transducers.

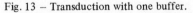

Fig. 13 – Transduction with one buffer.

CONCLUSION

I have shown that meta-rules are not essentially meta-rules in that they can do their appointed job without being applied to other rules. Instead they are taken as specifications of transducers that have the effect of making a string of constituents to which a derived rules could apply look to the relevant portion of the parser like a string to which a basic rule would apply. Since, in this scheme, meta-rules are not really meta-rules, the cost of acquiring a new context-free rule, or modifying or deleting an old one is very small. The cost of altering the stock of meta-rules is considerably more difficult to assess. To get the best performance from the generation and parsing machinery, the meta-rules must not only be transformed into transducers, but these must then be composed into a single transducer. If performance is a paramount consideration, then this composition step must be repeated whenever the stock of meta-rules changes. However, a number of tradeoffs are possible. Since composition is a pairwise process, it would be possible to preserve certain intermediate results to speed up possible later recompilation steps. Notice also that the parsing strategy suggested here does not require that the meta-rules be represented by a single transducer, or even that any composition of transducers is undertaken at all. It is therefore possible to imagine a number of strategies that a language learner might follow involving, for example, composing the transducers for an adjacent pair of rules only when they had proved themselves in the field for some time.

REFERENCES

Gazdar, G. (1979a) English as a context-free language. Mimeo, University of Sussex.

Gazdar, G. (1979b) Constituent structures. Mimeo, University of Sussex.

Gazdar, G., Pullum, G. and Sag, I. (1981) Auxiliaries and related phenomena in a restricted theory of grammar. Indiana University Linguistics Club.

Griffiths, T. V. and Petrick, S. R. (1965) On the relative efficiencies of context-free grammar recognizers, *Communications of the ACM,* **8**, 289–300.

Kay, M. (1967) Experiments with a powerful parser. In *2ème Conférence Internationale sur le Traitement Automatique des Langues,* Grenoble, also as Report RM-5452-PR, The Rand Corporation, Santa Monica, California.

Kay, M. (1977) Morphological and syntactic analysis. In A. Zampolli (ed.), *Syntactic Structures Processing.* Amsterdam: North-Holland.

Kay, M. (1980) Algorithm schemata and data structures in syntactic processing. Report CSL-80-12, Xerox PARC, Palo Alto, California.

Generalised phrase structure grammar, Earley's algorithm, and the minimisation of recursion

S. G. Pulman, University of East Anglia

I. Gazdar's (1981) demonstration that unbounded dependencies can, after all, be elegantly treated by context-free grammars makes available for plunder by linguists a large body of literature on context-free parsing; there exist automatic procedures for generating parsers for many such grammars (e.g. Pager, 1977), and their properties are, by comparison with current alternatives, well understood.

An alternative view is that this literature is not directly relevant to the area of the theory of parsing which has been most prominent recently: modelling human parsing strategies (Frazier and Fodor, 1978; Marcus, 1980, etc.). The computational linguistics literature is concerned with general and exhaustive algorithms, whereas the conclusion usually drawn about the human parsing mechanism is that it is relatively limited and specific, displaying a 'peculiar mix of blindness and intelligence' (Frazier and Fodor, 1978:324) and characterised by its seeming reliance on various heuristics and strategies (possibly imposed on it by its structure) which break down in certain circumstances.

The burden of this paper is that this conflict is only apparent: that if we take a general context-free parsing algorithm, make some modifications to it motivated originally on grounds of efficiency, make some assumptions about the form of the grammar it is parsing in ways likewise largely motivated by efficiency, the resulting behaviour approximates that observable in humans, to an interesting extent. Furthermore, the resulting framework can easily be adapted so as also to imitate various memory limitations or closure strategies: at the very least it offers a clear and practical way to implement and assess different proposals concerning these.

This approach was prompted by dissatisfaction with some aspects of heuristic-based parsers. It seems mildly paradoxical that they often provide a better account of failure than success: Frazier and Fodor, for example, say little or nothing about how their 'sausage machine' parser is able to recover from (some of) the errors caused by the narrowness of the 'window' of its first stage; where Marcus's PARSIFAL is led up the garden path some separately represented 'grammatical problem solving component' is invoked, involving a 'special packet of rules' producing phrasal packages which are in turn passed to a 'set of grammatical heuristics' (pp. 204–250). This extra machinery makes it difficult to motivate the claim that humans parse determinstically on grounds of economy of memory or computation. A more plausible picture may be one in which the parser is powerful enough to detect garden paths, multiple readings and so on, when necessary, but that it is too expensive (or unnecessary) to run it at full steam all the time in this way.

II. Our choice of algorithm will be minimally constrained by the folk-psychological requirement that it operate left to right, rather than completely breadth first. Furthermore, it should be at least tacitly predictive: at any particular point in a sentence, people know what syntactic possibilities are still open and which closed (as evidenced by judgements about possible sentence completions etc.). One candidate which meets these requirements is a variant of the well-known algorithm described by Earley (1970). In the version used here, this algorithm proceeds by constructing, for an input of length n, $n + 1$ states. A state consists of a set of 'configurations', each of which is uniquely identified, and which contain (i) a production of the grammar (ii) a marker, conventionally a dot, in the right-hand side of the production indicating how much of it has been parsed (iii) a statenumber: the number of the state in which the production was first entered (= the position at which recognition of its left-hand side began). The states are constructed by the following sequence of operations: (notice that the order of these is different from Earley's version making it, in effect, bottom-up).
    In state n:

(1) Scan: look at the next word, and for each lexical category α that the word can belong to, enter into state $n + 1$ a configuration of the form "$\alpha \rightarrow$ word. n"
(2) Predict: let $+$ = output of Scan.
    For each distinct left-hand side α in X, if there is a production of the grammar $\beta \rightarrow \alpha \cdots$ then put in state n a configuration of the form "$\beta \rightarrow . \alpha \cdots n$" if such a configuration has not already been entered.
    Now let X = output of Predict and repeat recursively until no more configurations can be entered.
(3) Complete: let $n = n + 1$, and let Y = state n (i.e. the output of Scan).
    For each configuration in Y with the marker at the end, and left-hand side α, go to the state indicated by its statenumber, and copy into state n every configuration of the form "$\cdots \alpha \cdots$" but with the marker to the right of α. Annotate α with the number of the configuration which caused this operation.
    Now let Y = output of Complete and repeat recursively until no more configurations can be completed.

The algorithm has successfully parsed a sentence when there are no more words in the input string and the final state contains at least one configuration with statenumber 0, with the marker at the end, and with a starting symbol of the grammar on its LHS. The parse tree is implicit in the annotations to the productions effected by Complete.

In a Generalised PSG, unbounded dependencies are introduced by linking rules, and the dependency is shown by passing 'slashed' category labels down a tree via rules derived from basic rules by a metarule. See Gazdar (1981) for details. We can somewhat laboriously parse such structures by treating linking and derived rules analogously to basic rules — i.e. as already present in the grammar — and adding to Complete a check to enable it to recognise 'gaps': when checking for a marker at the end of a configuration, check also for any α/α symbols to the *right* of a marker: if found, Complete them by moving the marker, and annotate α/α as 'gap'.

To illustrate, a run of the algorithm on the sentence 'Joe, nobody likes', is given (see Fig. 1): it uses the following simplified grammar (and for simplicity assumes that lexical entries are encoded as productions).

Basic rules	Linking rule	Derived rules
S → NP VP		
VP → V NP	TOPIC → NP S/NP	S/NP → NP VP/NP
NP → Joe, nobody		VP/NP → V NP/NP
V → likes		

State		Configuration	Statenumber	Introduced by:
0	1	S → . NP VP	0	P
	2	TOPIC → . NP S/NP	0	P
	3	S/NP → . NP VP/NP	0	P
1	4	NP → Joe .	0	S
	5	S → NP_4. VP	0	C
	6	TOPIC → NP_4. S/NP	0	C
	7	S/NP → NP_4. VP/NP	0	C
	8	S → . NP VP	1	P
	9	TOPIC → . NP S/NP	1	P
	10	S/NP → . NP VP/NP	1	P
2	11	NP → nobody.	1	S
	12	S → NP_{11}. VP	1	C
	13	TOPIC → NP_{11}. S/NP	1	C
	14	S/NP → NP_{11}. VP/NP	1	C
	15	VP → . V NP	2	P
	16	VP/NP → . V NP/NP	2	P
3	17	V → likes.	2	S
	18	VP → V_{17}. NP	2	C
	19	VP/NP → V_{17}. NP/NP	2	C
	20	VP/NP → V_{17}. NP/NP_{gap}.	2	C
	21	S/NP → NP_{11} VP/NP_{20}.	1	C
	22	TOPIC → NP_4 S/NP_{21}.	0	C

Fig. 1

The parse tree can now be traced from configuration 22; see Fig. 2.

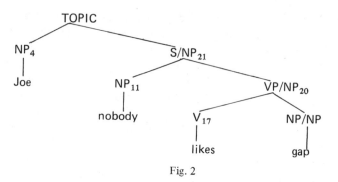

Fig. 2

We now have an algorithm which will parse a GPSG satisfactorily. It will find all the structures a string could possibly have assigned to it by a particular GPSG. If memory allocation — both for storage of the grammar, which may be very large when closed under the operation of meta-rules, and for workspace — is not a consideration (nor speed), it will cover a great deal of English syntax with only the faults of any other context-free parser.

Nevertheless, the drawbacks of such an algorithm should be obvious: in attempting to find all possible parses, it also considers many which turn out to be impossible ones. In the example given, and in others involving rightward movements of constituents (NP, PP, and REL), a large number of useless configurations are entered because the algorithm does not embody the obvious generalisations concerning when the derived rules passing along slashed categories become relevant. For leftward movements, if a linking rule configuration has been introduced into a state and the algorithm has begun recognition of the slashed category, it is only then that the remaining derived rules become necessary. The algorithm should ideally be capable of using the fact that it has recognised a 'filler' in order to introduce the appropriate derived rules anticipating a gap, and of course also to recognise that the basic rules are not appropriate here. For rightward movements the reverse should be the case: a gap or potential gap should be recognised and a filler expected.

It is possible to alter the algorithm so as to do this, although in the case of leftward movements the solution depends on the fact that fillers can always be recognised almost immediately as fillers. If there are languages where this is not so, this solution is not available for them. In the case of rightward moveable constituents the solution is optimal for cases of 'obligatory' gaps such as in

(1) I threw _ to the soldiers a large can of beer

but finds 'optional' gaps at every possible point, and in terms of the number of useless configurations entered is quite expensive.

The solution for leftward movements consists of a constraint on the operation of Predict: if there is in the current state a linking rule configuration of the form $\alpha \rightarrow \cdots . \beta/\gamma \cdots$ then if the normal operation of Predict yields a basic rule configuration of the form $\beta \rightarrow . \cdots$, enter instead the corresponding derived rule configuration(s) $\beta/\gamma \rightarrow . \cdots$. This means that the derived rules involving slashed categories need not be pre-stored, but can be computed as necessary during the course of parsing.

The solution for rightward movements (PP and REL extraposition, among others) is more complex. The first state examined by Complete operating in state n is always state $n-1$. We add to Complete a check on state $n-1$ for any configurations with a rightward moveable constituent α, (NP, PP or REL), to the right of a marker, such that there is no configuration in state $n-1$ or state n with statenumber $n-1$ and with α as its LHS. (If this is the case, it means that neither Scan nor Predict have recognised the beginning of an α.) If there are no configurations otherwise Complete-able then there is an 'obligatory' α gap: if there is at least one, then there is an 'optional' α gap. When such a gap is encountered, we have, in effect, to backtrack and add to the preceding states slashed versions of the configurations leading to that in which the gap was detected. Beginning with state $n-1$, we add to that state a slashed, Completed version of the configuration

$$\beta \rightarrow \cdots . \alpha \cdots, \text{i.e. } \beta/\alpha \rightarrow \cdots \alpha/\alpha_{gap} \cdots.$$

We then go to the state indicated by its statenumber and look for a configuration of the form $\gamma \rightarrow \cdots . \beta \cdots$ and add to that state a configuration $\gamma/\alpha \rightarrow \cdots . \beta/\alpha \cdots$ etc. We can repeat this process as far as is necessary: if we want to enforce the equivalent of bounded rightward movement then we stop at the first point at which a sentential category on a LHS is reached, say S. The slashed version $s/\alpha \rightarrow . \cdots$ is entered into the state along with the appropriate linking rules, e.g. $\Sigma \rightarrow . S/\alpha \, \alpha$.

This treatment of rightward movements is satisfactory for obligatory gaps, and in this case the Complete operation just described can *replace* configurations by their slashed equivalents in a state rather than add extra configurations to that state. Unless all linking rules introducing rightward movements are introduced earlier by allowing the normal operation of Predict to have access to them, something of the sort will be needed to prevent the parse from blocking at the point at which an expected constituent is not encountered. But the treatment of optional gaps is extremely profligate: every NP position, for example, will be treated as if it could be followed by a gap representing an extraposed REL, or an extraposed PP. This is both counter-intuitive and expensive and suggests that such a treatment may be along the wrong lines.

III. Examination of a range of examples reveals many ways, other than those already mentioned, in which this algorithm operates quite counter-intuitively:

that is to say, many more 'predictions' about possible analyses are made than are correct, and almost certainly many more than it is plausible to assume would be made by a hearer. There are five main inadequacies:

(i) Configurations with root sentence nodes as their LHS are introduced whenever any constituent that could begin a sentence is recognised, though this should only happen at the beginning of a sentence.

(ii) In a context-free grammar with no abbreviatory devices, optionality is expressed by pairs of n-tuples of rules: e.g. VP → V NP, VP → V NP PP, VP → V NP PP PP, etc. This is in this case descriptively inadequate since there is no limit to the number of modifiers which can appear in this position, and for an algorithm such as ours means that many different configurations — one for each member of the n-tuple — will be entered at the point at which constituents which can contain these modifiers are begun.

(iii) Constituents which begin with optional elements (again represented by n-tuples of rules, for example: NP → N̄, NP → Det N̄, etc.) are 'predicted' afresh even when such a configuration has already been entered in a preceding state. For example, a configuration incorporating the production NP → Det N̄ will be entered when a Det is encountered, but in the next state a configuration incorporating NP → N̄ will be entered as the beginning of the N̄ is recognised, as well as the correct N̄ → · · ·.

(iv) Left-recursive rules present two problems. As in all bottom-up parsers of this type, some arbitrary limit (in this case one) must be placed on the number of left-recursive configurations that can be entered in a particular state, to prevent an infinite loop. But this means that the parser will fail to recognise structures containing more than the limit: as does the following:

(2)   [[[John's] mother's] friend's] car ...

On the other hand, the parser will be over-cautious in many cases too, for it will predict that, given rules like NP → NP PP, *any* NP could be the left branch of a higher NP. As well as being expensive in terms of unnecessary space and computation, there are at least two arguments which suggest that this is an inaccurate description of how people parse: (i) 'Minimal Attachment' phenomena (Frazier and Fodor, 1978) — it is well known that the preferred interpretations of structures like

(3)   We took *the present* from Susan

(4)   We told *the girls* that ...

are not those on which the underlined NP has been parsed as the left branch of a higher NP. (ii) We do not regard the position after an NP as a 'possible gap' position in the same way that we do for sub-categorised NP positions, as in:

(5)   Joe read _ in the park (a book about physics)

(although as noted earlier, our treatment of rightward movements does regard all these positions as possible gaps).

(v) Right recursive rules (or sets of rules) likewise produce an effect which, though not fatal, does not seem either very efficient, or very plausible as a model of human parsing. Given an embedded structure like:

(6)   Joe thought [that Bill had said [that he would leave]]

the fact that *thought* is followed by an appropriate complement is only recognised (via Complete) at the very end of the sentence: moreover, this only happens *after* the complement of *said* is recognised as appropriate to that verb.

The solution to (ii), optional non-initial modifiers, is the most straightforward. We replace n-tuples of rules like VP → V NP, VP → V NP PP, VP → NP PP PP etc. by a rule of the form VP → V NP (PP)*, interpreted in the usual way. Then, following a suggestion by Earley in his original paper, we modify the Complete operation to produce from a configuration of the form $\alpha → X . (\beta)^* Y$, configurations of the form $\alpha → X . Y$ and $\alpha → X . \beta (\beta)^* Y$ which are then inspected and treated by Complete in the usual way.

The problems of (i) root sentences and (iii) optional initial elements of constituents can also be solved fairly simply on the assumption that root sentential categories are distinct from subordinate sentential categories, an assumption which does not seem very radical (see Gazdar, 1981: 162). We add to the algorithm the ability to maintain a list of 'active' constituents: a list of the LHS of all configurations which have been entered and have not yet been Completed. We then impose on Predict the constraint that no new configuration with LHS α can be entered into a state if α is on the active list.[1] It follows immediately that there can only be one instance of any configuration the LHS of which is a root category (a starting symbol of the grammar). It likewise follows immediately that given a pair of rules NP → Det N̄, NP → N̄ and a string consisting of, for example, "Det N", where N can begin an N̄, that a configuration with the rule NP → N̄ cannot be introduced if there is already one with NP → Det N̄ active — i.e. the situation described in (iii) can no longer arise.

However, this constraint has some rather drastic consequences for structures involving rules of the type in (iv) and (v): it will mean that configurations based on such rules can never be entered into a state at all. If the beginning of an NP is recognised, for example, then Predict will enter a configuration NP → . · · · and put "NP" on the active list. Thus no other configuration of that form, such as a left recursive one NP → . NP · · · can be entered until the first NP has been

Completed. Given the operation of the algorithm at present, in fact, such con-figurations will not be entered at this point either, and so such structures could never be parsed. Likewise, structures such as those in 6 will not be parsed since the configuration entered when the $\overline{S}$ complement of *thought* is begun will still be active when the complement of *said* is encountered.

Let us approach this problem by considering what the original linguistic motivation for recursive rules was, in particular rules like NP → NP PP and NP → NP REL. The original motivation was twofold: (a) they enabled a succinct statement of the distributional fact that wherever an NP can appear, an NP + PP or NP + REL can also appear (b) they allowed these complex NPs to behave just like simple NPs in transformations since the highest NP satisfied the structure index of T-rules automatically. In a non-transformational grammar these two considerations collapse into the distributional one, which is in fact equally well satisfied by invoking a meta-rule stating that for any rule in which an NP is introduced, there are to be further rules introducing an NP followed by PP or REL. Thus to a rule S → NP VP, there correspond rules S → NP PP VP, S → NP REL VP etc.

While in general parsing with meta-rules is not easy, in this case it is quite simple to implement the effects of such a meta-rule on the basic rules. Noticing that an NP can be modified by any number of REL or PP:

(7a) The man that you like that you saw yesterday . . .

(7b) The man from the house with the money . . .

we can, as a first attempt, prestore the derived rules as S → NP (PP)* VP, S → NP (REL)* VP etc.; and then, noticing that PP and REL can be combined, borrow some regular expression notation and store instead a combined rule S → NP (REL/PP)* VP, and likewise for other rules introducing NPs. We will have to modify the operation of Complete, in an obvious way, to accommodate this. What we have done, in effect, is to treat PP and REL modifiers after NPs as essentially like the PP and adverbial modifiers discussed earlier under (ii). If we now make the parallelism exact by allowing REL to occur in VP-final positions, or more generally, wherever PP can occur as a modifier, then we can parse extraposed REL and PP constructions quite straightforwardly, without the excessive prediction of possible gaps entailed by our earlier treatment. To see how this is so, consider a sentence like:

(8) We sent the clothes to the laundry that you were wearing yesterday

where the REL has been extraposed. Assume we have rules like VP → Vn NP (PP/REL)* PP (PP/REL)*, where Vn is the class of verbs which in a transforma-tional grammar would be subcategorised [+ _ NP PP] (see Gazdar and Pullum (1982) for details), where the first (PP/REL)* represents the operation of the meta-rule for NP modification and the second represents (in part) the possibili-ties for VP final modification. Since there is no REL found after the object NP, the relevant configuration at the point at which the extraposed REL is encountered will have the form VP → Vn NP PP. (PP/REL)*. No REL gap after NP will have been detected since the rule states that these modifiers are optional. However, the extraposed REL will be parsed in the same way as an optional PP would be at that point. The resulting structure will be:

(9)

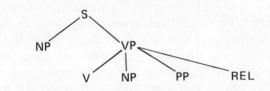

A potential difficulty arises, however, from the fact that at present there will be an alternative parse based on the fact that the meta-rule for NP modification, unless restricted, results in the PP rule having the form PP → P NP (PP/REL)*. Thus there will also be a parse of the form:

(10)

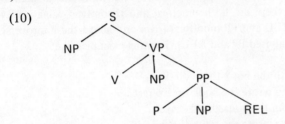

In fact, both (8) and (11) will receive both parses (9) and (10):

(11)   We gave the job to the girl who was pretty

even though (10) is more appropriate to (11), and (9) to (8). This is unsatisfactory in two respects: firstly, the constraint on Predict would never allow a sequence of two PPs (or analogously, two RELs) to be parsed as:

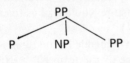

but only as:

Secondly, now that the flattened trees we get from these rules, for example,

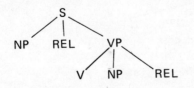

do not explicitly associate the RELs with the NPs they modify as did the recursive structures they replaced, we must assume that these RELs and PPs are associated with their NPs by some non-syntactic means. This in itself is uncontroversial: it has been recognised since the earliest days of work on formal syntax that a purely syntactic approach ascribes a great number of irrelevant and inappropriate analyses in cases such as this and provides no way of choosing between them (Chomsky, 1961: 128. Similar remarks apply to conjunction). But given that we therefore need some non-syntactic procedure to associate these constituents correctly with what they modify, then there is no point, and no motivation, for assigning more than one (flat) syntactic structure in these cases, since choice of one over the other has no semantic consequence. We would thus like to arrange things so that (9) was the only possible parse for sentences like both (8) and (11). This means that rules of the type PP → P NP (PP/REL)* must somehow be prevented from occurring.

On the assumption that some principled way can be found of achieving this latter restriction,[2] there are both practical and theoretical gains achieved by this treatment of REL and PP modifiers (over and above the improvement in the treatment of extraposed PP and REL). Treating examples like:

(12a)   The man with the book that you like . . .
(12b)   The man who wrote the book on Everest . . .
(12c)   The man from the house by the river . . .
(12d)   The man who wrote the book that you like . . .

as having a flat structure, with the various possible readings computed non-syntactically, avoids the combinatorial explosion associated with strings of PP and REL (see Martin, Church and Patil (1981) for discussion of the PP cases). Furthermore, as has often been pointed out, structures like this do not have the intonation contours predicted by a deeply embedded structure. Instead they are pronounced roughly as such a 'flat' structure would lead us to expect (Chomsky, 1965: 13–14; Langendoen, 1975: 544).

Similar remarks apply to deeply left-embedded structures involving possessive determiners. One rule for NP will be of the form NP → (NP   )*N̄ and will allow structures like   + poss

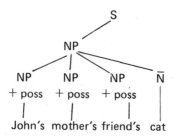

It will be noticed that we apparently have one level of recursion in a tree like this. There are two possible responses to this: we could regard possessive NPs as a sufficiently distinct type of NP for the constraint on Predict to be inapplicable. Technically speaking, if categories are bundles of features, this is already the case. Alternatively, we could interpret the intonational evidence — the relevant portions of sentences like these very nearly have a 'list' intonation — as suggesting that such a string of possessive NPs is not regarded as forming a single constituent at all (much less a deeply embedded one). We would then need a metarule to the effect that wherever an NP can appear, so can a sequence $(NP_{+poss})*\bar{N}$, giving structures like:

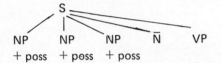

We come now to the question of right embedding of constituents. Notice that although in cases of multiple embedding the intonational evidence suggests that we are again dealing with a flat structure (Langendoen, 1975: 548):

(13)   John believes [that Joe thinks] [that Mary said] [that she would help]

we could not adopt a version of the proposal offered above for eliminating left recursion unless we were prepared to accept a grossly inappropriate structure for such sentences. However, when we view that proposal from a somewhat different angle, the natural solution begins to emerge. In the examples so far, by replacing a recursive structure with what is in effect an iterative structure, we have imposed a kind of 'closure': we have ensured that a sequence of, for example, PPs, must be parsed as

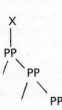

rather than

The result is the same as requiring a PP constituent to be closed as soon as possible: an incoming PP must be a new constituent and not part of the one currently being parsed.

If we now explicitly force closure of right-embedded complements on the parsing algorithm, then the recursive structures of sentences like (13) are no longer treated as recursive: 'Complement closure' can be implemented in the following way: when the beginning of sentential complement (for example $\bar{S}$) is recognised (i.e. a configuration $\bar{S} \rightarrow . \cdot \cdot \cdot$ is introduced into a state by Predict), and there is a configuration $\alpha \rightarrow \cdot \cdot \cdot \cdot . \bar{S}$ in the current state, Complete the second configuration with the first. If the resulting configuration is then one which has the marker at the end, Complete as normal. (In the simplest case we can now relabel the current state as 0 and proceed as if $\bar{S}$ were a starting symbol.) At this point the parser will have enough information to build a partial tree like:

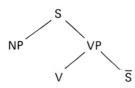

and can do so, clearing from memory the space in which previous states are stored: it will not have to wait until the end of the $\bar{S}$ has been reached. It will have been noticed in the illustration given earlier that there is otherwise a flurry of Completions in the final state, analogous to a sequence of POPs in a ATN; both this, and the counter-intuitive order in which the complements to verbs are recognised as appropriate is avoided here.

The advantages of closures to a parser with limited memory have been extensively discussed (Kimball, 1973, 1975; Frazier and Fodor, 1978; Church, 1980). There is much more to be said about the kind of closure just described, which may be a little too strong as it stands. (It should be pointed out, however, that in a system like this, where PP and Adverbial modifiers are attached non-syntactically, many of the arguments in the literature concerning the extent of closures and evidence for them, are not applicable). But it will be clear that the algorithm we have elaborated is quite capable of simulating various different kinds of closure: we can mimic the A-over-A closure discussed by Church (1980), or we can make closure dependent on the number of active configurations, or to the number of words encountered, or to some combination of these. At the very least, then, we have a useful framework for experimentation around these parameters.

IV. The constraint on Predict that has been described does not allow the algorithm to parse self-embeddings. Given that root nodes are distinct from subordinate nodes this correctly claims that sentences like:

(14) That [that the world is round is obvious] is false

should prove very difficult to parse. In a grammar which regards headed and headless REL as distinct, and yes/no and constituent indirect questions as distinct, structures like:

(15a) What the man who you saw yesterday was doing amused us
(15b) Whether John asked where Bill was isn't clear

will on the other hand be successfully parsed. However, as is well known, various other factors can affect the comprehensibility of self-embedded structures, including semantic or pragmatic constraints and some little understood considerations of length:

(16a) *The dog the cat the rat bit caught at the malt
(16b) The man that the girl who you saw yesterday dislikes so much has just arrived

It is thus more plausible to regard the number of configurations of a particular type which can remain on the active list as something which is not fixed, but can vary as non-syntactic or even non-linguistic factors affect the amount of 'memory' available.

There are various parallels between the parsing model described here, and suggestions made by Chomsky many years ago concerning the theory of performance: these parallels require further elaboration than can be given here. For example, the constraint on Predict that only one LHS of a given type can be on the active list at a time seems to be one way of realising Chomsky's speculation:

> that the perceptual device has a stock of analytic procedures available
> to it, one corresponding to each kind of phrase, and that it is organised
> in such a way that it is unable (or finds it difficult) to utilize a pro-
> cedure φ while in the course of executing φ. (1965: 14).

It remains to be seen whether this is what Chomsky had in mind: at first sight, it appears that there are differences, since the proposal here applies to all types of recursion, whereas the discussion preceding Chomsky's hypothesis makes it clear that that hypothesis is intended to distinguish self-embedding from left and right recursion (though it would not do so as stated).

A second parallel concerns the relation between context-free and finite-state languages. It is known (Chomsky, 1959) that for a context-free grammar with a finite degree of self-embedding there is a finite state machine (a finite automaton) which will parse the language it generates. It has usually been assumed that natural languages in principle allow unlimited self-embedding and that therefore a theory of competence must prescribe grammars of at least the power of context-free grammars. It has further been assumed, however, that the performance of a speaker—hearer must at some level be representable as a finite automaton:

> ... we must conclude that the *competence* of the native speaker cannot
> be characterised by a finite automaton . . .. Nevertheless, the *perfor-*
> *mance* of the speaker or hearer must be representable by a finite

automaton of some sort. The speaker–hearer has only a finite memory,
a part of which he uses to store the rules of his grammar (a set of rules
for a device with unbounded memory), and a part of which he uses for
computation in actually producing a sentence or "perceiving" its
structure and understanding it. (Chomsky, 1963: 390).

It would, of course, be possible, given Chomsky's proof just referred to and
given the observation that self-embedding is very restricted, to claim that the
human parsing device was a finite state machine parsing a finite state language.
But this has seemed implausible to most people, for one reason or another
(see Chomsky, 1959: 121, Chomsky and Miller, 1963: 470). Presumably this
was the reason why Chomsky, in an early statement of the scope of a theory of
grammar, required that in addition to a class of grammars, a universal phonetic
alphabet, and an evaluation measure, the theory of grammar should also specify
a function g (i, n) which should be a description of some finite automaton with
its capacity fixed by n, that assigns to a sentence the set of structural descriptions provided for it by a grammar Gi (Chomsky, 1959: 120). That is to say, the
first modest stage of a theory of performance should be the description of a
function which operates with finite state resources to parse a grammar of much
richer resources: Chomsky of course had in mind a transformational grammar,
whereas we have been dealing with a context-free grammar. It should be clear,
though, that the parsing algorithm we have described here is a function of
exactly the type in question: the role of the constraint on Predict, the subsequent enlarging of the part played by meta-rules, and the use of closures of right-
embedded constituents mean that we are parsing a context-free language with
what are essentially finite state resources, in a way in which the only loss of syntactic information — about attachment of modifiers — is of a kind which was in
any case insufficient and ultimately unnecessary for the task of understanding
the language. We have therefore, if the foregoing account withstands further
examination, achieved the first modest stage.

NOTES

1. This has to be stated more carefully so as to distinguish between configura-
    tions belonging to different parses of the same string, and to exclude useless
    configurations, once it is apparent that they are useless.
2. The restriction is simple enough to state: we only allow the meta-rule to
    apply to NPs which are sisters of VP or V.

BIBLIOGRAPHY

Chomsky, N. (1959) On the notion "rule of grammar". Reprinted in J. J. Katz
    and J. A. Fodor (eds), *The Structure of Language*. Englewood Clifts, New
    Jersey: Prentice-Hall, 1964.

Chomsky, N. (1963) Formal properties of grammars. In R. Luce, R. Bush and E. Galanter (eds) *Handbook of Mathematical Psychology* Vol. II. New York: Wiley.

Chomsky, N. (1965) *Aspects of the Theory of Syntax.* Cambridge Mass. MIT Press.

Chomsky, N. and Miller, G. (1963) Finitary models of language users. In Luce, Bush and Galanter (eds) *Handbook of Mathematical Psychology* Vol. II. New York: Wiley.

Church, K. W. (1980) On memory limitations in natural language processing. Report MIT/LCS/TR-245, Laboratory for Computer Science, MIT.

Earley, J. (1970) An efficient context-free parsing algorithm. *Communications of the ACM* **13**, 94–102.

Frazier, L. and Fodor, J. D. (1978) The sausage machine: a new two-stage parsing model, *Cognition* **6**, 291–325.

Gazdar, G. (1981) Unbounded dependencies and coordinate structure, *Linguistic Inquiry* **12**, 155–184.

Gazdar, G. and Pullum, G. D. (1982) Subcategorisation, constituent order, and the notion 'head'. In M. Moortgat, H. v.d. Hulst and T. Hoekstra (eds) *The Scope of Lexical Rules.* Dordrecht: Foris.

Gueron, J. (1980) On the syntax and semantics of PP extraposition. *Linguistic Inquiry* **11**, 637–678.

Kimball, J. (1973) Seven principles of surface structure parsing in natural language. *Cognition* **2**, 15–47.

Kimball, J. (1975) Predictive analysis and over-the-top parsing. In J. Kimball (ed.), *Syntax and Semantics,* Vol. 4, New York: Academic Press.

Langendoen, D. T. (1975) Finite-state parsing of phrase structure languages and the status of readjustment rules in grammar, *Linguistic Inquiry* **6**, 533–554.

Marcus, M. (1980) *A Theory of Syntactic Recognition for Natural Language.* Cambridge, Mass: MIT Press.

Martin, W., Church, K. and Patil, R. (1981) Preliminary analysis of a breadth first parsing algorithm: theoretical and experimental results, Report MIT/LCS/TR-261, Laboratory for Computer Science, MIT.

Pager, D. (1977) A practical general method for constructing LR(k) parsers. *Acta Informatica* **7**, 249–268.

Natural and unnatural language processing

M. Steedman, University of Warwick

1. INTRODUCTION

There are two respects in which natural language processors are unlike artificial language processors such as compilers. The first is in respect of their grammar. Transformationalists have argued that the grammar of human languages cannot usefully be captured using context-free rules alone. Although recent work, such as Gazdar (1981), has shed doubt on the stronger claim that natural languages *cannot* be captured in CF grammars, the fact remains that there are generalisations about the form of natural language constructions that appear to remain unexplained by CF grammar alone. In particular, the presence of "unbounded dependencies" between elements of "discontinuous constituents" raise difficulties for such accounts. An example of such a construction is an object relative clause, in which an arbitrary amount of material may separate the element of a VP (italicised).

(1)   (a man) *that* I think you *know 0*

Such phenomena have led to the introduction of major unbounded movement transformations, to the "hole inducing" schema or meta-rule and the associated apparatus of designated variables of Gazdar, and to the "partial combination" apparatus of Ades and Steedman (1982, discussed below). Computer languages, on the other hand, seem to manage quite well with only "ordinary" context-free rules.[†]

The second puzzle concerns the extreme local structural *ambiguity* of natural language. At any point in the passage of a left-to-right parser through a sentence, there will typically be several rules of grammar which might apply.

[†] It has frequently been noted that the grammar of computing languages like ALGOL cannot entirely be described using CF rules alone. However, the features in question are not typically handled by purely syntactic mechanisms.

The standard example is where a left-to-right parser has encountered the words *have the policemen* . . ., which could be the start of either an imperative or an interrogative.

(2a) Have the policemen (whom I invited) arrived?
(2b) Have the policemen (whom I invited) dismissed!

The remainder of the sentence may or may not restrict these alternatives to one, but typically the disambiguating information may be delayed for a considerable number of words or even constituents. Programming languages, on the other hand, typically do not involve such extreme local ambiguity: where the convenience of human users demands it, care is taken to make it very locally resolvable, typically by a look ahead of one word.

The puzzle is why natural languages appear both to use rules of grammar which seem more powerful than necessary, and to allow a degree of local ambiguity which is greater than would be tolerated in a language of our own designing. Both features have potentially disastrous consequences either for learnability and heritability or for efficiency of processing. And for example nothing seems easier than for languages to evolve in the direction of non-ambiguity. The two problems are logically independent. However, this note will conclude with a conjecture that both have a common functional origin.

2. THE PSYCHOLOGICAL MECHANISM FOR RESOLVING LOCAL AMBIGUITIES

By and large, recent proposals have assumed that the mechanism responsible for the resolution of local ambiguities is primarily structural in nature (examples are the compiler-like "limited lookahead" of Marcus (1980 and the "minimal attachment" strategy of Frazier (1979). Such studies have laid great emphasis upon "garden path" sentences as evidence. In such sentences, a local ambiguity seems to be irrevocably *mis*resolved by the mechanism, as in the following examples:

(3a) The horse raced past the barn fell
(3b) The boat floated down the river sank
(3c) The authors read in the garden stank.

However, on the one hand such mechanisms are notoriously subject to over-riding pragmatic influences, various of which such as definiteness (d), *a priori* plausibility (e) or more abstruse thematic aspects (f) may reduce or remove the garden path effect from structurally identical sentences like the following:

(3d) Boats floated down rivers sank
(3e) The articles read in the newspapers stank
(3f) The horse raced past the barn fell over the sacks of potatoes that I had carelessly left in its way.

And on the other hand there is a considerable amount of evidence that semantics can affect syntactic processing at an early stage (cf. Marslen-Wilson, 1973; Tyler and Marslen-Wilson, 1977; Marslen-Wilson and Tyler, 1980; Crain, 1980; Crain and Steedman, 1982).

Crain (1980) presents experiments in which reference and context are manipulated, and subjects' ability to comprehend "garden path" sentences is shown to depend on them. Crain and Steedman (1982) present these experiments in the context of a theory of ambiguity resolution based on reference and context distantly related to that of Winograd (1972), but extended to further varieties of indefinite and definite reference to a context, together with a hypothesis concerning the way in which reference and presupposition might interact with parsing processes. The basis of the account is the idea that differential costs are associated with accommodating the presuppositions[†] or entailments of various kinds of referring expressions within the hearer's mental model of the domain of reference. In particular, if presuppositions that concern the prior establishment of entities or sets of entities in the model or focus of discourse are not satisfied by that model, then the entities in question must be added to it, at some cost. If one interpretation implicates fewer such additions than another, then that interpretation is favoured. Using Crain's experiments manipulating definiteness and context (and hence presuppositions) to either produce garden paths where none had been before, or to prevent them where they are classically found, they argue that the so-called "null" or "neutral" context, used in many experiments (e.g. Frazier, 1979; Marcus, 1980; Ford *et al.*, 1982; *passim*) in support of the view that human syntactic processing is autonomous, is in fact far from neutral with respect to these processes, and favours certain analyses simply on the pragmatic grounds that they involve fewest unsatisfied presuppositions. For example, simple definite noun phrases like *the horse* carry fewer presuppositions or entailments about the context of discourse than complex definite noun phrases involving restrictive relative clauses. The simple NP reading of an ambiguous fragment like *the horse raced past the barn* is therefore easier to accommodate in a "neutral" context in which no mention of horses or racing has been made. Their conclusion is that what appears at first glance to be massive local ambiguity is in fact resolved by continual reference to context, carried out incrementally even while constituents remain incomplete, possibly almost word-by-word.[‡] These experiments are briefly reviewed below.

---

†It has been suggested that the concept of presupposition should be subsumed under the broader concept of entailment. However, we shall continue to use the term here in a common-language informal sense.

‡The often-quoted counter-argument from computational expense of inference that has been mounted by Woods (1973) may be bad news for the *practicality* of attempts to simulate human parsing, or (more likely) it may not. Either way, it is not relevant to the psychological question.

2.1 Experiments (Crain, 1980; Crain and Steedman, 1982)

2.1.1 *Experiment I: Removing Garden Paths*

The following sentences are structurally identical to *The horse raced past the barn fell* (3a).

(4a) The teachers taught by the Berlitz method passed the test.
(4b) The children taught by the Berlitz method passed the test.
(4c) Teachers taught by the Berlitz method passed the test.
(4d) Children taught by the Berlitz method passed the test.

Examples (a) and (b) illustrate how plausibility (that is, the likelihood of a particular reading in the light of real-world knowledge) can be manipulated in order to show its effect during parsing. Sentences (c) and (d) manipulate the definiteness, and hence the referential and presuppositional character, of the subject NPs in the same sentences. (Indefinite complex noun-phrases like *horses raced past barns* do not carry as many presuppositions about the prior discourse as the related definites carry.)

Sentences like these were presented visually one word at a time, and the subjects had to press a response key whenever they had any "difficulty" interpreting a sentence. "Difficulty" was defined as the occurrence of apparently missing or apparently unexpected words. Following Frazier (1979), a rather rapid presentation rate of 300 msec. per word was used, which is slow enough to allow each word to be seen accurately, but fast enough to pressure the subjects sufficiently to reveal differences in processing difficulty.

Subjects responded more often that sentences like (a) were difficult than they did for sentences like (b), showing a significant effect of semantic plausibility and general world knowledge on syntactic processing. This result confirms the observation by Bever (1970) that *a priori* plausibility of the local S reading affected the garden path effect in such variants of the garden path sentences as (4b). However, it was a relatively weak effect. A much stronger effect was that the presence of a bare plural nounphrase as in (c) and (d), removing the presuppositions or entailments concerning the reference sets inherent in (a) and (b), significantly increased the likelihood of a successful parse (i.e., no response). (For further details, see Crain and Steedman, 1982).

2.1.2 *Experiment II: Creating Garden Paths*

Consider the following sentences.

(5) The psychologist told the wife that he was having
　　　　trouble with　(a) to leave her husband
　　　　　　　　　　 (b) her husband

Contexts in which the complement clause reading of the ambiguous substring "The woman that he was having trouble with . . ." (for which (b) is an appropriate continuation) is felicitous are easy to come by. Since it is the reading with the fewest presuppositions, the so-called null context is one, a fact that has lent arguably spurious support to a number of structural disambiguation strategies such as Minimal Attachment. But other contexts favouring the relative clause reading (for which the appropriate continuation is (a)) can also be constructed, as in the following example. Under the present hypothesis, in such contexts the ambiguous substring should be assigned a relative clause analysis during processing, even before it is complete. If so, and if alternative (b) demanding a complement analysis is presented, then when the words "her husband" are encountered they should evoke a garden path effect. Conversely, in contexts where a complement clause analysis is felicitous, alternative (a) continuing "to leave her husband" should be unacceptable.

(6a) *Complement Inducing Context*
       A psychologist was counselling a married couple.
       One member of the pair was fighting with him but the other one was nice to him.

(6b) *Relative Inducing Context*
       A psychologist was counselling two married couples.
       One of the couples was fighting with him but the other one was nice to him.

(6c) *Complement Target Sentence*
       The psychologist told the wife that he was having trouble with her husband.

(6d) *Relative Target Sentence*
       The psychologist told the wife that he was having trouble with to leave her husband.

The target sentences in these two examples both contain completing phrases which will produce garden path effects if the inappropriate context is used to intervene in the syntactic analysis of the ambiguous substring "the wife that he was having trouble with". The presence of two married couples in the relative-inducing context establishes a set of wives from which to restrict. Therefore, the simple NP "the wife" does not succeed in referring, while the complex NP "the wife that he was having trouble with" does. In the complement-inducing context only one woman has been introduced, so the simple NP analysis is felicitous, and the complex is not.

Such pairs of contexts and target sentences in the four possible combinations CC, CR, RC, RR, were presented by Crain in an experiment again using an RSVP paradigm. The complement target sentence (c) when preceded by the complement context (a) (CC condition) induced garden path responses only 12% of the time. This low proportion of garden paths is not surprising, since the complement analysis is also preferred in the so-called null context. However, the same target (c) when preceded by the relative inducing context (b) (RC condition) produced garden path effects 54% of the time. When the same relative-inducing context (b) was succeeded by the relative target sentence (d) (RR condition), only 28% of responses indicated garden pathing. However, when this same relative target (d) was preceded by the complement-inducing context (a) (CR condition), subjects garden pathed 50% of the time. In short, people took a garden path that they could not recover from roughly equally often in both contexts when the completing phrase was inconsistent with the context. As hypothesised, the contexts produced significantly different syntactic analyses, implying that referential context is made use of during parsing to resolve local ambiguities.

Since response times were taken for the judgements of difficulty, it was also possible to determine whether subjects made their syntactic decisions before or after the target sentences were completed. Where the critical word, (in the example, "to" or "her"), appeared between four and nine words prior to the end of the sentence, 59% of the subjects' responses occurred before the sentence was completed. This result appears to support the contention that appeals to semantics and reference can intervene while syntactic processing is still incomplete.

3. THE PSYCHOLOGICAL GRAMMAR

It has also been argued by Ades and Steedman (1982) that the logically independent peculiarities of natural language grammar (in particular the "discontinuous constituents" that caused transformationalists to posit "unbounded" extractions and dependencies) also suggest that entities corresponding to what are in classical terms incomplete constituents are created during the operation of the psychological sentence processor.

In their scheme, the generalisations that have in the past been captured in various "unbounded movement" transformations are captured instead by augmenting a Categorial Grammar of context-free power (Ajdukiewicz, 1935; Bar Hillel *et al*, 1960) with a novel type of rule schema called "partial combination", which has the effect of including in the grammar as a kind of constituent certain incomplete fragments of sentences and phrases like *She must have, She might have been, She might have been dreaming she loved* and so on.[†] It is only by treating such fragments as in some sense constituents that the context-free apparatus of Categorial Grammar can be generalised to handle the apparent discontinuity of constituency in constructions like Topicalisation, as in

(7)   [[*that man*] [she might have been dreaming she *loved*]]

The arguments for generalising Categorial Grammar in this way are purely linguistic. However, Ades and Steedman point out that the grammar is directly compatible with a class of processors known as "Shift and Reduce" parsers,

[†] The scheme of Gazdar (1981) also represents certain similar "hole categories" within the grammar. The relation between these theories is discussed in Ades and Steedman (1982).

and that the schema in question can be viewed as a rule of processing. They show that the partial combination rule can be associated with a well-defined semantic operation of "function composition" which will allow such a parser to perform an immediate word-by-word assembly of a fully interpreted semantic representation of such a fragment. For example, if the semantic entity corresponding to the fragment *she might* expresses the fact that it needs to combine with an infinitival VP complement, then it can be thought of as a function from VP interpretations onto S interpretation. Similarly, the semantic entity corresponding to the verb *have* is a function from the interpretation of a past-participial phrase onto that of a VP. The two functions, like any others, can be "composed" using this rule into a function from the interpretation of a past-participial phrase onto that of an S, the semantic entity corresponding to the fragment *She might have*. Similarly, this function can in turn be composed using the "partial combination" rule with the interpretation of the past participle *eaten*, which is presumably a function from NP meanings onto past-participial phrase interpretations. Each of the composed functions that results from the operation of "partial combination" is a fully interpreted semantic entity, which can be applied to an argument without any further stage of interpretation. The operation (unlike certain other augmentations of CF grammar) is therefore as compatible with fully-non-autonomous syntactic processing as the more usual context-free apparatus, and the potential usefulness of such fully interpreted fragments in the resolution of local syntactic ambiguities by appealing to context, even while constituents like the verb-phrase remain incomplete, is striking.

4. WHY ARE NATURAL LANGUAGES LIKE THIS?

It has been argued above that both the aforementioned peculiarities of grammar and local ambiguity resolution in natural language are to be explained as the concomitants of a processor that non-autonomously assembles semantic interpretations immediately and often word by word. It is tempting to speculate further that the involvement of such processors in psychological sentence comprehension stems in turn from a functional need for the comparatively slow medium of spoken natural language to be understood rapidly in a world which may not wait for the end of the sentence to change in ways that may drastically affect the hearer, and from the nature of discourse focus.

Once such a capability is added to the basic apparatus of context-free syntax and semantics, two things seem to happen. The first is that just a few extra constructions become possible, over and above the ones that are defined by a straightforward semantics and the corresponding context-free syntax. These additional constructions seem to be of exactly the kind that are so peculiarly widespread among the languages of the world (notably ones involving unbounded extractions). The second is that the same capability can be used for local ambiguity resolution. It is so powerful in this respect that a degree of syntactic ambiguity that with any other means would give rise to intolerable inefficiency can be handled with no extra cost.

5. CONCLUSION

It remains to be seen whether the generalisation of Categorial Grammar outlined above will handle all the constructions found in English and other natural languages.[†] It also remains to be seen whether *anything* in the way of structural criteria in addition to the powerful resources of semantics and reference is used for local ambiguity resolution by the psychological parser. Crain's experiments described above question various related structural criteria that have been implicated in the garden path sentences under the names of "Closure" (Kimball), "Minimal Attachment" (Frazier) and "Limited Lookahead" (Marcus). The other main strategy, which has gone under the name of "Right Association" (Kimball), "Late Closure" (Frazier) and "Final Arguments" (Ford *et al.*) remains to be investigated. But if the argument that has been put forward here is correct, then the way forward in modelling human parsing may be to refine techniques for representing context and focus in discourse, rather than structural parsing techniques. It follows that the outlook for building practical working parsers for natural language may be, not bleak, but rather boring. On the one hand, building a practical parser that really works as humans do, and in the way that the language is "designed" to work, may (given existing practical inference systems) be unreasonably demanding of computing resources. And on the other hand there may be cheap structural tricks, like limited lookahead, which work fine a lot of the time, but for rather un-psychological and non-explanatory reasons.

REFERENCES

Ades, A. E. and Steedman, M. J. (1982) On the order of words. *Linguistics and Philosophy* **4**, 517–558.

Ajdukiewicz, K. (1935) Die syntaktische Konnexität. *Studia Philosophica* **1**, 1–27. English translation in S. McCall (ed) *Polish Logic 1920–1939*, 207–231, Oxford: Oxford University Press.

Bar-Hillel, Y., Gaifman, C. and Shamir, E. (1960) On categorial and phrase structure grammars. *The Bulletin of the Research Council of Israel* **9F**, 1–16; reprinted in Y. Bar-Hillel, *Language and Information*. Reading, Mass: Addison-Wesley, 1964.

Bever, T. (1970) The cognitive basis for linguistic structures. In J. R. Hayes (ed) *Cognition and the Growth of Language*. New York: Wiley.

Crain, S. (1980) Pragmatic Constraints on Sentence Comprehension, Ph.D. Thesis, University of California at Irvine.

†Cf. Steedman (1982) for a discussion of how the theory copes with "intersecting dependencies", whose existence in natural languages has been regarded as a conclusive argument for the inclusion of transformations in natural language grammars.

Crain, S. and Steedman, M. J. (1982) On not being led up the garden path: the use of context by the psychological parser. In D. Dowty, L. Karttunen and A. Zwicky (eds) (Title to be announced). Cambridge: Cambridge University Press. To appear.

Ford, M., Bresnan, J. and Kaplan, R. (1982) A competence-based theory of syntactic closure. In J. Bresnan (ed), *The Mental Representation of Grammatical Relations,* Cambridge, Mass: MIT Press.

Frazier, L. (1979) On Comprehending Sentences: Syntactic Parsing Strategies. Ph.D. Dissertation, University of Connecticut. Indiana University Linguistics Club.

Gazdar, G. (1981) Unbounded dependencies and constituent structure. *Linguistic Inquiry* **18**, 155–184.

Kimball, J. (1973) Seven principles of surface structure parsing in natural language. *Cognition* **2**, 15–47.

Marcus, M. P. (1980) *A Theory of Syntactic Recognition for Natural Language.* Cambridge, Mass: MIT Press.

Marslen-Wilson, W. D. (1973) Linguistic structure and speech shadowing at very short latencies. *Nature* **244**, 522–523.

Marslen-Wilson, W. D. and Tyler, L. K. (1980) The temporal structure of spoken language understanding: the perception of sentences and words in sentences. *Cognition* **8**, 1–74.

Steedman, M. J. (1982) On the generality of the nested dependency constraint and the reason for an exception in Dutch. In B. Butterworth, B. Comrie and O. Dahl (eds) *Explanations for Language Universals.* The Hague: Mouton. To appear.

Tyler, L. K. and Marslen-Wilson, W. D. (1977) The on-line effects of semantic context on syntactic processing. *Journal of Verbal Learning and Verbal Behaviour* **16**, 683–698.

Winograd, T. (1972) *Understanding Natural Language.* Edinburgh: Edinburgh University Press.

Woods, W. (1973) Transition network grammars, in R. Rustin (ed) *Natural Language Processing.* Courant Computer Science Symposium 8, New York: Algorithmics Press.

PART V

Semantic problems in parsing

Request-based parsing with low-level syntactic recognition

A. **Cater**, University College, Dublin

This paper argues that effective parsing of English can be achieved by the use of "requests" which operate on low-level syntactic constituents, embedded in a nondeterministic preference-directed framework. This approach has been used successfully for several years as the basis of the AD-HAC analyser: fuller descriptions can be found in Cater (1980, 1981). The description given here mirrors that implementation.

1. THE BASIC STRATEGY

The analyser used in AD-HAC delivers a representation of the meaning, rather than of the form, of individual sentences. This representation is modelled upon Schank's Conceptual Dependency (Schank, 1972, 1973), using basically the same set of "conceptual primitives". While there are differences between Conceptual Dependency and the representation scheme used here, they do not significantly affect the actual parsing process, and so these differences will be ignored in the present paper.

The analysis process uses information of various kinds: syntactic constituents — noun groups, verb groups, prepositional phrases etc. — are recognised by an ATN (Woods, 1970); within these constituents, the head noun or the main verb is easily identified, and may have associated "requests" or "features"; the requests (usually associated with verbs) specify a gross syntactic framework, and specify also preferred features of surrounding noun groups; the features of noun-groups found by the ATN are compared with these preferences, and affect the "preference score" (Wilks, 1973a, b) of a particular course of analysis. There are many sources of potential ambiguity, which can give rise to multiple partial analyses: the request-application procedure selects the most promising partial analysis on the basis of its "preference score", holding the others in abeyance while this one proceeds. Each partial analysis proceeds in a left-to-right fashion.

The basic organisation is diagrammed in Fig. 1.

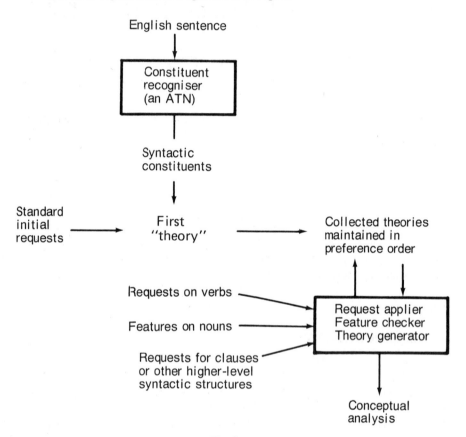

Fig. 1.

The "partial analyses" are termed theories: they contain several pieces of information, notably

(a) A conceptual structure for the phrases read so far
(b) A set of requests specifying what constituents are expected, together with actions to be performed if they are found
(c) A numeric measure of the degree of "fit" with past predictions
(d) The constituents still to be accounted for by this theory.

The analyser operates by selecting the most-preferred theory, and selecting those of its requests which are applicable; each applicable request specifies actions to be performed, and causes the construction of a new theory. This process of theory expansion continues until the theory selected has no further constituents to account for: its conceptual structure is then given as the meaning representation of the sentence.

2. THE SYNTACTIC COMPONENT

Rudimentary morphological processing is performed while the sentence is being read: with a sufficiently small vocabulary, even this could be bypassed. The recognition of syntactic constituents then requires only the ability to determine the syntactic class (or classes) of a word. Since no attempt is made to determine the structure of clauses, no further information is needed. Thus, for example, it is unnecessary to distinguish transitive and intransitive verbs.

The explicit syntactic processing merely involves recognising and labelling several types of constituent: verb groups, noun groups, prepositional phrases, and conjunctions. The constituents found by this process are placed in a tree structure which permits the representation of alternative syntactic analyses: the words "HER MONEY", for instance, may be parsed as either one noun group, or as two in sequence. More complex examples of the nondeterministic nature of this task are easily found.

The labelling of the constituents permits the requests to operate at a level higher than the word-by-word level, exemplified by Riesbeck's early work. In particular, the use of an ATN to group words together removes the need for requests attached to determiners, adjectives and auxiliary verbs. The requests used here can operate on entire groups of words functioning as a unit.

3. THE REQUESTS

The use of requests in conceptual parsing was introduced by Riesbeck (1973). His requests had just two elements, a predicate and an action: when the predicate part of a request succeeded, the action was performed and the request was then removed from the active list.

This approach was tried during the early development of the analyser described here, and was found awkward in two ways.

(i) There was only one way a request could be removed: its predicate had to succeed, and its action had to be performed. In Riesbeck's work, this led to the introduction of request with a "True" predicate, and with an action which depended on some further condition. Such a programming trick, while workable, renders the basic mechanism suspect.

(ii) It became apparent that there were several distinct kinds of request: some requests caused an embedding of the analysis process, some caused an unembedding, some inspected a word (in Riesbeck's case; a constituent in mine) of the input sentence, some interrogated a pre-stored structure, etc. It seemed desirable to exploit these regularities, particularly since there was a correlation between the kind of request and the opportunities for nondeterminism.

Consequently, the notion of "request" has been expanded. Requests now have a main predicate and an action, as in Riesbeck's work; but they also have a "keep predicate" and a request class. The request class is used to impose an ordering on the application of requests, which is achieved by having theories state which request class should be tried when this theory is expanded. The keep predicate is used when a request of a given class has not been used in the expansion of a theory, even though the theory was looking for that class of request: if the request's keep predicate fails, the request is discarded.

4. THE ANALYSIS PROCESS

The first step in analysing a sentence is to read in the words, performing simple morphological operations in the process, and building the tree of syntactic constituents. This tree, together with a standard set of initial requests, and initial preference score and registers holding temporal information, forms the first theory.

This theory is then "expanded": it states that USE-class requests are to be applied, so the first constituent is taken from the tree, and the predicates of the USE-class requests are evaluated. Typically, the first constituent will be a noun group, and one of the requests will succeed; its action is to store away that noun group as the subject of the sentence, and to add a further request seeking a verb group. Meanwhile, the other initial requests − seeking a leading auxiliary, or an imperative verb, or whatever − will not succeed, and the failure of their keep predicates will cause those requests to be discarded from the new theory.

In the case of an uncomplicated declarative sentence, the next constituent will be a verb group. This causes the existing request to succeed, signalling acceptance of the verb group: this request has an empty action part, and plays no further role in the analysis. The dictionary definition of the main verb, however, provides a set of requests: these are loaded, and direct the further processing of the sentence. Typically, they will direct that a skeleton conceptual structure should be built; that the "subject" should be placed into a specified slot of that structure; that the preference score should be modified to reflect the agreement between the subject's *actual* and *expected features*; and that various direct objects, prepositional phrases, and embedded clauses should be expected.

The definitions of verbs play a central role in the analysis of a sentence. The initial requests serve only to set the stage, accounting for regularities of sentence-level syntax. The view of parsing embodied in this approach is that each verb has idiosyncratic requirements, both at the semantic and the syntactic level: there are certain regularities, but these fall naturally into place in a verb-centred analysis model such as this.

There are further regularities, for instance the ability of noun-groups to be postmodified by prepositional phrases and relative clauses; and there are regularities in embedded clauses also. These regularities are captured by the use of macro requests. Thus the verbs are defined in terms of packages of parameterised requests. These macro requests can be used, for example, to seek a clause with no surface subject and with a finite verb: the verb in that embedded clause will specify its own syntactic framework.

5. AMBIGUITY

The parser outlined here can construct parallel theories, and does so in response to various forms of ambiguity. Referential ambiguity, however, is not tackled by the parser: there is an inference mechanism which takes the conceptual structures produced by the analyser, and which performs pronoun resolution and question answering as well as producing numerous inferences.

Category ambiguity (e.g. "SAW" can be noun or verb) can be handled in two ways: in some cases, the surrounding words can be used by the ATN constituent recogniser to give it top-down predictions — for example the word "MY" must be followed by a noun; in other cases, the ambiguity will be reflected in the presence of several constituents in competition. In this last case, several competing theories will be formed at the point in the analysis, and usually only one will satisfy the predicate of a request. Several theories may be carried along in parallel if more than one such constituent satisfies the predicates of requests.

Sense ambiguity (e.g. the noun "CROOK", as "CRIMINAL" or "STICK") will cause the production of two competing theories when a USE-class request encounters the corresponding constituent. Typically, one of the senses will give a better match of actual versus expected features, and this will cause one of the theories to have a higher preference score than the other: other things being equal, this will discriminate in favour of the "correct" sense. In the case of sense-ambiguous verbs, there will typically be several distinct syntactic frameworks, or differences in expected features of surrounding noun or prepositional phrases. Either of these differences will help to distinguish the intended sense of the verb. (Sense ambiguity may co-occur with category ambiguity, though no further problems arise.)

Structural ambiguity (e.g. the attachment of prepositional phrases, the scoping of conjunctions) reduces, in this approach, to the problems of when processing should be embedded and unembedded. In the case of PP-attachment, the general feature-matching and preference-manipulating operations suffice, since verbs can be quite specific about the objects of particular prepositions.

The scoping of conjunctions seems adequately handled by a simple heuristic: embed as soon as possible, and unembed as late as possible. When this heuristic is combined with the ability to carry along multiple competing theories, the heuristic can be reformulated as: reward a theory for embedding, and penalise it for unembedding. Then the ordinary process of selecting for expansion the most-preferred theory will permit the correct parsing of a sentence like

> "A MAN WAS KILLED WHEN THE CAR IN WHICH HE WAS RIDING SWERVED OFF THE ROAD AND STRUCK A TREE"

6. CONCLUSION

The parser outlined here uses a combination of syntactic and semantic knowledge in order to build a conceptual representation of individual sentences. The approach depends upon the specification of syntactic frameworks for individual verbs, which to a large extent direct the analysis process for individual clauses. There is explicit knowledge of syntax at the level of constituents, and this is exploited to facilitate the definitions of verbs in terms of syntactic frameworks. There is also implicit knowledge of higher-level syntactic constructs, though no syntactic structures are created.

Various syntactic and semantic cues affect the preference score attached to a theory (or partial analysis), thereby influencing the parser's choice between parallel competing analyses. The semantic cues are simple, being computed by comparing "features" of nouns — and hence of noun phrases — with features expected by the main verb of a clause. Nevertheless, the integrated treatment of semantic cues and syntactic cues corresponds with Marcus' proposal for the comparability of semantic and syntactic "biases". The reliance upon parallel theories, of course, flies in the face of current fashion.

There are many outstanding problems with the current implementation of this approach to parsing: the syntactic coverage must be extended; adjectives are simplistically assumed to have one meaning only; compound nominals are not properly analysed; metaphors are taken literally; and work is only now beginning on the handling of abstract nouns. Balanced against these defects, we may note that the analyser does handle several forms of ambiguity, does have a fair vocabulary (about 450 roots), does handle conjunctions, and does provide a deep analysis of a wide variety of sentences.

REFERENCES

Cater, A. W. S. (1980) Analysing English text: a nondeterministic approach using limited memory", *Proceedings of the AISB-80 Conference on Artificial Intelligence*.

Cater, A. W. S. (1981) Analysis and inference for English. Ph.D. Thesis, Computer Laboratory, University of Cambridge.

Riesbeck, C. (1973) Computational understanding: analysis of sentences and context. Report STAN-CS-73-337, Computer Science Dept., Stanford University.

Schank, R. C. (1972) Conceptual Dependency: a theory of natural language understanding. *Cognitive Psychology* **3**, 552–631.

Schank, R. C. (1973) Identification of conceptualisations underlying natural language. In *Computer models of thought and language* (eds. Schank and Colby), San Francisco: Freeman.

Wilks, Y. A. (1973a) Preference semantics. Report STAN-CS-73-377, Artificial Intelligence Laboratory, Stanford University. In *Formal semantics of natural language* (ed. Keenan), Cambridge: Cambridge University Press, 1975.

Wilks, Y. A. (1973b) An artificial intelligence approach to machine translation. In *Computer models of thought and language* (eds. Schank and Colby), San Francisco: Freeman.

Woods, W. A. Transition network grammars for natural language analysis. *Communications of the ACM* **10**, 591–606.

Incremental semantic interpretation in a modular parsing system

C. S. Mellish, University of Sussex

MAINTAINING A DISTINCT SYNTACTIC COMPONENT

Most researchers accept that basic word order and grouping information must be taken into account in successful natural language parsing. The disagreements occur partly when decisions are made to classify this information as primarily "syntactic" or "semantic". They also occur, however, when decisions are made to ascertain this structure more or less separately from the other activities associated with meaning extraction.

Theoretical advances in linguistics led to a very strong, independent syntactic component (and separate semantic component) in some of the early systems (Woods *et al.*, 1972; Winograd, 1972). Reacting against this, a variety of frameworks have been proposed in which all processing is clearly seen as serving the main goal of meaning extraction and all consideration of information or representations that might have only syntactic relevance is carefully avoided (Wilks, 1975; Riesbeck and Schank, 1976; Burton, 1976). However, it is fair to say that none of these "semantically based" approaches has succeeded in producing anything like the clear, communicable framework that seems to be offered by a syntactic parser sitting together with a semantic interpreter. As a result, people are continuing to write new and better syntactic parsers (Marcus, 1979; Mark and Barton, 1980) and more and more complete grammars to be used with them in two-part natural language processing systems (Robinson, 1982). The advantages of modularity (different people can work on the different sections) and portability to new application areas seem to outweigh any other arguments that there may be.

THE INDEPENDENCE OF CONTROL STRATEGY

This trend towards maintaining separate syntactic and semantic modules in natural language parsers could hamper scientific progress significantly if it was always accompanied with the simple Lunar-style "two pass" control strategy. First of all, such a strategy is unlikely to lead to any good models of how human beings process language, given the evidence (Marslen-Wilson, 1976) that people "understand as they read". Second, there may well be engineering reasons why syntactic/semantic interaction could increase the efficiency of the system as a whole (as Winograd argued). Fortunately, there is no reason why, just because we choose to *describe* the analysis of a fragment of natural language in terms of two separate components, the actual execution of our programs need reflect this in any significant way. That is, the way we think about rules and generalisations can be essentially *independent* of what control strategies our programs use to decide what to do when. Given a clear description of our grammar and semantic interpretation rules, we can sit down as a separate exercise and decide how those rules are to be interpreted in such a way that a working program results. There is a close analogy here with Kowalski's notion of "Algorithm = Logic + Control" (Kowalski, 1979).

SEMANTICALLY BASED PARSERS AS OPTIMISATIONS

Flexible control structures can enable us to capture some of the advantages of "semantically based" parsers whilst still retaining a clean syntax/semantics module structure. Indeed, we would like to try and view a class of "semantically based" parsers (including perhaps ELI (Riesbeck and Schank, 1976) and Semantic Grammars (Burton, 1976)) as carrying out equivalent operations to two-part parsers, but with cleverly optimised code. The optimisations that are involved are such that redundant structures are not created and unnecessary computations are avoided. We would like to suggest that researchers should be aiming for a system where such optimisations are carried out *automatically*, either by having a language fragment description pass through an intelligent compiler or by having a clever interpreter which adjusts the execution dynamically to reflect the constraints of processing. Having one's two-part description pass through such a system might lead to an execution trace that looked very much like that of ELI, for instance. But the advantage would be that a clean, modular description of the rules used by the program would be available and that the program writer would not have to worry about sorting out all the optimisations himself.

Here is a very simple example, to try to make these ideas a bit clearer. Consider the following partially-instantiated "plan" to understand a sentence beginning with the word "the man . . .". We have adopted a variant of Sacerdoti's notation, (Sacerdoti, 1975), where necessary orderings between actions are shown by lines between the relevant boxes, but where all other orderings are unspecified. In this informal diagram (Fig. 1), boxes with dotted edges represent goals to be activated and boxes with solid edges represent actions to be performed.

The task here has been conceived in a traditional way in terms of activities at each of three levels — syntactic, semantic and pragmatic. However, this is a description of the understanding process at quite an abstract level. We might decide to drive an actual computer program in many different ways. The most straightforward (but probably least interesting) way would involve imposing

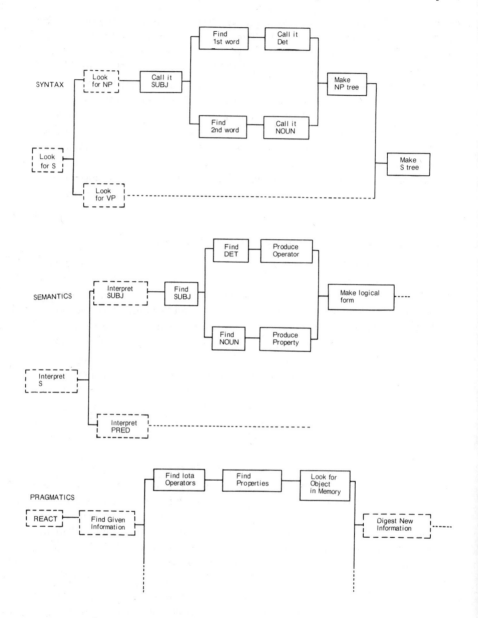

Fig. 1.

extra ordering constraints so that the three levels are dealt with sequentially —
pragmatic processing follows semantic processing which follows syntactic
processing. A more interesting way might be to drive the execution by principles of dataflow (Gurd, Watson and Glauert, 1980). That is, the only reason
for performing any action at some point in time would be that its necessary
input data was available. Conversely, if at any time the inputs for some action
were available then that action would be performed then. Such a scheme would
obviously depend on at least pseudo-parallelism, to handle the case where
multiple actions are enabled simultaneously.

In this example, once the "syntactic" level has identified that it is about to
obtain the subject of the sentence ("Call it SUBJ"), the "semantic" level can
prepare to interpret it, knowing that there actually is a subject in the sentence
("Find SUBJ"). It cannot proceed any further, though, because the determiner
and noun have not yet been ascertained. When a syntactic level action labels a
word "DET", the semantic level can jump in again and produce a relevant
operator (here an iota operator for the word "the")' The production of this
operator enables the analysis at the pragmatic level to proceed by one step,
since it is looking out for such operators being produced. Nothing can now
happen until the syntactic level has identified the "NOUN" of the noun phrase.
However, the discovery of the word "man" leads to an activity in each of the
other levels, so that the system may be starting to look for "the man" in its
world model before any other words are read. The "critical path" of actions
that leads most quickly to the satisfaction of the highest level goal ("REACT")
looks something like Fig. 2. Notice that some actions do not appear on this

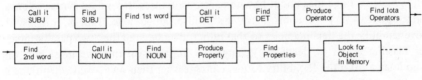

Fig. 2

path — for instance, those which would build structures that are not used
elsewhere. These actions could either be ignored by the control strategy, or
they could be carried out in parallel, where they would not interfere with the
efficiency of the system as a whole. In addition, some labels (e.g. "SUBJ")
serve only to highlight the points of communication between actions, and
could be dispensed with by the system in favour of more "hard wired" communications channels (such as subroutine calling). If we were to write a program
that carried out precisely those actions on the "critical path", with these optimisations borne in mind, it would have little apparent similarity with the modular description that we started with. This program would be, in a very strong
sense, performing only those actions that were motivated by the requirements

of meaning extraction. Its actions would therefore look a great deal like those performed by a "semantically based" parser.

This example has glossed over many important details and can be considered as no more than suggestive of the kinds of arguments one might make about controlling parsing. In particular, we have not discussed how one would handle choices at the various levels, or indeed exactly how the various actions would communicate their results to others.

PARALLEL MODELS FOR PARSING

This paper is obviously not the first to suggest that in parsing, although syntactic and semantic modules may be conceptually distinct, nevertheless their processing can be interleaved in interesting ways. Hearsay (Lesser *et al.*, 1974) provided an example of different levels of analysis interacting in flexible ways, but unfortunately did not cover language of any complexity. Woods' conception of cascaded ATN grammars (Woods, 1980) also suggests promising lines of research, assuming that the various levels of analysis are well expressed in terms of ATNs. This may not be the case if the order of inputs to a certain level has no significance (as may happen, for instance, in a case frame interpreter). It may be valuable in this context for natural language researchers to draw on some of the ideas in computer vision, for instance those embodied in the Sussex POPEYE project (Sloman and Hardy, 1976).

TOWARDS INCREMENTAL SEMANTIC INTERPRETATION

If we keep a fixed idea about how semantic structures depend on syntactic ones, attempts to "vary the control strategy" will produce little. That is, it is easy to oversimplify the dependencies so that either little beyond the "two pass" strategy is feasible at all (a deadlock occurs). To improve on this, we must give the modules a lot more flexibility to make progress on their own, even when there is a degree of uncertainty about their inputs. In order to do this, the modules must be able to represent and reason about incomplete information provided, rather than being frozen into inactivity or forced into a premature decision about its overall significance. We can see aspects of this in the "wait and see" strategies of Marcus (Marcus, 1979) and also in Brady's vision program (Brady and Wielinga, 1977). Brady sums up his philosophy by saying:

> . . . a vision program should explicitly represent partially-formed percepts, and should operate by incrementally refining such partial percepts by looking at each stage for what seems to be the information which can be computed most cheaply.

When applied to the domain of semantic interpretation, this leads to the goal of *incremental semantic interpretation*.

Bobrow and Webber's PSI-KLONE framework (Bobrow and Webber, 1981) is an elegant illustration of what incremental semantic interpretation can look like. The system is capable of gradually narrowing down the analysis of a sentence within a space of interpretable syntactic—semantic patterns as evidence from the syntactic parser appears, bit by bit. Unfortunately, the PSI-KLONE system does not incorporate "discourse level" processing, such as reference evaluation, in the same way. Our own work can be seen as an attempt to achieve incremental semantic interpretation in the area of reference evaluation. We have tried to capture in this the idea that what is chosen as the referent of a phrase can be affected by the analysis of other phrases, which may appear before, or even quite a long time after, the phrase in question. Therefore at certain intermediate stages, the referent is only partially identified. Nevertheless, even a partial description of a referent can serve as a useful guide for resolving other syntactic and semantic ambiguities. For instance, a system understanding the fragment

The president of the US . . .

can only have a partial representation of who is being talked about, at least until a continuation like ". . . in 1962" is encountered. Likewise, the knowledge of what "it" refers to in:

A bell is suspended from a light string.
It . . .

can only gradually be refined as continuations like ". . . has a mass of 50 lbs" or ". . . passes over a smooth pulley" are read. In order to tackle the problem of incremental reference evaluation, we have cast it in the form of a constraint satisfaction task. We have then investigated solutions involving Waltz-style filtering (Mellish, 1981a) and a "call by need" style inference mechanism (Mellish, 1981b). In a more recent development, we have developed a framework in which the type of an unknown object (for instance, a pronoun referent) can be incrementally determined as the semantic interpretation proceeds (Bundy *et al.*, 1982).

CONCLUSIONS

As an easily understood and maintained framework for building natural language parsing systems, the two-part conception is unrivalled. However, the adoption of such a framework need not necessarily involve sacrificing some of the aims that the "semantically based" parsers have. This is because by altering the way in which the syntactic and semantic processing is interleaved we can obtain a variety of different behaviours.

If we wish to pursue the idea of syntactic and semantic units cooperating in the parsing of a sentence, then we are likely to get a more flexible system (and one less liable to deadlocks) if one of these units is in the position to continue with only partial information. For this reason, we believe that the concept of incremental semantic interpretation is of great importance.

REFERENCES

Bobrow, R. J. and Webber, B. L. (1981) PSI-KLONE: Parsing and Semantic Interpretation in the BBN Natural Language Understanding System. Bolt, Beranek and Newman Inc., Cambridge, Mass.

Brady, J. M. and Wielinga, B. J. (1977) Reading and Writing on the Wall. Department of Computer Science, University of Essex.

Bundy, A., Byrd, L. and Mellish, C. S. (1982) Special Purpose, but Domain Independent, Inference Mechanisms. *ECAI-82: Proceedings of the 1982 European Conference on Artificial Intelligence*, 67–74.

Burton, R. (1976) Semantic Grammar: An Engineering Technique for Constructing Natural Language Understanding Systems. Report 3433, Bolt, Beranek and Newman Inc., Cambridge, Mass.

Gurd, J. R., Watson, I. and Glauert, J. R. W. (1980) A Multilayered Data Flow Computer Architecture (3rd issue). Internal Report, Department of Computer Science, University of Manchester.

Kowalski, R. (1979) Algorithm = Logic + Control. *Communications of the ACM* 22, 424–431.

Lesser, V. R., Fennell, R. D., Erman, L. D. and Reddy, D. R. (1974) Organisation of the Hearsay II Speech Understanding System. IEEE Symposium on Speech Recognition.

Marcus, M. P. (1974) *A Theory of Syntactic Recognition for Natural Language*. Cambridge, Mass: MIT Press.

Mark, W. S. and Barton, G. E. (1980) The Rusgrammar Parsing System. Research Report GMR-3243, General Motors Research Laboratories.

Marslen-Wilson, W. (1976) Linguistic Descriptions and Psychological Assumptions in the Study of Sentence Perception. In Wales, R. J. and Walker, E. (eds) *New Approaches to Language Mechanisms*. Amsterdam: North-Holland.

Mellish, C. S. (1981a) Coping with Uncertainty: Noun Phrase Interpretation and Early Semantic Analysis. Ph.D. Thesis, University of Edinburgh.

Mellish, C. S. (1981b) Controlling Inference in the Semantic Interpretation of Mechanics Problems. Paper presented at the Workshop on Logic Programming for Intelligent Systems, Los Angeles.

Riesbeck, C. and Schank, R. (1976) Comprehension by Computer: Expectation-Based Analysis of Sentences in Context. Research Report 78, Department of Computer Science, Yale University.

Robinson, J. J. (1982) DIAGRAM: A Grammar for Dialogues. *Communications of the ACM* 25, 27–47.

Sacerdoti, E. D. (1975) The Non-Linear Nature of Plans. *Advance Papers of the Fourth International Joint Conference in Artificial Intelligence,* 206–214.

Sloman, A. and Hardy, S. (1976). Giving a Computer Gestalt Experiences. Proceedings of the AISB Conference, Edinburgh.

Wilks, Y. A. (1975) An Intelligent Analyser and Understander of English. *Communications of the ACM* **18,** 264–274.

Winograd, T. (1972) *Understanding Natural Language.* Edinburgh: Edinburgh University Press.

Woods, W. A. *et al.* (1972) The Lunar Sciences Natural Language Information System: Final Report. Report 2378, Bolt, Beranek and Newman Inc., Cambridge, Mass.

Woods, W. A. (1980) Cascaded ATN Grammars, *American Journal of Computational Linguistics* **6,** 1–12.

Parsing, how to

E. Charniak, Brown University

In this paper I will argue for a model of the parsing process as illustrated in Fig. 1.

For the most part I will be concerned with evidence to support the overall structure, and will spend little time on the details of the individual components. The sole exception here will be the last section, in which I will argue that we should be expecting much more from our syntactic parsers than they are currently providing. In all cases, my arguments will be the curious stew of pop psychology, computational considerations, and common sense which we all recognise as Artificial Intelligence.

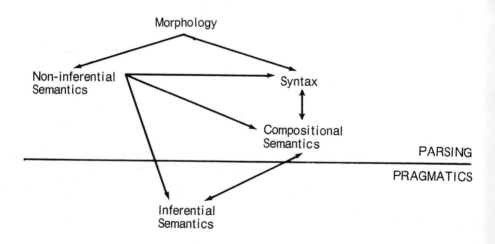

Fig. 1

1. PARALLEL SYNTAX AND SEMANTICS

Let me start by arguing for a model in which syntactic parsing and some form of semantic processing go on in parallel, with some communication between the two.

People are able to parse sentences which make no sense, or in which all open class words are replaced by nonsense.

Furious ideas color sleeplessly.
The frobbels from the werp grambed a sterp.

At the same time, we are able to piece together collections of nouns with no syntactic structure at all, e.g. "lecture student confusion question". As superficial as such examples are, the most natural explanation is that there are two responsible processes which proceed independently of each other. This in turn suggests that they proceed in parallel.

Also, some work by Prather and Swinney (1977) indicates that when we initially access the meaning of words, we do so independently of their parts of speech. The basic idea of such experiments is to get a word which can serve as both noun and verb, and where the meanings differ slightly (the example they give is "watch"). The word is used in a sentence in such a way as to clearly indicate the part of speech. Immediately after hearing the word, a second word is presented visually. The subject is asked to determine if the word is a word of English. Naturally, half the time the subject is given a nonsense string, just to keep everyone honest. A well-known result is that people are faster in situations where the world is semantically related to the one just heard in the sentence than if the word is unrelated. That is, if we just heard the word "cow", we would be faster in recognising that, say, "milk" was a word of English, than, say, "leaf". If one then presents the subjects with words related to both uses of "watch" (the ones used were "seconds" and "observe") one finds that the subjects are faster with both than they are with a word which is not related to either, "college". This is independent of how the word "watch" is used in the sentence. The conclusion is that both parts of speech are accessed, independently of syntactic context. If this result holds up, we might then conclude that the process of determining meaning happens prior to the completion of syntactic processing.

Some recent work by Milne (forthcoming) suggests why this sort of parallel processing might be beneficial. In his experiments he presented subjects with sentences in which certain nouns are followed by a second word which can either be a noun or a verb. If the subject interprets it as a noun, then he sees a noun noun combination, while if he sees it as a verb, he sees a noun followed by the beginning of the verb phrase of the sentence. For example

This research was supported in part by the Office of Naval Research under contract N00014-79-C-0592, and in part by the National Science Foundation under contract IST-8013689.

The sentry stands are green. (noun noun) Garden path
The sentry stands on guard. (noun verb)
The granite rocks were by the sea shore. (noun noun)
The granite rocks during the earthquake. (noun verb) Garden path

As the above examples indicate, semantic considerations dictate that certain pairs are more likely to be interpreted as noun noun combinations while others tend to be seen as an np vp combination. Furthermore, he found that if the sentence could only be syntactically parsed in one way, then a mismatch between the syntax and semantics led to greatly increased parsing time, suggesting that the subjects found the sentences to be mild garden paths. The most obvious interpretation is that semantics is being used to guide syntax by deciding whether the word in question is a noun or a verb. Obviously, if we are to use semantics in this fashion, we cannot require syntax to have already told semantics the correct part of speech.

2. WHY COMPOSITIONAL SEMANTICS AFTER SYNTAX

In my initial model I have split semantics in three. One part operates in parallel with syntax, as argued in the previous section. We will return to the nature of this semantic processing in the next section. Now I want to look at the part which immediately follows syntax which I call "compositional semantics". This is the process of creating the logical form of the sentence. My belief is that this typically goes after syntactic parsing, in the sense that we do a little syntax, followed by a little compositional semantics, much in the way that Montague grammar, and its followers, dovetail the two processes. However, it is a dovetail in which the syntax always comes first, so, in the limited vocabulary of block diagrams, I have chosen to indicate that syntax precedes semantics.

As this process is currently understood, one wants to map the verb of the sentence into a semantic predicate, and the noun phrases of the sentence into the arguments of that predicate. (This is oversimplified, but it is good enough for our purposes.) One of the major ambiguities which must be resolved in this process is which noun phrase corresponds to which argument. It is well known that syntax is one of, if not the, major factors in this process. Active/passive sentence structure reverses the roles played by the subject and object:

The boy killed the dragon.
The dragon killed the boy.

Rules governing so called "deletions" decide if a missing argument is to be equated with the existing subject or object:

The boy asked the girl what to eat. (the boy does the eating)
The boy told the girl what to eat. (the girl does the eating)

The examples are endless. If logical form depends on knowing such things, and it is syntax which tells us, then the construction of logical form must occur after syntax.

3. NON-INFERENTIAL SEMANTICS

What happens after parsing is, naturally, beyond the bounds of this paper. However, I do need to emphasise one rather obvious fact. Virtually every model I know of has this section doing some form of inference (though not necessarily deduction), and inference requires logical form (it is hard to infer who is now dead if you have not decided who killed whom). Thus, inferential semantics can only occur after we have made guesses as to the case roles of the noun phrases in the sentence. If, as our model suggests, we typically only have this after syntax, any semantic processing prior to syntax (or in parallel with it) must be non-inferential in nature.

Thus I have called that semantic processing which occurs in parallel with syntax, "non-inferential semantics". All suggestions as to what this might be can be generically clumped as some sort of path-following in a semantic network.

One of the oldest and most popular of this sort of process is "spreading activation". The "classical" model of this is that by Collins and Quillian (1969). For my thoughts on this model, see Charniak (1981a). In the spreading activation model, we "activate" the content words in a sentence as we hear them. This in turn will cause the concepts associated with the words to be activated, and then using the semantic relations between concepts as pathways, we access other concepts which are semantically related. We do this in the hope of finding intersections between two spreading waves of activation. When we find such an intersection, it often indicates a semantic relatedness between two words in the sentence. By looking at the two paths leading to the intersection we can get valuable information on which sense of an ambiguous word is intended.

This dog barks at the moon.
The tree had sections of its bark missing.

We asume that in one case the path from "bark" to the intersection would go through the sense meaning "make a loud sound", while in the second example it would be the "skin of a tree" sense which leads to an intersection. As this example also indicates, spreading activation can help determine if a noun or verb usage is intended (since the "skin" sense has no verb counterpart, it must be a noun).

Furthermore, a process like spreading activation can help resolve what might have bothered some readers as a latent contradiction in my previous discussion. In the last section we noted that syntax is a mighty aid in determining the case roles of noun phrases, and therefore the creation of logical form occurs after syntax (if, nevertheless, interleaved with it). However, in my early example of how we could understand without syntax,

lecture student confusion question,

it seems clear that one thing which makes us feel that we have understood is that we have determined the case relations between the nouns. It is the student who is confused, and who asked the question. The student is located at the lecture. But spreading activation may well be able to handle this as well. If "confusion" requires an animate experiencer, and "students" are animate, then a path from "student" to "confusion" might well trace out this relation. Thus, our paths may indicate case relations as well, and once we have such relations, even if they are not provided by syntax, logical form, and then inference, can follow.

I have used spreading activation to illustrate how non-inferential semantics can do the things which seem to be required. But spreading activation is not the only semantic path tracing scheme which could do this. Wilks' ideas on parsing which go under the general label of "preference semantics" (Wilks, 1975) do not exactly fit my mould, since they mix syntax and semantics in a more complicated fashion than I am willing to consider, but I do not believe we do them too much injustice to say that they get much of their power from a path tracing model in which the paths such as that from "student" to "confusion" are used to predict case relations. The reason most would not normally classify these two schemes (spreading activation, and preference semantics) as similar is because they differ widely in the kinds of paths they consider, and the method used for constructing paths. In spreading activation we create relatively long paths and place little control on where we go next from a given node in the semantic network. In Wilks' scheme, we tightly control the paths to certain links at each point, and all paths are shallow. Thus the latter does not really look like a search (it seems to know where to look), while spreading activation is a search of the most costly kind.

I myself tend toward spreading activation. For one thing, the meaningful relations we may have between two concepts do not seem very constrained. So we can relate "suicide" in many different ways to other nouns:

                  pills

                  victim

suicide   note

                  depression

                  death

And while the paths illustrated here are not very long, the relation "pills taken in excess to cause death, which, in turn, is suicide" is not terribly direct either.

However, with completely undirected search, and with long paths, one will often get false intersections, such as that between "pills" and "death" corresponding to the idea "a person died from an illness for which he was taking pills". Perhaps this is reasonable if we had not seen "suicide" but once we have it should not be considered. For this reason we want some control over paths.

4. MORPHOLOGY FIRST

The only aspect of my model which I have not discussed is the proposal to put morphology prior to non-inferential semantics. Everyone assumes that we strip off plurals from nouns and endings from verbs before we do syntax. If we do not do this before non-inferential semantics we would have to have different nodes in our network for "watching" and "watched". Somehow this seems unlikely. A reasonable alternative would be that what is prior is not morphology, but rather some form of word recognition, which notes the "watch" in both forms, without knowing anything about endings in English. While this is possible, it would also predict that we would see "rasp" (a coarse file) in "raspberry". Introspection says we don't, but introspection has been wrong before. Alternatively, we might hypothesise something between the two (it knows, say, that word endings are a maximum of three characters or so). However, it seems easiest to assume that we are doing morphology first, and that is what I will do.

5. DESIDERATA IN SYNTAX

Having laid out the basic scheme, I should now ideally specify in greater detail what goes into each of the three components (four, including morphology) which make up my parsing model, "syntax", "non-inferential semantics" and "compositional semantics". However, as of late I have been thinking most about syntax, so I will ignore the other two, and spend what remains of this paper talking about syntactic parsing.

In particular, I have been looking at two current models of parsing, the old standby, the ATN parser (Woods, 1973) and a relative newcomer, Marcus' Parsifal (Marcus, 1980). What I find is that both have advantages and disadvantages. While there are any number of things one would like from a syntactic parser, from a plausible neural implementation, to the prediction of linguistic universals, I have been concentrating on the following set of goals:

(1) Rules of syntax must be isolatable entities
One would like to be able to look at the grammar and point to local portions which completely capture some grammatical rule. More generally, one wants rules which "capture the relevant generalisations". In Parsifal, most rules are isolated entities, but this is not usually true for grammars written for ATN parsers. Consider a rule like "there insertion"

Twenty paintings have been stolen from Italian churches this year.
There have been twenty paintings stolen from Italian churches this year.

In current ATN grammars (e.g., the one currently in use at BBN (Bates, 1981)) "there insertion" is not expressed as a single rule covering all typical cases, and the rule is spread over several different parts of the grammar, with one part noting the "there", while another attends to the fact that the subject appears after the auxiliary.

(2) Ambiguous words are automatically processed

The grammar should not require anything to handle words which are ambiguous between, say, a noun sense and a verb sense. In this respect ATN grammars are definitely superior to Parsifal. Because Parsifal does not use backtracking, it must explicitly consider all cases where ambiguity can lead the grammar down the wrong path. So, Marcus' grammar for Parsifal has three rules to decide if the word "that" is being used as a determiner e.g. "I don't believe that story", or a "wh" word e.g. "I don't believe that Jack went home". In an ATN this is not required, since it can simply assume the first, and if it does not pan out, then try the second.

(3) Constituents should only be created if they have a reasonable chance of being needed

Parsifal is somewhat better here, but neither parser wins any prizes. In an ATN grammar one creates a constituent whenever that constituent might appear at that place in the sentence, and due to rule ordering, we decide to explore that possibility. So, at the start of a sentence we might try, in turn, looking for np's, pp's, adverbial phrases (e.g. "the day before yesterday"), vp's (if the subject was deleted, as in imperatives), not to mention several variations of each one. Parsifal only creates a constituent if (a) it could be used, and (b) if there are currently words in the buffer which could start that kind of constituent. Thus Parsifal is more parsimonious in its creation of new constituents. However, this is at a price. In my attempt to remove all ad hoc rules of a Parsifal-like grammar (Charniak, 1981b) I found that the most recalcitrant were about nine rules which had no other purpose in life than deciding if the words in the buffer warranted the creation of a certain kind of constituent. I would like to get rid of these rules.

(4) Syntax must be compatible with semantics

The grammar should interface nicely with some semantic component which will give it advice about how to proceed, and uses its results to construct the logical form of the sentence. At first glance there are no startling weaknesses with either ATNs or Parsifal since both have convenient ways to both call semantic routines at appropriate places, and use the results thereof. There is, however, one difficulty with both, concerning the well known problem of prepositional phrases placement. The prototypic example is

I saw the man on the hill with a telescope.

Syntax typically allows terminal prepositional phrases to be attached to any one of a number of locations on the tree, and hence it must be semantics which makes the decision. One important fact about such decisions is that they seem to be comparative in nature. That is, semantics does not seem to decide on some absolute basis where the prepositional phrase can or cannot go, but rather decides which of the possibilities works best. For example:

I saw the man with a club.
I hit the man with a club.

There is nothing wrong with "with a club" modifying "man", as demonstrated by the first of these sentences, but since "hit" likes "with a club" as its instrumental phrase very much, this is the preferred reading of the second sentence. Unfortunately, with both Parsifal, and current implementations of ATNs, it requires ad hoc rules to allow such a process. In both grammars, the normal decision would be, can this prepositional phrase fit at a certain place in the tree, "yes or no". It is not hard to fix this with a special rule, but in the best of all possible parsers, nothing of this sort would be needed.

I have some ideas on all four of these issues, and am currently working on a parser which uses backup, but whose rules look more like those in Parsifal, than the typical rules of an ATN. Thus I hope to get the best of both worlds. However, this work is quite preliminary at this point.

6. REFERENCES

Bates, M. (1981) ATN grammar. Unpublished Computer Listing.

Charniak, E. (1981a) Passing markers: a theory of contextual influence in language comprehension, Report TR-80, Department of Computer Science, Brown University.

Charniak, E. (1981b) A parser with something for everyone, Report TR-70, Department of Computer Science, Brown University.

Collins, A. and Quillian, M. R. (1969) Retrieval time from semantic memory, *Journal of Verbal Learning and Verbal Behavior* 8. 240–248.

Marcus, M. P. (1980) *A Theory of Syntactic Recognition for Natural Language.* Cambridge, Mass: MIT Press.

Milne, R. W. (forthcoming) Predicting garden path sentences, *Cognitive Science*.

Prather, P. and Swinney, D. (1977) Some effects of syntactic context upon lexical access. Presented at a meeting of the American Psychological Association.

Wilks, Y. A. (1975) An intelligent analyzer and understander of English, *Communications of the ACM* 18(5) 264–174.

Woods, W. A. (1973) An experimental parsing system for transition network grammars. In *Natural Language Processing,* ed. R. Rustin, New York: Algorithmics Press.

So what about parsing compound nouns?

K. Sparck Jones, University of Cambridge

THE PROBLEM

Compound nouns, and more generally, complex nominals, are a problem we have turned away from. But any serious natural language program, whether practically or theoretically motivated, has got to tackle it.

Three processes apply to compound nouns. They have to be bracketed: 'wicker (bread basket)' vs '(wholemeal bread) basket'; they have to be lexically disambiguated: 'bread = loaf' vs 'bread = money'; and they have to be given a meaning characterisation: 'basket for bread' vs 'basket with bread'.

Various strategies, or rather non-strategies, have been adopted to deal with compound nouns. One, for example, is to put compound nouns in the lexicon. A second is to assume that restrictions on the possible interpretations of the constituents, for a specific universe of discourse, will force an appropriate interpretation on the whole. A third is not to attempt a full characterisation of the whole. And a fourth is to disregard elements which cannot be processed. These are all unsatisfactory, for obvious reasons. We cannot put all the compounds, even for a limited domain, in the lexicon. We cannot rely on sense restrictions to give us an acceptable interpretation. We cannot assume that an explicit characterisation is unnecessary. And we cannot always throw parts of the input away.

If we accept, therefore, that more serious approaches to compound noun processing are required, what does this imply?

Processing compound nouns has implications for system capacity, and for system structure.

The essential problem about compound nouns is that interpreting them requires inference, and specifically pragmatic inference, in an unpredictable way. Various attempts have been made to characterise compound nouns in terms of general semantic relations, for example PRODUCT, CAUSE, RESEMBLANCE

(Warren, 1978; Levi, 1978). But many compounds cannot be characterised in this way (Downing, 1977), and the particular relations underlying those that can have still to be discovered, for which inference may be required. Moreover, while more than one alternative interpretation of a compound may be tolerated, others may have to be rejected. Equally, though inexplicit representations may serve for some purposes, explicit meaning representations may be required even for apparently text- rather than knowledge-oriented tasks, like translation as opposed to question-answering, and to provide these inference may be necessary.

AN ILLUSTRATION

To emphasise these points, consider "border plants" in

"These border plants have to be replaced"
("These plants in the border have to be replaced")

and in

"These border plants are expensive"
("These plants for the border are expensive").

We can say that the general semantic relations underlying "border plants" in these two sentences are LOCATION and PURPOSE respectively. But even if "border plant" figured in the lexicon with these two meanings, we might have to use pragmatic inference to establish which of the two meanings applied in each sentence; and as it is unlikely to appear in the lexicon, we will very probably have to use inference. That is, we cannot assume that we will have standard semantic patterns which will collocate 'plant' and 'replace' for LOCATION and 'plant' and 'expensive' for PURPOSE. Nor can we assume that our pragmatic knowledge base will contain low-level, directly applicable facts about border plants needing replacement, etc. We should expect to have to make inferences from more general facts about plants, or even living things, deteriorating or getting old or dying, about ornamental objects typically being items of purchase, and so on.

Notice, moreover, that we have no reason to suppose that domain-specific knowledge structures will help us in any straightforward way here: both sentences could naturally occur in a 'Gardening' frame. We will have to rely at least on techniques for exploiting several frames concurrently, and almost certainly on applying local textual context information as well.

The refined inference operations needed to sort out the two interpretations of "border plants" just given are equally needed if we accept that "border plants" in the first sentence can mean either 'plants located in the border' or 'plants belonging to the border'. They will also be needed for a text-oriented task like translation, to select appropriate output prepositions in French, say, as much as for a knowledge-oriented task for which referents for "these border plants" have to be found.

If we extend the example to consider e.g. "perennial border plants", or "park border plants" (and, further, "blue border plants"), we have a bracketing problem; and as "park border plants" can be bracketed either as "park (border plants)" − those flowers I saw yesterday − or as "(park border) plants" − those favourites of municipal gardeners, it is highly likely that inference would be needed to establish the correct reading. Equally, as soon as we consider the other senses of the words involved, it is not clear that yet more inference will not be required. We could presumably eliminate 'plant = factory, installation' with more or less standard semantics; but distinguishing 'border = bed' from 'border = edge' is more of a challenge. (What, moreover, would standard semantics do to "The IRA have done so much bombing recently all the border blants need replacing"?)

What the example suggests, therefore, is that while syntactic, semantic and pragmatic information can contribute to the interpretation of compound nouns, their relative contribution for any given compound is unpredictable. Or, to put the point more strongly, the problem for a natural language processor is that it is possible that rather little effective work can be done on an input noun string unless pragmatic inference is invoked. What does this imply for the design of a natural language interpreter?

COMPOUNDS AND SYSTEM ARCHITECTURES

First, it is clear that there are problems about the conventional natural language program in which the contents of clearly demarcated information boxes labelled syntax, semantics, and pragmatics are applied in successive processing steps. At the high level relevant here it does not matter whether the sequence of steps is followed only for complete input sentences, or for within-sentence constituents, though the detailed consequences of the choice made on this will differ. The essential problem for sequential processing is that at each stage before the pragmatic one, compound nouns may be handed over in a very poorly analysed state. Thus syntax may not be able to do much more than label the rightmost element as the head of the compound. For richer complex nominals, some bracketing constraints on the way adjectives and nouns can be grouped may apply, but noun strings as such can generally be bracketed any way, so the syntactic processor is obliged to hand over, implicitly or explicitly, all the alternatives. Moreover if the word forms involved can have other syntactic functions, for example as verbs, we can get yet more options for the semantic processor to consider.

A semantic processor using any kind of pattern matching in turn has the problem that the location of the units to be related in matching is uncertain.

Thus if it is not clear, given a multiple noun string, what its constituent groups and their heads are, there is more complex pattern matching to do. The result is likely to be many alternative semantic analyses which are handed forward for weeding to the pragmatics component. These semantic interpretations may of course have been obtained by semantic inference rather than by simple pattern matching. Further, since we cannot expect even semantic inference to select or reach interpretations for all compound nouns, we are likely to be left with non-interpretations as much as with alternative interpretations for the pragmatic component to sort out.

As long as we are not concerned with psychological modelling, the fact that alternative analyses are carried forward may not matter in principle; but it is likely to be very inconvenient in practice, in the limit so inconvenient as to undermine the idea of effective processing on which the staged program is based. There is perhaps some difficulty too at the level of principle about reconciling compound interpretation as selection with compound interpretation as construction of a specific meaning relationship. But even if this is not an issue of principle, there is certainly a practical problem in managing the two.

The natural reaction to these practical difficulties is to modify the rigidly sequential system architecture, to allow for more flexible processing in which different types of information and procedure can be called at more than one point in the overall attack on the input sentence. A variant of this scheme is that advocated by Charniak (1981), where word-based network processing is carried out in parallel with the normal processing, and is allowed to feed its results into any ordinary processing stage. The kind of network-based compound noun resolution apparently developed by McDonald (1981) would seem to fit in here.

The advantage of an approach like this is that sentence processing is orderly, indeed the assumption underlying it is that sentence processing *is* basically orderly. However, if enough interaction between, and cycling over, process stages is allowed, it is not clear that the whole notion of processing steps has any meaning. It would be better then to face this fact and go for the radical alternative of non-sequential, and hence word-driven, processing. This looks very attractive as a solution to the compound noun problem: we let all kinds of process, syntactic, semantic, and pragmatic, do their bit, as the individual input words stimulate them. Logically, processing can be parallel, so pragmatic inference can be brought to bear on compound noun string interpretation just as soon as syntactic processing.

Unfortunately, things are not so simple. It is not clear how far word-driven interpretation can capture those gains in applying patterns and rules which come from explicitly working with higher-level constituents. A word-driven interpreter which works implicitly with constituents is obviously subject, if only in a variable, specific way, to those 'staging binds' which occur globally in the modular system. However a word-driven interpreter of a purer sort is also likely to be subject to staging binds. Any interpreter at any time is going to have to pursue one processing path rather than another, simply because life is too exigent even in principle for full parallelism, and can therefore find itself, for compound nouns at least, in a situation where some other processor has not supplied the information a given processor needs.

The difference between the two interpreter architectures, in other words, is not that staging binds will occur in one case and not the other, but that they will occur systematically in one case and unsystematically in the other.

IMPLICATIONS FOR PARSING

These architecture ramifications of compound noun processing point up the limitations of conventional views of parsing and its importance. Conventionally, parsing means syntactic processing; and conventionally it is used to drive everything else. The real problem with compound nouns (and of course even more with complex nominals) is in interfacing the different interpretive processes within the system as a whole. Syntax can do something with compound nouns, and their sentence environments, but not much. The real interest in dealing with compounds is in the rest of the interpreter: how to apply semantic and pragmatic procedures to them. Applying semantics and pragmatics in relation to weakly informative syntax depends on this.

Compound nouns show that either system model — sequential or parallel — presents problems; but they equally show that concentrating on sentence parsing in its own right is of limited utility. It is the entire complex system, with syntactic processing in a subsidiary role, which counts: we must start with a view of what text interpretation is, and hence of the system as a whole, before we think about how syntactic parsing contributes to interpretation, and so about how a parser should be constructed.

ACKNOWLEDGEMENT

This paper was stimulated by discussions with John Tait.

REFERENCES

Charniak, E. (1981) Passing markers: a theory of contextual influence in language comprehension. Technical Report CS–80, Department of Computer Science, Brown University.

Downing, P. (1977) On the creation and use of English compound nouns. *Language* **53**, 810–842.

McDonald, D. B. (1981) Compound: a program that understands noun compounds. *Proceedings of the Seventh International Joint Conference on Artificial Intelligence,* 1061.

Warren, B. (1978) *Semantic patterns of noun–noun compounds,* Gothenburg Studies in English 41, Göteborg: Acta Universitatis Gothenburgensis.

PART VI

Semantics-directed parsing

Semantic parsing and syntactic constraints (Mark IV)

J. I. Tait, University of Cambridge

1. INTRODUCTION

This paper considers ways in which semantic parsers can exploit a particular example syntactic constraint which has semantic consequences. By semantic parsers I mean programs which convert natural language sentences into some representation of their meaning. The main conclusion is that there are significant disadvantages in attempting to do semantic parsing without complete syntactic processing of the input. It will also be suggested that for a certain class of existing parsers the constraint can only be implemented by means of a rather odd division between syntactic and semantic processing.

Two semantic parsers are considered. One is that of Cater (1982); the other is that of Boguraev (1979). I have selected these two because, from the point of view of this paper, they are reasonable representatives of two styles of parsing. In one style little syntactic analysis is done: processing is based on semantics-driven programs associated with particular words. Cater's program is the representative of this style. Other programs written in this style include Small (1980), Riesbeck (1975) and Birnbaum and Selfridge (1979). The other style, represented by Boguraev's program, involves complete syntactic processing of input sentences, with semantic processing more or less decoupled from it. Others in this style include Woods (1973) and Winograd (1972).[†]

Another reason for the choice of these parsers is that I am very familiar with them. I have maintained and developed both of them. Such familiarity is important here because the essence of my argument is that in practice the

---

[†] Note that it is the *logical* separation of syntax and semantics which is at issue here. I am ignoring important issues of processing architecture for the moment, in particular, whether syntactic analysis should precede semantic analysis or operate in parallel with it.

implementation of the exploitation of the constraint in Cater's parser is beset with technical difficulties. Moreover, these difficulties are products of the style of parsing, with its odd division between syntactic and semantic processing, and not infelicities in Cater's program. Thus the discussion proceeds at a rather technical level.

The syntactic constraint considered in this paper is the well-known no-crossing-of-branches rule and, in particular, its application to prepositional phrase attachment.[‡]

Consider, for example:

(E1)   The man saw the woman in the park with the telescope.

The constraint prohibits any reading of this sentence corresponding to:

(E2)   The man in the park saw the woman, who had the telescope.

In general the constraint places significant restrictions on the possible readings of sentences with optional prepositional postmodifiers and, as in (E1), it can eliminate possible readings which are perfectly plausible on semantic grounds.

In order to simplify the discussion, throughout this paper it is assumed that there is no difference between prepositional postmodification of the subject of a sentence and prepositional postmodification of the main verb. Thus, for (E1), it is assumed that any reading corresponding to a paraphrase containing "the man in the park" as its subject will equally correspond to a paraphrase containing "the seeing . . . done by the man was done in the park". Making such a crude assumption is justified here because a motivated treatment of this distinction would merely obscure the primary concern of this paper: the use which may be made of cross-constituent syntactic constraints by semantic parsers.

2. THE STRUCTURE OF THE TWO PARSERS

Boguraev's parser operates by interleaving syntactic and semantic processing. It uses a large ATN grammar for English which invokes so-called semantic specialists whenever a noun phrase or clause can be syntactically terminated. The semantic specialists are handed partial syntactic analyses in the form of constituents to be assembled. The specialists exploit a semantic primitive system to determine if the constituents they are handed form a semantically plausible whole. If they do, a case-labelled dependency structure is built to represent them. Otherwise the associated syntactic parsing is blocked. The simplicity of

‡ See, for example, Radford (1981). But also see McCawley (1982) for a discussion of some cases where the rule may not apply. I will ignore these for the purposes of the present discussion, since it seems that they cannot be used to argue against the existence of semantically important cross-constituent syntactic constraints, the main point at issue here.

this description masks the complexity in Boguraev's system of the ATN-based syntactic processing and the semantic pattern matching.

Cater's parser operates by breaking the input sentence into a set of constituent units, like basic noun phrases, prepositional phrases and verb groups, and then performing semantic processing of these constituents using an expectation-based mechanism not dissimilar to Riesbeck (1975). That is, the fundamental operation of the semantic processing is the application of rules of the form: if the current word is X then it is likely that either constituent A, or constituent B, or constituent C, and so on, follows. This is implemented by attaching coroutines, called requests, to words in the lexicon. As a constituent enters the semantic processor any requests attached to words in the constituent are activated. In general a word-activated request loads other requests which examine the input constituent stream for constituents which are expected to follow the original word whose occurrence caused the activation of the first request. For example, one of the requests associated with "give" loads two pairs of requests: one pair deals with two noun phrases following the verb phrase; the other pair will operate if the verb phrase is followed by a single noun phrase and then a prepositional phrase whose preposition is "to". Note that the semantic processing runs through the sequence of constituents in a primarily left to right direction. The requests also build semantic representations of the constituents they analyse.

If attention is restricted to one reading of part of a sentence, at any point in the processing of the sequence of constituents there will be one active routine with a pointer to a particular place in the constituent string. The coroutines which analysed the parts of the sentence to the left of the active coroutine's pointer will have handed it a partially built meaning representation and a set of so-called registers into which arbitrary values can be placed. These registers form the primary means by which coroutines intercommunicate. They are used for such diverse things as passing forward the syntactic subject of a sentence until a main verb is found, passing around temporal information derived from verb tense analysis, and recording constraints on the way partially-built structures may be modified by subsequent processing. The parser produces, as its output, representations in a development of Conceptual Dependency Theory (Schank, 1975).

In summary, from the point of view of this paper the essential difference between Boguraev's and Cater's parsers is that Boguraev's completely processes a sentence syntactically, so that any syntactic information required by the semantic specialists may be given to them, whereas Cater's only uses explicit syntactic information to group input words into small constituents.

3. INCORPORATING THE CONSTRAINT INTO BOGURAEV'S PARSER

Boguraev's parser explicitly uses the no-crossing-of-branches constraint to restrict the readings which may be found for sentences like (E1). Two implementations have been used. The original version of the program, that described in Boguraev (1979), used a rather complicated technique, which will not be discussed here. More recently I have completed an implementation of Boguraev's parser which exploits the constraint in an entirely straightforward way.

The implementation operates with an ATN which is written in such a way that it only discovers those syntactic analyses (of prepositional phrase post-modification) which could be generated by a Phrase Structure Grammar under the standard rewrite interpretation. Such grammars cannot generate analyses which violate the no-crossing-of-branches constraint. Both the noun phrase and verb phrase subnetworks consider, optionally, processing postmodifying pre-positional phrases syntactically before calling their semantic specialists. For example, in (E1) for the noun phrase containing "the woman", the syntactic constituent analyses produced are "the woman", "the woman in the park" "the woman (in the park) (with the telescope)" and "the woman (in the park (with the telescope))"; and the sentence-level clause specialist is handed struc-tures corresponding to "The man saw", "The man saw with the telescope", "The man saw (in the park) (with the telescope)" "The man saw (in the park (with the telescope))". The semantic speciaiists simply check to see if they have been handed a constituent analysis which contains such optional post-modifiers, and if they have, they construct dependency structures for all the semantically plausible ways the prepositional phrases may modify the head noun of the noun phrase or main verb of the clause.[†]

4. INCORPORATING THE CONSTRAINT INTO CATER'S PARSER

Cater's parser is a particularly suitable vehicle for discussion in this paper be-cause it is one of the few in its class which is designed to take account of the possibility of structural, rather than lexical, ambiguity in its input. However it has never actually been used to produce multiple meaning representations for single sentences, and does not exploit the constraint. Therefore this section is rather more hypothetical than the preceding one.

In Cater's system optional postmodifiers are handled by attaching requests to the relevant prepositions. Disregarding the constraint for the moment, if the present implementation were extended to produce all of the six semantically plausible readings for (E1) (a fairly straightforward matter), it would proceed as follows. A coroutine would be started by the word "in". It would have been handed the representation built for "The man saw the woman", and would

---

[†]Experience with this system of prepositional phrase attachment suggests (perhaps not unexpectedly) that it is probably inefficient to postpone the initiation of semantic pro-cessing until after all possible prepositional postmodifiers at a level have been processed syntactically. It would, perhaps, be better to invoke semantic specialists after the *first* possible end of a noun phrase or clause, and then again after each possible postmodifying constituent at a level, in order to eliminate semantically implausible constituent/post-modifier pairs at an earlier stage in syntactic processing.

construct a suitable representation for the prepositional phrase. It would then generate two daughter coroutines. In one of them the structure would represent "The man, who was in the park, saw the woman"; in the other the structure would represent "The man saw the woman, who was in the park". When "with" was read both the existing coroutines would spawn daughters which would attempt to find a prepositional phrase and attach it to all existing nominals in their parent's structure. Coroutines would be spawned by these third generation prepositional phrase attachment coroutines. In the structures in the fourth generation, representing the set of possible readings of the sentence as a whole, the representation for "with a telescope" would be attached to all the semantically plausible points. Six coroutines would therefore be generated, including one in which the structure would reflect the constraint violating reading (E2).

It is possible to see how the no-crossing-of-branches constraint might be introduced into Cater's parser. There are a number of techniques which might be adopted to implement it. Perhaps the most elegant is to set up, for all noun phrases, an expectation that they may be modified by a prepositional phrase at some point in the clause in which they occur. If such an expectation is satisfied, then an expectation should be set up that the original noun phrase may be modified by a further prepositional phrase. At the same time any similar requests associated with noun phrases to the right of the modified one in the sentence should be eliminated. The processing of the request-based part of Cater's parser will then be as described below.

In the example, "↑" indicates the position of the cursor in the input constituent stream; "{" and "}" enclose the representations of portions of the text which have already been processed; "[" and "]" enclose descriptions of prepositional phrase attachment requests: no other requests are shown; large parentheses are used to associate partially-built structures with the corresponding requests; nested large parentheses are used to indicate that the processing associated with the outermost level of large parentheses has caused the reactivation of some previously suspended requests and their associated structure: the result of the application of the requests (which may be done without moving the cursor) is indicated in an inner set of large parentheses. Requests representing unsatisfiable expectations are not shown.

An expectation is introduced that at some point a prepositional phrase may modify "The man".

The man saw the woman in the park with the telescope.
↑

$$\left\{ \begin{array}{l} \{(\text{The man})\} \\ [\text{Expect PP to modify "The man"}] \end{array} \right\}$$

Another is added expecting the prepositional phrase to modify "the woman". (The possibility that a prepositional phrase may modify "saw" is ignored here: see section 1.)

The man saw the woman in the park with the telescope.

$$\left\{ \begin{array}{l} \{(\text{The man}) \text{ saw (the woman)}\} \\ [\text{Expect PP to modify "The man"}] \\ [\text{Expect PP to modify "the woman"}] \end{array} \right\}$$

When the cursor moves over the prepositional phrase "in the park" three theories are created. One builds a partial structure in which "The man" is modified by "in the park". As this structure is built, a check is made on whether there are any prepositional phrase requests which are associated with a noun phrase to the right of the one being modified. In this case there is (for "the woman"): it is removed from the theory. This removal constitutes the enforcement of the no-crossing-of-branches constraint. In the second theory, a partial structure is built in which it is "the woman" which is modified by "in the park". In the third an expectation that "the park" may be modified by a further prepositional phrase is introduced; until this expectation is satisfied attempts to find modifiers associated with "The man" and "the woman" are suspended and their associated structure (corresponding to "The man saw the woman") removed from consideration. This does not occur until the cursor reaches the end of the sentence.

The man saw the woman in the park with the telescope.

$$\left\{ \begin{array}{l} \{(\text{The man (in the park))} \text{ saw the woman}\} \\ [\text{Expect another PP to modify "The man"}] \end{array} \right\}$$

$$\left\{ \begin{array}{l} \{\text{The man saw (the woman (in the park))}\} \\ [\text{Expect a PP to modify "The man"}] \\ [\text{Expect another PP to modify "the woman"}] \end{array} \right\}$$

$$\left\{ \begin{array}{l} \{\text{the park}\} \\ [\text{Expect a PP to modify "the park"}] \end{array} \right\}$$

When the cursor reaches the end of the sentence, five theories will exist. They correspond to all the expectations in the above three theories being satisfied: but in mutually exclusive ways. The third theory above, which is to allow for prepositional phrases which modify "the park", involves slightly more complex processing. When a prepositional phrase is discovered which may modify "the park", the partial structure built to represent that part of the sentence to the right of "the park" will be reinstated, all previously suspended requests will be reactivated and allowed to operate without the cursor being moved. Here the suspended expectations (which are not illustrated) are one attempting to find a prepositional postmodifier for "The man", and another attempting to find a prepositional postmodifier for "the woman", both of which may build structures.

The man saw the woman in the park with the telescope.
                                                    ↑

{(The man (in the park) (with the telescope) saw (the woman)}
{(The man (with the telescope)) saw (the woman (in the park))}
{(The man saw (the woman (in the park) (with the telescope))}

$$\left\{ \begin{array}{l} \{(\text{the park (with the telescope)})\} \\ \left\{ \begin{array}{l} \{(\text{The man (in the park (with the telescope)))}\} \\ \text{saw (the woman)}\} \end{array} \right\} \\ \left\{ \begin{array}{l} \{(\text{The man) saw} \\ \text{(the woman (in the park (with the telescope)))}\} \end{array} \right\} \end{array} \right\}$$

Thus only the five syntactically legitimate analyses are discovered.

The processing done to achieve this seems to me to be a precisely syntactic analysis of the whole sentence, something Cater wishes to avoid *as a principle* in his system. Examples like the above demonstrate that this position is untenable. However, even if the principle of no syntactic analysis of complete sentences is abandoned, the position one has to adopt to justify the building of an implementation, such as that described above, seems to me to be rather odd.

The above proposed implementation is effectively based on a claim that there are two entirely different sorts of syntactic rule. The first sort are rules which deal only with local word order. The second sort are rules which deal with syntactic phenomena which do not exhibit themselves purely through local word order effects. Examples of the first sort of rule are that determiners may only be followed by nouns, adjectives and then nouns, and so on. The no-crossing-of-branches rule is an example of the second sort.

Such a claim is difficult to justify. It requires one either claim that a rule which states that nouns may be directly followed by prepositional phrases is quite different from a rule which states that nouns may be preceded by determiners; or claim that the mechanism by which nominals may be directly post-modified by prepositional phrases is quite different from the mechanism by which prepositional phrases occurring at the end of a clause may modify the subject. Furthermore, in either case, Cater seems to have to claim that the no-crossing-of-branches rule is more closely related to a rule which states that "only sentient beings may be displeased" than to a rule which states that "determiners may be followed by nouns".[†]

Such separation of like information and association of unlike information is inelegant, and, I believe, computer systems constructed from an inelegant theory are likely to be difficult to maintain and extend.

[†]It should be pointed out that Cater's position in this area is a reworking of that of Wilks (1975) which explicitly supports the separation of word-order based syntax from higher-level syntactic analysis, and the merger of higher-level syntax with semantic processing. However, Wilks gives no justification for his position other than the relative success of his machine translation system.

Of course, this argument would not hold if simple word-order syntactic rules were not separated from the other parts of the system at all, as is done in the CA system of Birnbaum and Selfridge (1979). However, CA does not produce multiple readings for sentences like (E1), nor can it produce different readings in different contexts. It also appears that the implementation of the no-crossing-of-branches constraint would involve the manipulation of rather more explicit syntactic information than is done in the system described in Birnbaum and Selfridge (1979). Thus it is not clear to what extent it is possible to avoid the criticisms levelled at Cater within the CA framework.

5. CONCLUSIONS

There is a widespread belief in the semantic parsing community that sentence analysis is most easily achieved by using syntactic rules which deal only with local word-order effects, applying semantic processing on the structures created by such rules and expressing any syntactic information not concerned with local word-order effects by means of quasi-semantic rules. Consideration of a fairly straightforward non-local syntactic rule, the no-crossing-of-branches constraint applied to prepositional phrases, leads one to conclude that such a position is tenable only if one is willing to accept a fairly arbitrary distinction between the different sorts of syntactic rules. No such inelegance is introduced in a system which performs complete syntactic processing of its input.

This is not to support systems in which complete syntactic processing of input strings is performed *before* semantic, pragmatic and contextual processing is applied to the input. Strings which are judged grammatical only in certain contexts, the processing of noun phrases containin large numbers of prepositional phrase postmodifiers, and the processing of sentences containing a number of categorially ambiguous words, present severe problems for such systems. Other phenomena presenting difficulties for approaches based on decoupled syntactic processing are not hard to find.

In conclusion, I would like to suggest that semantic parsers which do not perform complete syntactic processing will consider entirely illegitimate interpretations of their input. Further, if such processing is done without a directly represented grammar of English it is likely to lead to computer systems which are difficult to maintain and extend.

ACKNOWLEDGEMENTS
I would like to thank E. J. Briscoe, Dr. K. Sparck Jones and especially Dr. B. K. Boguraev for their advice and assistance during the preparation of this paper.

REFERENCES
Birnbaum, L. and Selfridge, M. (1979) Problems in Conceptual Analysis of Natural Language. Research Report No. 168, Department of Computer Science, Yale University.

Boguraev, B. K. (1979) Automatic Resolution of Linguistic Ambiguities. Technical Report No. 11, Computer Laboratory, University of Cambridge.

Cater, A. W. S. (1981) Analysis and Inference for English. Technical Report No. 18, Computer Laboratory, University of Cambridge.

McCawley, J. D. (1982) Parentheticals and Discontinuous Constituent Structure. *Linguistic Inquiry* **13**, 91–106.

Radford, A. (1981) *Transformational Syntax*. Cambridge: Cambridge University Press.

Riesbeck, C. K. (1975) Conceptual Analysis. In R. C. Schank (ed) *Conceptual Information Processing*. Amsterdam: North-Holland.

Schank, R. C. (1975) *Conceptual Information Processing*. North-Holland, Amsterdam.

Small, S. (1980) Word Expert Parsing: A Theory of Distributed Word-based Natural Language Understanding. Report TR–954, Department of Computer Science, University of Maryland.

Winograd, T. (1972) *Understanding Natural Language*. Edinburgh: Edinburgh University Press.

Wilks, Y. A. (1975) An Intelligent Analyser and Understander of English, *Communications of the ACM* **18**, 264–274.

Woods, W. A. C. (1973) An Experimental Parsing System for Transition Network Grammars. In Rustin, R. (ed.) *Natural Language Processing*. New York: Algorithmics Press.

Some problems for conceptual analysers

K. Riesbeck, Yale University

Every few years, someone points me to interesting work that has gone on in or near the field of linguistics, e.g. McCawley, Lakoff, Marcus, and Gazdar, to drop a few names. Each time I hope that at last help is on the way. I don't consider linguistics to be the handmaiden of AI, but I would like to go next door and borrow a cup of sugar once in a while. More accurately, I look for help in dealing with some knotty piece of text that my work on a natural language system has run afoul of.

Unfortunately, knottiness in linguistics seems to mean knottiness in the structure of a sentence, or knottiness in the explanation of what appears to be, on the surface, a simple phenomenon. While I don't expect any linguist to drop what he or she is doing and come to my rescue, I would like to spend some time on some texts where I have failed to come up with what I consider reasonable solutions.[†]

An important caveat must precede these confessions of failure. The problem with them is not that I have no idea at all on how to do them. It's that the ideas I have are either too vague to be programmed (and much too vague to be formalised), or that the ideas do not mesh in any uniform way with what I consider to be normal processing. Nor are these all the kinds of failures I have run into. There are also the standard problems, such as ambiguity and anaphoric reference, for which I have only the standard solutions, and others, such as metaphor, for which I have no solutions at all.

Several years ago, I was working on the understanding of directions, i.e. texts that told you how to get some place (Riesbeck, 1980). I was able to handle many cases with a simple analyser called McELI (Schank and Riesbeck, 1981). The analyser I used broke things into fairly small phrases, relying on semantics to put them together in a reasonable way. I still believe that, for texts like

---

[†] I could pick the set of texts for which others think I have failed to find reasonable solutions, but this is much too large to go into here.

directions, which are often quite fragmentary, this is a good model of how people deal with them.

The analyser also had a few speech act rules to enable it to realise that "I can't remember what's on the right" was a relevant comment about spatial layout, not about memory, and that "You can't miss it" was a comment about the apparent non-clarity of the directions.

The analyser was quite limited. It had nothing for handling passives, sub-clauses, or complex questions. This didn't bother me since had these forms appeared in the texts, I had ways (messy, to be sure) to deal with them. But the following text is typical of failures that did bother me, because the texts were common and important to the task at hand.

It's hard to describe but I'll try anyway.

1. Turn *at the park* off Happy Valley Rd onto Seaside Scenic.

2. Park as close as you can to the last row of the brown shingled condos.

3. 3388 is the *third unit on your right* (on the east side) as you walk in from the street.

4. When you get lost, ask someone or call.

Fig. 1

Consider the first sentence in Fig. 1:

It's hard to describe but I'll try anyway.

What's hard to describe? Normally, my analyser assumes that "it" refers to "where you are going," as in "Go 2 blocks and it's on your right." Hence, the analyser assumes that the destination is hard to describe, which is a perfectly reasonable thing to say, as in

It's hard to describe but I'll try anyway. It's a big house with a lot of wings . . .

But "it" in the real text refers to the route to be followed, not the destination. Why? Was getting this right important for my program? Yes, because I was trying to make a point about how judgements of the clarity of directions were made.

Now, one way to find what the "it" refers to is to use syntactic information to understand the sentence "It's hard to describe but I'll try anyway" as meaning the same thing as "It's hard to describe (an object) but I'll try (to describe that object) anyway." Then the program needs to infer from the "I'll try" clause that the text that follows will describe the object. This is a textual prediction based on the meaning of the sentence. So the first sentence really means "It's hard to describe the object that the text that follows will describe".

But if the program stopped the analysis at this point, because it knew what the "it" referred to, it would be missing the point of this sentence, which is

"Be aware that the following description is not up to standard". That is, the text should be read carefully, and, when actually following the directions, the reader should be aware that there may be problems. The sentence is like those "Manufacturer not liable for damage due to use of this product" statements.

When you get lost, ask someone or call.

In the original research, I dealt with one idiomatic meta-comment, the classic "You can't miss it." But the above falls into the general class of *warnings,* which includes such other encouragements as "It gets tricky here," "Everyone misses this turn," and "They don't believe in having very many street signs in Boston". As you can see, to handle these requires being able to recognise many different ways of describing trouble. The sentence structures are the least of my worries.

Here's another set of directions, to make another point:

The Inn is north from the airport, on Rte. 1−5, at the La Jolla Village Drive Turnoff, going west. Arrangements will be made to transport participants between the Inn and the UCSD campus for workshop sessions.

The problem here is in recognising that the second sentence does not have anything to do with the directions. This is probably the most pervasive problem I (and other developers of text understanders) run into: recognising when something is not what you're looking for. I rarely get (nor do normal readers need) a warning that the next sentence is different in kind from the previous one.

Currently, I am working on newspaper articles about the U.S. economy, particularly about causes and cures for high inflation, interest rates, and unemployment. Here's an example text:

A second economic Laetrile is the balanced budget. How often have we heard that budget deficits are the fundamental source of inflation? Mechanically, balanced budgets are no more a panacea than mechanical monetary rules. The budget affects inflation primarily through its effect on economic slack.

One obvious problem arises from the metaphoric references to Laetrile and panacea. The complete article had a running metaphor of "snake-oil" cures for economic ills. Adding a metaphoric sense-extender to normal semantic routines is like adding nitroglycerine to your gas tank. The increase in energy output is likely to be correlated with an increased randomness in your car.

Another problem text is the second sentence which is a question. The reader has to realise when a question in a text is answered by the rest of the text and when it is not. For example, is this question answered in this text? Yes, it is. Is this one? It can make a difference in how you interpret the next sentence. This is the "Is the sentence what I was looking for?" problem again.

Notice that the text talks first about "budget deficits", and "balanced budgets", but concludes with the effect of "the budget". I don't want the analyser to decide that it is only the U.S. budget that is limited to affecting inflation through slack, but I don't want the analyser to be insensitive to such differences in the text either. Why does it seem reasonable to assume that "the budget" should really be read as "any budget"?

Here is another text:

> With high growth choked off by high interest rates, budget deficits are going to be bigger, not smaller. The result: more demands for credit and higher interest rates.

This shows how syntactic structures knot up with argument structures. The 'with' clause is setting up the antecedent cause of the increase in deficits. I don't know if the second sentence is grammatical, but the phrase "the result:" clearly signals the conclusion of the argument, and allows the writer to dispense with the need for a main verb.

I hope that the reader can see now what I mean by knotty texts. The knots are not in the syntax of the sentence, but in the ties between the syntax, the semantics, the text, the speech acts, and so on. In AI (at least my brand) compromise and simplification is the order of the day. But texts like these break through the neat wall that I try to construct. And that, of course, is why texts like these will probably be, in the long run, the most important ones of all.

REFERENCES

Riesbeck, C. (1980) You can't miss it: judging the clarity of directions. *Cognitive Science* **4**, 285–303.

Schank, R. and Riesbeck, C. (1981) *Inside Computer Understanding*. Hillsdale, NJ: Lawrence Erlbaum Associates.

Does anyone really still believe this kind of thing?

Y. Wilks, University of Essex

This brief paper restates a proposition that I have always believed, and still do, even though it may be getting more difficult: that parsing is fundamentally a matter of mapping texts onto semantic structures, and doing so without the need for a separate, identifiable, syntactic component. Where by "semantic structures" I include both the sorts of semantic/conceptual structure found in preference semantics/conceptual dependency work of the early seventies, as well as the factual and stereotypical event structures to be found in frames and plans (of which more below).

I can see much more clearly the ways in which all of these can be cleaned up (and could have been years ago), with the aid of better formalisms and (even) model-theoretic semantics. But I am still sure that these are no more than tidying up matters and *not* matters of substance. Tidying-up theories do not provide substantive claims about the nature of language and its organisation but are compatible with virtually any sets of such claims.

The general drift in linguistics and AI in the last 10 years has made the above position both better and worse *a priori*: worse in that

(a) the collapse of generative semantics to some extent dragged the very similar work in AI down with it;

(b) the work of Marcus and Kaplan has been taken by many to suggest that constraints, in Chomsky's *Universal Grammar* sense, can be given procedural form, and therefore there are important generalisations, having nothing whatever to do with meaning, that any parsing system must take account of, and which cannot be expressed at all in the approach defended here.

Conversely, things look *a priori* better in that

(c) Chomsky's position (to name but one) has drifted about so much on the issue of the relation of syntax to semantics that virtually all heat has gone out of such once-passionate disputes as to what sort of entity NOUN, CAUSE, HUMAN, MOVE are on a syntax-semantics spectrum;

(d) "procedural semantics" may not yet be a clear doctrine but it offers a real possibility for the defence of abstract entities like those just capitalised without the need to root them in either a syntactic or a model-theoretic semantic framework;

(e) recent "themes" etc. in Chomsky's *Government and Binding* work all look pretty familiar to those who worked in general AI semantics/case paradigm.

The three last reasons support those who simply want to go on with semantics-orientated AI in the belief that much of contemporary linguistic syntax will get to look more, rather than less, like what they have been doing, so the best thing is just to carry on regardless.

In what follows, I shall:

(i) make a few remarks about (a) and (b) above,

(ii) restate certain claims about language that still seem to me important and awkward,

(iii) concede a crucial point by looking back for a moment at the sort of work that was actually done under the banner of semantic parsing.

(i) I need an acronym in order to be able to refer to the thesis being defended here: I shall call it SP (semantic parsing). There is still much confusion about what it is/was. It certainly never claimed that syntactic information was not used in parsing — it was only necessary to point out that a parser was likely to need to know that adjectives normally followed determiners in English to show that SP proponents could hardly have denied *that*. What was argued was that such information could be expressed in semantic terms and, whether or not it was more efficient, no separate syntactic analysis module was required. This claim, even in its modified form, was and is quite incompatible with mainstream generative linguistics.

It was for this reason that the collapse of generative semantics was significant: mortally wounded by Katz's observation that *arms* and *weapons* were synonymous, but:

(1a) Here are three   (*arms)
(1b)   (weapons)

where *arms* is taken to have the appropriate "synonymous" sense. I have never seen the, to me obvious, thesis argued that, on the contrary, the two words are not at all synonymous and one might well expect the meaning/knowledge structures that represent them to be different in ways above and beyond the +COUNT feature that distinguished them, and which was in question in the above dispute. On an SP view, the two concepts might well be expected to represent different perspectives on the world (in the KRL sense) in virtue of "massness". The only point of view from which they are even plausibly synonymous is that of a crude model-theoretic semantics, the very view that Katz of all people should have been wary of!

Let me turn to point (b) briefly: the work of Marcus and others has marvellously sharpened what it is SP has to show to stay in business. Consider the Marcus/trace account of a sentence like:

(2) The lecture was believed to have been given yesterday

It seems to me that any SP account can deal with this, given plausible assumptions about the semantic preferences for filling the slots involved: e.g. that *believe* prefers a full proposition (clause) to an entity as object, if it can get one, etc. This must be taken together with general heuristics about what kinds of slot (e.g. subjects) hold or cede their contents during reorganisation. Any theory, from the selection rule of case grammar, through forms of SP, to Chomsky's recent work on case and theme, will have some form of those. The problem for SP comes with more "semantically symmetrical" versions of (2), such as:

(3) John was believed to have been loved by his sister

where the properties of the entities cannot possibly, taken alone, determine how the slots of *believe* and *love* are to be filled, since they are too similar. Ah ha, just so, say syntacticians, didn't we tell you that you had to have the kinds of generalisations we offer? I shall come back to this point later (not conceded by SP, I maintain) but indeed it must be won, because all the psychological evidence is on SP's side. All I have done here, I hope, is sharpen the issue of what SP must be able to do to survive as an account of how to parse such sentences.

(ii) Some more assertions about language. First, it seems to me obvious, though worth repeating, that text does not consist of the ten-word sentences normally found in linguistics papers, including this one, but of much longer items. It is these that have to be parsed, and almost all syntactically-motivated approaches underrate the importance of the location of phrase and clause boundaries (I exempt chart-based approaches to some degree here). It seems to me clear that these boundaries are not only psychologically (clicks and all that) fundamental, but their recognition is equally vital to keep down the search space for computational parsing (if indeed those two notions can be distinguished here).

I think generative linguistics has lost sight (because of its concentration on a particular type of example) of the degree to which most text sentences are long flat concatenations of phrase and clause items, whose boundaries can be reliably identified by a combination of key words and SP slot-filling. I say that not to defend the utterly naive fragmentation routines of my own past parsers, but to remind myself that the *principle* was correct. The counter-examples to what I have just said, are potentially infinitely deep embeddings, and that is precisely why they are never used by speakers and writers.

Secondly, all the syntax-based approaches I know are crucially dependent on assumptions about English word order that are factually false (so are some SP variants, see below). That applies as much to Marcus as to Gazdar's recent and highly ingenious claim that a PSG for English, and perhaps all languages, has no rule pairs in which (right-hand side) constituents appear in reverse order. This seems to me plainly inconsistent with the facts of English, ones which cannot be just written off as "syntactic variants". (4) below is as common and natural as (5), and arguably more so:

(4) Climbing over the wall was a sturdy well-built youth

(5) A sturdy well-built youth was climbing over the wall

As I wrote earlier, and will return to below, certain SP variants (with strong and unrevisable expectations on linear order) would have trouble with this last sentence (and that it is not a contrived example, see the enormous quantity of data in Green (1977)), but any SP based strongly on semantic slot filling has no such trouble.

Thirdly, a crucial weakness of Marcus' and cognate approaches is their assumption that complete noun groups can be either assumed (as in all basic presentations of his work) or reliably detected by an enlargement of his "buffer window". Milne has shown that that is almost certainly not so, and I think we have to remind ourselves that the location of novel, and semantically coherent, noun-noun groupings is an unsolved but vital matter for parsing (the best known work being Finin's (1980)). Examples are gratuitous here, from the all-time favourite

(6) Japanese push bottles up Chinese,

comprehensible, on acceptable terms at least, only within a sense structure for battles rather than bottles, right down to the detection of the difference between *soup spoon* (for soup) and *silver spoon* (of silver), given a state of a parsing dictionary in which neither has been coded as an idiom.

I take it as obvious that only if structure can be imposed on such noun strings can structure be imposed on the sentence as a whole and, moreover, that such structure can only be imposed using semantic criteria. Of course, this claim could be made for noun phrases that are not merely strings of apparent nouns (viz. *Analyse d'une méthode dynamique spécifique d'établissement de balance matériel d'une installation de retraitement de combustion nucléaire par simulation*. Puzzle, is, what does *par simulation* depend on?). Nonetheless, it is clear that strings of apparent nouns present special problems.

There is a growing literature on this issue, but few concrete suggestions for semantic hypotheses. I offer one for what it is worth: if we code words in a semantic dependency structure of primitive concepts (the trees in the Appendix are updated versions of my own formulas) then a hypothesis worth trying is that the case linking a dependent to the head noun is the one on the *highest node* in the semantic structure for the head noun that dominates the appearance in that structure of the main primitive appearing in the semantic structure for the dependent noun. I think the diagram in the Appendix makes that obscure form of words clear. This seems a correct rule for range of cases and certainly worth a try in a parsing program.

Fourthly, I think that frame and script structures have an important role in parsing, but not the one that those who developed them believed. I argued when such structures first appeared (Wilks, 1977) that frames could not be simply matching skeletons that would "appear" in texts to be parsed, and this seems now to be accepted even by enthusiasts. Where they do have a role in parsing (I argued in Wilks, 1978) is to deal with the fact that the slot expectations of word semantics are, in real text, violated as often as observed, and this is seen as much in

(7) John ran a mile,

an apparently syntactic example (of violation of intransitivity), as in apparently idiomatic examples like

(8) My car drinks petrol

In both cases, I argued, it is only by reference to a frame-like structure that shows, at a low level of detail, what is normally associated with such actions, that we can reliably infer the most appropriate representational structure. It is in that sense that I believe that representational structures like frames are fundamental to parsing, while not accepting that access to a stereotypical story line or plan *is* in the same sense fundamental.

Fifthly, and lastly, parsing cannot be done without access to models of the belief structures of participants in a dialogue, or those described in a narrative text. The literature of speech acts is full of persuasive examples. In semi-conventional cases like

(9) Can you pass the salt?

a group of syntacticians were persuaded by Searle that there were firm conventions that could be expressed in generative syntactic terms and could provide an appropriate structure for such sentences. In less conventional cases like

(10) I would like you to leave me your house when you die

it would seem to make sense to see parsing this as a choice between pre-established and "underlying" syntactic structures: e.g. a request versus a statement.

There are simply no clear conventions, syntactic or otherwise, covering such cases. Such situations can only be understood by computing an interpretation of such an utterance with respect to an individual's model of the world (including the beliefs and intentions of other individuals). It may be said that that is not parsing, but since such a process will achieve the same effect (though by different means) as those systems that *did* assume parsing (9) was a choice between, say, an underlying request and a surface question, then this, too, should be considered parsing by such standards (see Wilks and Bien, 1982).

It should be noted that this view of what parsing is also tells against much that has been called SP: since parsing with such belief structures cannot be modelled by simply matching a text or dialogue against a frame or script structure. Any representation achieved will be distributed round a number of participants' world models, and there may be no single representation of a text.

(iii) I would like to end with a brief, and possibly gratuitous, note that may remove some of whatever plausibility the foregoing has. Much early SP did not quite live up to the assumptions I have attributed to it. My question here is how could it do better: what kind of heuristics should be employed that are not merely general control structures but revealing about the structure of language?

I argued in Wilks (1976) that Riesbeck's SP, in its treatment of (among other phenomena) the English indirect object, would often go wrong. It had a firm and unshakeable conviction that, if what followed *give* immediately was ANIMATE then it was an indirect object, which gets

(11)   John gave his sister to the Sheik of Araby

wrong.

Now it can well be argued that other productions could be added to the system to get this right and that I do not deny (they almost certainly have been in later Yale parsers). My case remains that the generalisations are then those of production systems themselves which, like old-fashioned TG, can do anything, and as Peters and Ritchie pointed out in the latter case, therefore say nothing specific at all about language (as opposed to, say, the mating habits of pigeons!).

My alternative had been what I called a "preference" approach, one on which the first item after a verb like *give* was attached directly to and made dependent on the verb, while the next appropriate item, if any, was made the object. The "semantic densities" were compared in the two cases. If there was no indirect object, as in

(12)   John gave his rabbit, and Mary her hamster

the more dense structure won out as always, because (for reasons that need not detain us) being an object counted for more than being an indirect object. Thus in all cases the structure was imposed by a single, simple, "greatest density" rule. There was only one problem: there was nothing particularly semantic about the whole business (except that the dictionary codings were uniform and in that sense semantic). It was just slot-filling and counting.

The relevant psychological evidence, for what it is worth, and I am making it up from memory but it is more or less right, is as follows:

(13a)　The boy gave the girl a toy
(13b)　The girl gave the toy a boy
(13c)　The boy gave the woman a man

where (13a) is understood much the fastest, and the other two much slower, with (13c) marginally the slowest (cf. Steedman and Johnson-Laird, 1976). If that is roughly how it is, then both syntactically-motivated approaches, *and my version of SP for these constructions* are implausible because they both get all of them right and in the same way and at the same rate. (Worse still, 13b, is often understood, wrongly in fact, as having a deleted *to* in it).

What kind of procedures should an SP theory have for such constructions, and would they have wider significance? I suggest we need a notation of "sticky" slots, in which (if we think of words coming in from the right) anything that fits an object slot (by being, preferably, a PHYSOBJ, say) stays there, unless bumped out by a better candidate coming in. A little work and space would show that such an approach is a real SP one (unlike my old one above), and gets the constructions (13) right in about the right order of effort (and might even predict mistakes). The hard task will be programming "reluctance to disgorge slot-fillers" in a standard programming language.

The last section is purely speculative but, after all, this is only intended to be a position paper. Its message is that SP is still viable, though recent work in computational syntax has made it clearer what SP must show to survive, which I do not take to include the so-called "universal generalisations", since I believe these to be unnecessary for parsing any given language, and not *seriously* universal in any case, nor intended as such. I have also suggested that much early SP was not really as semantic as its proponents claimed, though it could be rendered so.

REFERENCES

Finin, T. (1980) Noun—noun compounds, *Proceedings of the AAAI*.

Green, G. M. (1977) Do inversions in English change grammatical relations? *Studies in the Linguistic Sciences*.

Schank, R. C. (1975) *Conceptual Information Processing*, Amsterdam: North-Holland.

Steedman, M. and Johnson-Laird, P. (1976) A programmatic theory of linguistic performance, Ms, University of Sussex.

Wilks, Y. A. (1975) An intelligent analyzer and understander of English. *Communications of the ACM* 18, 264—274.

Wilks, Y. A. (1976) Processing case. *American Journal of Computational Linguistics*, Microfiche 56.

Wilks, Y. A. (1977) Frames, scripts, stories and fantasies, *Pragmatics Microfiche*.

Wilks, Y. A. (1978) Making preferences more active. *Artificial Intelligence* **11**, 197–223.

Wilks, Y. A. and Bien, J. (1981) Beliefs, points of view and multiple environments. Report CSCM-6, Cognitive Studies Centre, University of Essex. To appear in *Cognitive Science*.

APPENDIX

soup spoon = spoon FOR soup

silver spoon = spoon OF silver

The rule is to take the **top-most** available node

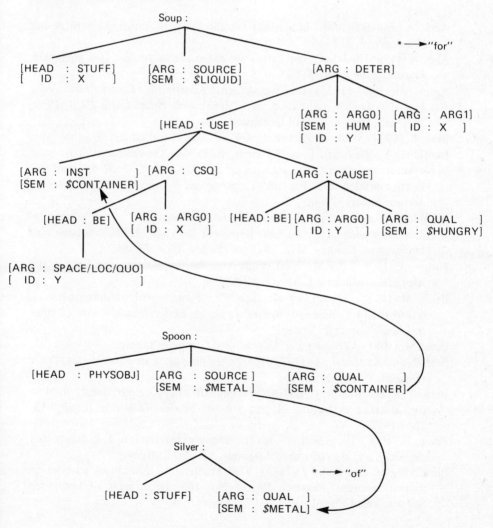

Bibliography

Ades, A. and Steedman, M. (1982) On the order of words. *Linguistics and Philosophy* **4**, 517–558.

Aho, A. (1968) Indexed grammars – an extension of context-free grammars. *Journal of the ACM* **15**, 647–671.

Ajdukiewicz, K. (1935) Die syntaktische Konnexität. *Studia Philosophica* **1**, 1–27. English translation in S. McCall (ed) *Polish Logic 1920–1939.* 207–231, Oxford: Oxford University Press.

Bach, E. (1974) *Syntactic Theory.* New York: Holt, Rinehart and Winston.

Bar-Hillel, Y., Gaifman, C. and Shamir, E. (1960) On categorial and phrase structure grammars. *The Bulletin of the Research Council of Israel* 9F, 1–16; reprinted in Y. Bar-Hillel *Language and Information,* Reading, Mass.: Addison-Wesley, 1964.

Bar-Hillel, Y. and Shamir, E. (1960) Finite state languages: formal representations and adequacy problems. Reprinted in Y. Bar-Hillel *Language and Information.* Reading, Mass.: Addison-Wesley, 1964, 87–98.

Barton, E. (1980) Psychological reality and the propriety of abstraction. Ms, Artificial Intelligence Laboratory, MIT.

Bates, M. (1978) The theory and practice of augmented transition network grammars. In L. Bolc (ed) *Natural Language Communication with Computers,* Berlin: Springer-Verlag.

Bates, M. (1981) ATN grammar. Unpublished Computer Listing.

Bear, J. and Karttunen, L. (1979) PSG: a simple phrase structure parser, *Texas Linguistic Forum* **15**, 1–46.

Berwick, R. and Weinberg, A. (1982) Parsing efficiency, computational complexity, and the evaluation of grammatical theories. *Linguistic Inquiry* **13**, 165–191.

Bever, T. (1970) The cognitive basis for language structures. In J. R. Hayes (ed) *Cognition and the Growth of Language.* New York: Wiley.

Birnbaum, L. and Selfridge, M. (1979) Problems in conceptual analysis of natural language. Research Report No. 168, Department of Computer Science, Yale University.

Blackwell, S. A. (1981) Processing conjunctions in an ATN Parser. M.Phil. dissertation, University of Cambridge.

Bobrow, R. J. and Webber, B. L. (1981) PSI–KLONE: parsing and semantic interpretation in the BBN natural language understanding system. Cambridge, Mass.: Bolt, Beranek and Newman.

Boguraev, B. K. (1979) Automatic resolution of linguistic ambiguities. Technical Report No. 11, Computer Laboratory, University of Cambridge, Cambridge.

Brady, J. M. and Wielinga, B. J. (1977) Reading the writing on the wall. Department of Computer Science, University of Essex.

Bresnan, J. (1978) A realistic transformational grammar. In M. Halle, J. W. Bresnan and G. A. Miller (eds) *Linguistic Theory and Psychological Reality*. Cambridge, Mass.: MIT Press.

Bresnan, J., Kaplan, R., Peters, S. and Zaenen, A. (1982) Cross-serial dependencies in Dutch. *Linguistic Inquiry* **13**, 613–635.

Bronnenberg, W. J. H. C., Bunt, H. C., Landsbergen, S. P. J., Scha, R. J. H., Schoenmakers, W. J. and van Utteren, E. P. C. (1980) The question-answering system PHLIQA 1. In L. Bolc (ed) *Natural Language Question-answering Systems*. Munich: Carl Hanser Verlag.

Bundy, A., Byrd, L. and Mellish, C. S. (1982) Special purpose but domain independent inference mechanisms. *ECAI–82: Proceedings of the 1982 European Conference on Artificial Intelligence*, 67–74.

Burton, R. R. (1976) Semantic grammar. Report no. 3453, Bolt, Beranek and Newman Inc., Cambridge, Mass.

Cater, A. W. S. (1980) Analysing English text: a nondeterministic approach using limited memory, *Proceedings of the AISB–80 Conference on Artificial Intelligence*.

Cater, A. W. S. (1981) Analysis and inference for English. Ph.D. thesis, Computer Laboratory, University of Cambridge. Technical Report No. 18, Computer Laboratory, University of Cambridge.

Charniak, E. (1981) Passing markers: a theory of contextual influence in language comprehension. Report TR–80, Department of Computer Science, Brown University.

Charniak, E. (1981) A parser with something for everyone. Report TR–70, Department of Computer Science, Brown University. To appear in M. King (ed) *Natural Language Parsing*, New York: Academic Press, 1983.

Chomsky, N. (1957) *Syntactic Structures*. The Hague: Mouton.

Chomsky, N. (1963) On the notion "rule of grammar". Reprinted in J. J. Katz and J. A. Fodor (eds.) *The Structure of Language*. Englewood Cliffs, N.J.: Prentice-Hall, 1964.

Chomsky, N. (1963) Formal properties of grammars. In R. D. Luce, R. R. Bush, and E. Galanter (eds) *Handbook of Mathematical Psychology*, Volume II. New York: Wiley.

Chomsky, N. (1965) *Aspects of the Theory of Syntax*. Cambridge, Mass: MIT Press.

Chomsky, N. and Miller, G. (1963) Finitary models of language users. In R. Luce, R. Bush and E. Galanter (eds) *Handbook of Mathematical Psychology* Volume II. New York: Wiley.

Christaller, T. (1981) Cascaded ATNs and their implementation. Unpublished memo, Research Center for Software, Linköping.

Christaller, T. (1982) An ATN programming environment. In L. Bolc (ed) *ATN Interpreters, Compilers and Editors*. Heidelberg: Springer.

Church, K. W. (1980) On memory limitations in natural language processing. Report MIT/LCS/TR–245, Laboratory for Computer Science, MIT.

Cleaveland, J. and Uzgalis, R. (1975) *Grammars for Programming Languages: What Every Programmer Should Know About Grammar*. New York: Elsevier.

Collins, A. and Quillian, M. (1969) Retrieval time from semantic memory. *Journal of Verbal Learning and Verbal Behavior* **8**, 240–248.

Colmerauer, A. (1970) Les Systèmes-Q ou un formalisme pour analyser et synthétiser les phrases sur ordinateur. Internal publication 43, Projet de Traduction Automatique, University of Montreal.

Cooper, R. (1975) Montague's semantic theory and transformational syntax. Ph.D. dissertation, University of Massachusetts at Amherst.

Cooper, R. (1979) Model theory for a fragment of English. Ms, University of Madison at Wisconsin.

Crain, S. (1980) Pragmatic constraints on sentence comprehension. Ph.D. thesis, University of California at Irvine.

Crain, S. and Steedman, M. J. (1982) On not being led up the garden path: the use of context by the psychological parser. In D. Dowty, L. Karttunen and A. Zwicky (eds) (Title to be announced), Cambridge: Cambridge University Press.

Dahl, Ö. (1981) Bound pronouns in dislocated constituents – the case of contextually interpreted variables. Mimeo, University of Stockholm.

Dahl, Ö. (1982) Converting in bound pronouns: the problem and its solution. Mimeo, University of Stockholm.

deJong, G. F. (1979) Skimming stories in real time: an experiment in integrated understanding. Research Report No. 158, Department of Computer Science, Yale University.

Downing, P. (1977) On the creation and use of English compound nouns. *Language* **53**, 810–842.

Dowty, D. (1978) Governed transformations as lexical rules in a Montague grammer. *Linguistic Inquiry* **9**, 393–426.

Dowty, D., Wall, R. and Peters, S. (1981) *Introduction to Montague Semantics*. Dordrecht: Reidel.

Dresher, E. and Hornstein, N. (1976) On some supposed contributions of Artificial Intelligence to the scientific study of language. *Cognition* **4**, 321–398.

Dresher, E. and Hornstein, N. (1977) Reply to Schank and Wilensky. *Cognition* **5**, 147–150.

Dresher, E. and Hornstein, N. (1977) Reply to Winograd. *Cognition* **5**, 377–392.

Earley, J. (1970) An efficient context-free parsing algorithm. *Communications of the ACM* **13**, 94–102.

Ejerhed, E. (1980) A context-free phrase-structure parser for English auxiliaries. Paper presented to the Fourth Groningen Round Table Conference on Auxiliaries, Groningen, Holland, July 1980.

Elster, J. (1978) *Logic and Society: Contradictions and Possible Worlds.* New York: Wiley.

Engdahl, E. (1980) The syntax and semantics of questions in Swedish. Ph.D. dissertation, University of Massachusetts at Amherst.

Engdahl, E. (1982) Constituent questions, topicalization, and surface structure interpretation. In D. Flickenger, M. Macken and N. Wiegand (eds) *Proceedings from the First Annual West Coast Conference on Formal Linguitics,* 256–267.

Engdahl, E. (1982) A note on the use of lambda-conversion in generalized phrase structure grammars. *Linguistics and Philosophy* **4**, 505-515.

Finin, T. W. (1977) An interpreter and compiler for augmented transition networks. Report T–48, Coordinated Science Laboratory, University of Illinois.

Finin, T. (1980) Noun–noun compounds. *Proceedings of the AAAI.*

Fodor, J. (1982) Phrase structure parsing and the island constraints. *Linguistics and Philosophy.* To appear.

Fodor, J. (1982) How can grammars help parsers? Paper presented at the Conference on Syntactic Theory and How People Parse Sentences, Ohio State University, May 14–15, 1982.

Fodor, J. A., Bever, T. and Garrett, M. (1974) *The Psychology of Language.* New York: McGraw-Hill.

Ford, M., Bresnan, J. and Kaplan, R. (1982) A competence based theory of syntactic closure. In J. Bresnan (ed) *The Mental Representation of Grammatical Relations,* Cambridge, Mass.: MIT Press.

Frazier, L. (1981) On comprehending sentences: syntactic parsing strategies. Ph.D. dissertation, University of Connecticut. Indiana University Linguistics Club.

Frazier, L. and Fodor, J. D. (1980) The sausage machine: a new two stage parser. *Cognition* **6**, 291–325.

Friedman, J. (1978) Computational and theoretical studies in Montague grammar at the University of Michigan. *SISTM Quarterly* **1**, 62–66.

Friedman, J. (1981) Expressing logical formulas in natural language. In J. Groenendijk, T. Janssen and M. Stokhof (eds) *Formal Methods in the Study of Language.* Mathematical Centre Tracts, Amsterdam, 113–130.

Friedman, J., Moran, D. and Warren, D. (1978) An interpretation system for Montague Grammar. *American Journal of Computational Linguistics,* microfiche 94, 23–96.

Friedman, J. and Warren, D. (1978) A parsing method for Montague grammars. *Linguistics and Philosophy* **2**, 347–372.

Fuchi, K. (1981) Natural language and its formal representation: a case study of translation in Montague style from a programmer's point of view. Paper presented to the First Colloquium on Montague Grammar and Related Topics, Kyoto, February 1981.

Gawron, J. M., King, J., Lamping, J., Loebner, E., Paulson, A., Pullum, G. Sag, I. and Wasow, T. (1982) The GPSG linguistics system. *Proceedings of the 20th Annual Meeting of the Association for Computational Linguistics,* 74–81. Also distributed as Hewlett Packard Computer Science Technical Note CSL–82–5.

Gazdar, G. (1979) English as a context-free language. Mimeo, University of Sussex.

Gazdar, G. (1979) Constituent structures. Mimeo, University of Sussex.

Gazdar, G. (1980) A cross-categorial semantics for coordination. *Linguistics and Philosophy* **3**, 407–409.

Gazdar, G. (1980) A phrase structure syntax for comparative clauses. In T. Hoekstra, H. v.d. Hulst and M. Moortgat (eds) *Lexical Grammar.* Dordrecht: Foris Publications, 165–179.

Gazdar, G. (1981) Unbounded dependencies and coordinate structure. *Linguistic Inquiry* **12**, 155–184.

Gazdar, G. (1981) On syntactic categories. *Philosophical Transactions of the Royal Society* Series B **295**, 267–283.

Gazdar, G. (1982) Phrase structure grammar. In P. Jacobson and G. Pullum (eds) *The Nature of Syntactic Representation.* Dordrecht: D. Reidel, 131–186.

Gazdar, G. and Pullum, G. (1981) Subcategorization, constituent order and the notion "head". In M. Moortgat, H. v.d. Hulst and T. Hoekstra (eds) *The Scope of Lexical Rules.* Dordrecht: Foris Publications, 107–123.

Gazdar, G. and Sag, I. (1981) Passive and reflexives in phrase structure grammar. In J. Groenendijk, T. Janssen and M. Stokhof (eds) *Formal Methods in the Study of Language.* Mathematical Centre Tracts, Amsterdam, 131–152.

Gazdar, G., Pullum, G. and Sag, I. (1982) Auxiliaries and related phenomena in a restrictive theory of grammar. *Language* **58**, 591–638.

Gazdar, G., Pullum, G., Sag, I. and Wasow, T. (1982) Coordination and transformational grammar. *Linguistic Inquiry* **13**, 663–676.

Georgeff, M. (1979) A framework for control in production systems. Memo AIM–322, Artificial Intelligence Laboratory, Stanford University.

Graham, S., Harrison, M. and Ruzzo, W. (1980) An improved context-free recognizer. *ACM Transactions on Programming Languages and Systems* **2**, 415–462.

Green, G. M. (1977) Do inversions in English change grammatical relations? *Studies in the Linguistic Sciences.*

Griffiths, T. V. and Petrick, S. R. (1965) On the relative efficiencies of context-free grammar recognizers. *Communications of the ACM* **8**, 289–300.

Grinder, J. and Elgin, S. (1973) *Guide to Transformational Grammar.* New York: Holt, Rinehart and Winston.

Grosz, B. *et al.* (1982) DIALOGIC: a core natural language processing system. In *COLING 82,* Proceedings of the Ninth International Conference on Computational Linguistics. Amsterdam: North-Holland.

Gueron, J. (1980) On the syntax and semantics of PP extraposition. *Linguistic Inquiry* **11**, 637–678.

Gunji, T. (1981) Toward a computational theory of pragmatics – discourse, presupposition, and implicature. Ph.D. dissertation, Ohio State University.

Gunji, T. and Sondheimer, N. (1980) The mutual relevance of model-theoretic semantics and artificial intelligence. *SMIL: Journal of Linguistic Calculus* **3**, 5–42.

Gurd, J. T., Watson, I. and Glauert, J. R. W. (1980) A multilayered data flow computer architecture (3rd Issue). Internal report, Department of Computer Science, University of Manchester.

Hakes, D. (1972) Effects of reducing complement constructions on sentence comprehension. *Journal of Verbal Learning and Verbal Behavior* **11**, 278–286.

Hakes, D., Evans, J. and Brannon, L. (1976) Understanding sentences with relative clauses. *Memory and Cognition* **4**, 283–290.

Harman, G. (1963) Generative grammars without transformation rules: a defense of phrase structure. *Language* **39**, 597–616.

Hendrix, G. G. (1977) The LIFER manual: a guide to building practical natural language interfaces. Technical Note 138, SRI International.

Heny, F. (1970) Semantic operations on base structures. Ph.D. dissertation, University of California at Los Angeles.

Hobbs, J. and Rosenschein, S. (1978) Making computational sense of Montague's intensional logic. *Artificial Intelligence* **9**, 287–306.

Hopcroft, J. and Ullman, J. (1979) *Introduction to Automata Theory, Languages, and Computation.* Reading, Mass.: Addison-Wesley.

Huybregts, M. A. C. (1976) Overlapping dependencies in Dutch. *Utrecht Working Papers in Linguistics,* **1**, 24–65.

Ishimoto, I. (1982) A Lesniewskian version of Montague grammar and its application to computational linguistics. In J. Horecký (ed) *Proceedings of*

Ninth International Conference on Computational Linguistics. Amsterdam: North-Holland. To appear.

Jameson, A. (1980) Ein Compiler für einen rekursiven ATN-Interpreter. In J. Petöfi and D. Metzing (eds) *Jährlicher Bericht zum Projekt Textverarbeitung,* University of Bielefeld.

Janssen, T. (1976) A computer program for Montague grammar: theoretical aspects and proofs for the reduction rules. *Amsterdam Papers in Formal Grammar* 1, 154–176.

Janssen, T. (1977) Simulation of a Montague Grammar. *Annals of System Research* 6, 127–140.

Janssen, T. (1980) On problems concerning the quantification rules in Montague grammar. In C. Rohrer (ed) *Time, Tense, and Quantifiers.* Tübingen: Max Niemayer, 113–134.

Joshi, A. (1982) How much context-sensitivity is required, if any, for assigning reasonable structural descriptions? Paper presented at the Conference on Syntactic Theory and How People Parse Sentences, Ohio State University, May 14–15, 1982.

Joshi, A. and Levy, L. (1980) Phrase structure trees bear more fruit than you would have thought. Revised and expanded version of a paper presented at the 18th Annual Meeting of the Association for Computational Linguistics, University of Pennsylvania, Philadelphia, June 1980.

Kaplan, R. M. (1972) Augmented transition networks as psychological models of sentence comprehension. *Artificial Intelligence* 3, 77–100.

Kaplan, R. M. and Bresnan, J. (1982) Lexical-functional grammar: A formal system of grammatical representation. In J. Bresnan (ed) *The Mental Representation of Grammatical Relations.* Cambridge, Mass.: MIT Press.

Kaplan, R. M. and Kay, M. (1981) Phonological rules as finite state transducers. Presented at the Winter Meeting of the Linguistic Society of America, New York.

Kaplan, R. M. and Kay, M. (1982) Word recognition. Technical Report, Xerox PARC, Palo Alto, California. To appear.

Kay, A. and Goldstein, A. (1974) SMALLTALK. Xerox PARC, Palo Alto, California.

Kay, M. (1967) Experiments with a powerful parser. In 2ème Conférence Internationale sur le Traitement Automatique des Langues, Grenoble; also as Report RM–5452–PR, The Rand Corporation, Santa Monica, California.

Kay, M. (1977) Morphological and syntactic analysis. In A. Zampolli (ed) *Syntactic Structures Processing.* Amsterdam: North-Holland.

Kay, M. (1980) Algorithmic schemata and data structures in syntactic processing. Report CSL–80–12, Xerox PARC, Palo Alto, California.

Keenan, E. and Faltz, L. (1978) Logical types for natural language. *UCLA Occasional Papers in Linguistics 3.*

Kimball, J. (1973) Seven principles of surface structure parsing in natural language. *Cognition* 2, 15–47.

Kimball, J. (1975) Predictive analysis and over-the-top parsing. In J. Kimball (ed) *Syntax and Semantics,* Volume 4, New York: Academic Press.

Klein, E. (1980) A semantics for positive and comparative adjectives. *Linguistics and Philosophy* **4**, 1–45.

Klein, E. (1981) The interpretation of adjectival, nominal, and adverbial comparatives. In J. Groenendijk, T. Janssen and M. Stokhof (eds) *Formal Methods in the Study of Language.* Mathematical Centre Tracts, Amsterdam, 381–398.

Klein, E. (1981) The syntax and semantics of nominal comparatives. In M. Moneglia (ed) *Atti de Seminario su Tempo e Verbale Strutture Quantificate in Forma Logica.* Florence: Presso l'Accademia della Crusca, 223–253.

Klein, E. (1982) The interpretation of adjectival comparatives. *Journal of Linguistics* **18**, 113–136.

Klein, W. (1979) Wegauskünfte, *Zeitschrift für Linguistik und Literaturwissenschaft* **9**, 9–57.

Konolige, K. (1980) Capturing linguistic generalizations with metarules in an annotated phrase-structure grammar. *Proceedings of the 18th Annual Meeting of the Association for Computational Linguistics,* 43–48.

Kowalski, R. (1979) Algorithm = logic + control. *Communications of the ACM* **22**, 424–431.

Kwasny, S. C. (1980) Treatment of ungrammatical and extra-grammatical phenomena in natural language understanding systems. Indiana University Linguistics Club.

Lakoff, G. and Thompson, H. S. (1975) Introducing cognitive grammar. In *Proceedings of the First Annual Meeting of the Berkeley Linguistics Society.* Berkeley Linguistics Society.

Lakoff, G. and Thompson, H. S. (1975) Dative questions and cognitive grammar. In *Papers from the Parasession on Functionalism.* Chicago Linguistic Society.

Landsbergen, J. (1981) Adaptation of Montague grammar to the requirements of parsing. In J. Groenendijk, T. Janssen and M. Stokhof (eds) *Formal Methods in the Study of Language.* Mathematical Centre Tracts. Amsterdam, 399–419.

Langendoen, D. T. (1975) Finite-state parsing of phrase structure languages and the status of readjustment rules in grammar. *Linguistic Inquiry* **6**, 533–554.

Langendoen, D. (1977) On the inadequacy of type-2 and type-3 grammars for human languages. In P. J. Hopper (ed) *Studies in Descriptive and Historical Linguistics.* Amsterdam: John Benjamin, 159–171.

Lesser, V. R., Fennall, R. D., Erman, L. D. and Reddy D. R. (1974) Organisation of the Hearsay II speech understanding system. IEEE Symposium on Speech Recognition.

Levi, J. N. (1978) *The Syntax and Semantics of Complex Nominals.* New York: Academic Press.

Maling, J. and Zaenen, A. (1982) A phrase structure account of Scandinavian extraction phenomena. In P. Jacobson and G. Pullum (eds) *The Nature of Syntactic Representation*. Dordrecht: D. Reidel, 229–282.

Marcus, M. P. (1980) *A Theory of Syntactic Recognition for Natural Language*. Cambridge, Mass.: MIT Press.

Mark, W. S. and Barton, G. E. (1980) The Rusgrammar parsing system. Research Report GMR–3243, General Motors Research Laboratories.

Marslen-Wilson, W. (1973) Linguistic structure and speech shadowing at very short latencies. *Nature* 224, 582–583.

Marslen-Wilson, W. (1976) Linguistic descriptions and psychological assumptions in the study of sentence perception. In R. J. Wales and E. Walker (eds) *New Approaches to Language Mechanisms*. Amsterdam: North-Holland.

Marslen-Wilson, W. and Tyler, L. (1980) The temporal structure of spoken language understanding: the perception of sentences and words in sentences. *Cognition* 8, 1–71.

Marslen-Wilson, W. and Welsh, A. (1978) Processing interactions and lexical access during word recognition in continuous speech. *Cognitive Psychology* 10, 29–63.

Martin, W., Church, K. and Patil, R. (1981) Preliminary analysis of a breadth first parsing algorithm: theoretical and experimental results. Report MIT/ LCS/TR–261, Laboratory for Computer Science, MIT.

Masumoto, Y. (1981) Software implementation of Montague grammar and related problems. In S. Iguchi (ed) *Formal Approaches to Natural Language: Proceedings of the First Colloquium on Montague Grammar and Related Topics*. Kyoto: Kyoto Working Group of Montague Grammar, 148–158.

Matsumoto, Y. (1982) A Montague grammar of Japanese with special regard to meaning adjustment. Paper presented to the Second Colloquium on Montague Grammar and Related Topics, Kyoto, March 1982.

McCawley, J. D. (1982) Parentheticals and discontinuous constituent structure. *Linguistic Inquiry* 13, 91–106.

McCloskey, J. (1979) *Transformational Syntax and Model Theoretic Semantics*. Dordrecht: Reidel.

McCord, M. (1982) Using slots and modifiers in logic grammars for natural language. *Artificial Intelligence* 18, 327–367.

McDermott, D. V. (1976) Artificial intelligence meets natural stupidity. *SIGART Newsletter* 57, 4–9.

McDonald, D. B. (1981) Compound: a program that understands noun compounds. *Proceedings of the Seventh International Joint Conference on Artificial Intelligence*, 1061.

Mellish, C. S. (1981) Coping with uncertainty: noun phrase interpretation and early semantic analysis. Ph.D. thesis, University of Edinburgh.

Mellish, C. S. (1981) Controlling inference in the semantic interpretation of mechanics problems. Paper presented at the Workshop on Logic Programming for Intelligent Systems, Los Angeles.

Metzing, D. (1982) Dialogue interaction in a task domain: model and some problems of application. In U. Hein and S. Hägglund (eds) *Models of Dialogue*. München: Hauser-MacMillan. To appear.

Milne, R. W. (forthcoming) Predicting garden path sentences. *Cognitive Science*.

Milne, R. W. (in preparation) Resolving lexical ambiguity in a deterministic parser. Ph.D. thesis, Department of Artificial Intelligence, University of Edinburgh.

Montague, R. (1974) *Formal Philosophy*. New Haven: Yale University Press.

Moon, D. and Weinreb, D. (1981) *Lispmachine Lisp manual*. Cambridge, Mass.: Symbolics Inc.

Moran, D. B. (1980) Dynamic partial models. Ph.D. dissertation, University of Michigan.

Nishida, T., Kiyono, M. and Doshita, S. (1981) An English–Japanese machine translation system based on formal semantics of natural language. In S. Iguchi (ed) *Formal Approaches to Natural Language: Proceedings of the First Colloquium on Montague Grammar and Related Topics*. Kyoto: Kyoto Working Group of Montague Grammar, 104–147.

Nishida, T.-A. and Doshita, S. (1982) An English–Japanese matching translation system based on formal semantics of natural language – a progress report. Paper presented to the Second Colloquium on Montague Grammar and Related Topics, Kyoto, March 1982.

Pager, D. (1977) A practical general method for constructing LR(k) parsers. *Acta Informatica* 7, 249–268.

Partee, B. and Rooth, M. (1982) Generalized conjunction and type ambiguity. In A. von Stechow *et al.* (eds) *Meaning, Use and Intepretation*. Berlin: de Gruyter. To appear.

Postal, P. (1964) Limitations of phrase structure grammars. In J. A. Fodor and J. J. Katz (eds) *The Structure of Language: Readings in the Philosophy of Language*. Englewood Cliffs, N.J.: Prentice-Hall, 137–151.

Prather, P. and Swinney, D. (1977) Some effects of syntactic context upon lexical access. Presented at a meeting of the American Psychological Association.

Psathas, G. and Kozloff, M. (1976) The structure of directions. *Semiotica* **17**, 111–130.

Pullum, G. (1982) Free word order and phrase structure rules. In J. Pustejovsky and P. Sells (eds) *Proceedings of the Twelfth Annual Meeting of the North Eastern Linguistic Society*. Graduate Linguistics Student Association, University of Massachusetts, Amherst, Mass, 209–220.

Pullum, G. and Gazdar, G. (1982) Natural languages and context-free languages. *Linguistics and Philosophy* **4**, 471–504.

Radford, A. (1981) *Transformational Syntax*. Cambridge: Cambridge University Press.

Riesbeck, C. (1973) Computational understanding: analysis of sentences and context. Report STAN–CS–73–337, Computer Science Dept., Stanford University.

Riesbeck, C. K. (1975) Conceptual analysis. In R. C. Schank (ed) *Conceptual Information Processing*. Amsterdam: North-Holland.

Riesbeck, C. (1980) "You can't miss it", judging the clarity of directions. *Cognitive Science* **4**, 285–303.

Riesbeck, C. and Schank, R. (1976) Comprehension by computer: expectation-based analysis of sentences in context. Research Report 78, Department of Computer Science, Yale University.

Ritchie, G. (1978) Augmented transition network grammars and semantic processing. Report CSR–20–78, University of Edinburgh.

Ritchie, G. (1980) *Computational Grammar – an Artificial Intelligence Approach to Linguistic Description*. Hassocks, Sussex: Harvester Press.

Ritchie, G. and Hanna, F. K. (1982) AM: a case study in AI methodology. Technical Report 18, Department of Computer Science, Heriot-Watt University.

Robinson, J. (1980) Computational aspects of the use of metarules in formal grammars. Research Proposal No. ECU 80–126, SRI International, Menlo Park, California.

Robinson, J. (1982) DIAGRAM: a grammar for dialogs. *Communications of the ACM* **25**, 27–47.

Root, R. (1981) SMX: a program for translating English into Montague's intensional logic. Ms, Department of Linguistics, University of Texas at Austin.

Ross, K. (1981) Parsing English phrase structure. Ph.D. dissertation, University of Massachusetts at Amherst.

Sacerdoti, E. D. (1975) The non-linear nature of plans. *International Joint Conference on Artificial Intelligence*, 206–214.

Sag, I. (1982) Coordination, extraction, and generalized phrase structure. *Linguistic Inquiry* **13**, 329–336.

Sag, I. (1982) On parasitic gaps. In D. Flickinger, M. Macken, and N. Wiegand (eds) *Proceedings from the First Annual West Coast Conference on Formal Linguistics*, 35–46. Also to appear in *Linguistics and Philosophy*.

Sagvall Hein, A.-L. (1978) Finnish morphological analysis in the reversible grammar system. In *Proceedings of the 7th International Conference on Computational Linguistics*. COLING, Bergen.

Saheki, M. (1982) A software program for a language like natural language. Paper presented to the Second Colloquium on Montague Grammar and Related Topics, Kyoto, March 1982.

Sampson, G. R. (1983) Deterministic parsing. In M. King (ed) *Parsing Natural Language*. New York: Academic Press.

Sawamura, H. (1981) Intensional logic as a basis of algorithmic logic. Paper presented to the First Colloquium on Montague Grammar and Related Topics, Kyoto, February 1981.

Schank, R. C. (1972) Conceptual dependency: a theory of natural language understanding. *Cognitive Psychology* **3**, 552–631.

Schank, R. C. (1973) Identification of conceptualisations underlying natural language. In R. C. Schank and K. M. Colby (eds) *Computer Models of Thought and Language*. San Francisco: Freeman.

Schank, R. C. (1975) *Conceptual Information Processing*. Amsterdam: North-Holland.

Schank, R. C. and Riesbeck, C. (eds) (1981) *Inside Computer Understanding*. Hillsdale, N. J.: Lawrence Erlbaum Associates.

Schank, R. C. and Wilensky, R. (1977) Response to Dresher and Hornstein. *Cognition* **5**, 133–145.

Schubert, L. and Pelletier, J. (1982) From English to logic: context-free computation of "conventional" logical translations. In J. Horecký (ed) *Proceedings of the Ninth International Conference on Computational Linguistics*. Dordrecht: North-Holland. To appear.

Shortliffe, E. (1976) *Computer-Based Medical Consultations: MYCIN*. New York: Elsevier.

Sloman, A. and Hardy, S. (1976) Giving a computer gestalt experiences. *Proceedings of the AISB Conference*, Edinburgh.

Small, S. (1980) Word expert parsing: a thory of distributed word-based natural language understanding. Report TR–954, Department of Computer Science, University of Maryland.

Sondheimer, N. and Gunji, T. (1978) Applying model-theoretic semantics to natural language understanding: representation and question-answering. *Proceedings of the Seventh International Conference on Computational Linguistics*, Bergen.

Steedman, M. (1982) On the generality of the nested dependency constraint and the reason for an exception in Dutch. In B. Butterworth, B. Comrie and O. Dahl (eds) *Explanations for Language Universals*. The Hague: Mouton. To appear.

Steedman, M. and Johnson-Laird, P. (1976) A programmatic theory of linguistic performance. Ms, University of Sussex.

Stenning, K. (1977) On remembering how to get there: how we might want something like a map. In A. M. Lesgold, J. W. Pellegrino, S. D. Fokkera and R. Glaser (eds) *Cognition and Instruction*. New York.

Stucky, S. (1981) Word order variation in Makua: a phrase structure grammar analysis. Ph.D. dissertation, University of Illinois at Urbana-Champaign.

The Royal Society (1981) *The Psychological Mechanisms of Language. Philosophical Transactions of the Royal Society*. Series B, Volume 295. London: The Royal Society.

Thompson, H. S. (1981) Joint Royal Society/British Academy Meeting on the Psychological Mechanisms of Language: A critical report. *AISB Quarterly* **10–41**, 16–19.

Thompson, H. (1981) Chart parsing and rule schemata in PSG. *Proceedings of the 19th Annual Meeting of the Association for Computational Linguistics*, 167–172.

Thompson, H. (1982) Handling metarules in a parser for GPSG. Research Paper No. 175. Department of Artificial Intelligence, University of Edinburgh. To appear in J. Horecký (ed) *Proceedings of the Ninth International Conference on Computational Linguistics.* Dordrecht: North-Holland.

Thompson, H. and Ritchie, G. (1983) Implementing a natural language parser: two techniques. In M. Eisenstadt and O'Shea, T. (eds) *Artificial Intelligence Skills,* New York: Harper & Row.

Tyler, L. K. and Marslen-Wilson, W. (1977) The on-line effects of semantic context on syntactic processing. *Journal of Verbal Learning and Verbal Behaviour* **16**, 683–692.

van Oirsouw, R. R. (1980) Deletion processes in coordinate structures in English. Ph.D. thesis, University of Cambridge.

Wanner, E. R. and Maratsos, M. (1978) An ATN approach to comprehension. In M. Halle, J. Bresnan and G. A. Miller (eds) *Linguistic Theory and Psychological Reality.* Cambridge, Mass.: MIT Press.

Wanner, E. R., Kaplan, R. M. and Shiner, S. (1975) Garden paths in relative clauses. Ms. Harvard University.

Warren, B. (1978) *Semantic Patterns of Noun–noun Compounds.* Gothenburg Studies in English 41, Göteborg: Acta Universitatis Gothenburgensis.

Warren, D. (1979) Syntax and semantics in parsing: an application to Montague grammar. Ph.D. dissertation, University of Michigan.

Welin, C. W. (1979) *Studies in Computational Text Comprehension.* Stockholm: Institute of Linguistics.

van Wijngaarden, A. (1969) Report on algorithmic language ALGOL68. *Numerische Mathematik* **14**, 79–218.

Wilks, Y. A. (1967) Transformational grammars again. Memo SP–2936. System Development Corporation, Santa Monica, California.

Wilks, Y. A. (1973) Preference semantics. Report STAN–CS–73–377, Artificial Intelligence Laboratory, Stanford University. In E. L. Keenan (ed.) *Formal semantics of natural language.* Cambridge: Cambridge University Press, 1975.

Wilks, Y. A. (1973) An artificial intelligence approach to machine translation. In R. C. Schank and K. M. Colby (eds) *Computer Models of Thought and Language.* San Francisco: Freeman.

Wilks, Y. A; (1975) An intelligent analyser and understander of English. *Communications of the ACM* **18**, 264–274.

Wilks, Y. A. (1976) Processing case. *American Journal of Computational Linguistics,* Microfiche 56.

Wilks, Y. A. (1977) Frames, scripts, stories and fantasies. *Pragmatics Microfiche.*

Wilks, Y. A. (1978) Making preferences more active. *Artificial Intelligence* **11**,

197–223.

Wilks, Y. A. and Bien, J. (1981) Beliefs, points of view and multiple environments. Report CSCM–6, Cognitive Studies Centre, University of Essex. To appear in *Cognitive Science*.

Winograd, T. (1972) *Understanding Natural Language*. Edinburgh: Edinburgh University Press.

Winograd, T. (1977) On some contested suppositions of generative linguistics about the scientific study of language. *Cognition* **5**, 151–197.

Woods, W. A. (1970) Transition network grammars for natural language analysis. *Communications of the ACM* **13**, 591–606.

Woods, W. A. (1973) An experimental parsing system for transition network grammars. In R. Rustin (ed) *Natural Language Processing*. New York: Algorithmics Press.

Woods, W. A. (1980) Cascaded ATN grammars. *American Journal of Computational Linguistics* **6**, 1–12.

Woods, W. A. *et al.* (1972) The lunar sciences natural language information system: final report. Report 2378, Bolt Beranek and Newman Inc., Cambridge, Mass.

Wunderlich, D. (1978) Wie analysiert man Gespräche? Beispiel Wegauskünfte. *Linguistische Berichte* **58**, 41–76.

Zwicky, A., Friedman, J. Hall, B. and Walker, D. (1965) The Mitre syntactic analysis procedure for transformational grammar. Proceedings of the Fall Joint Computer Conference, *AFIPS Conference Proceedings* **27**, 317–326.

Index

Index